CAN YOU KEEP
A SECRET?

Can You Keep A Secret?

J.M. Doe

Can You Keep A Secret?

© 2020 by J.M. Doe

All rights reserved. No portion of this publication may be reproduced, stored in a retrieval system, or transmitted by any means—electronic, mechanical, photocopying, recording, or any other—except for brief quotations in printed reviews, without the prior written permission of the publisher.

Edited by Matt Jordan, Liesel Schmidt, and Regina Cornell
Cover design by Robin Vuchnich
Interior design by Nikkita Kent

Indigo River Publishing
3 West Garden Street, Ste. 718
Pensacola, FL 32502
www.indigoriverpublishing.com

Ordering Information:
Quantity sales: Special discounts are available on quantity purchases by corporations, associations, and others. For details, contact the publisher at the address above.

Orders by US trade bookstores and wholesalers: Please contact the publisher at the address above.

Printed in the United States of America

Library of Congress Control Number: 2020930432
ISBN: 978-1-950906-48-2 (paperback) 978-1-950906-49-9 (ebook)

First Edition

With Indigo River Publishing, you can always expect great books, strong voices, and meaningful messages.
Most importantly, you'll always find . . . words worth reading.

I dedicate this book to Elaine and her parents; without their help my life would have had a different outcome.

In honor of my family who passed before my story was written—my father, my oldest sister and her husband, and my oldest brother. And my dear friends who recently passed: Bob, Glo, Kathleen, and Nikki. All of you encouraged and supported me for years to tell my story.

I have lived by the poem "Footprints." God, however you define him or her, definitely carried me when I could not face one more obstacle.

I am thankful to all of the angels along our path.
You know who you are.
Bless you all.

Contents

PREFACE I
PROLOGUE III

Part One: Meeting My Prince

GOING TO SAUDI ARABIA 3
HOSPITAL LIFE 21
MEETING MY PRINCE 29
VACATION 39
MARRIED IN CYPRUS, AND OUR HONEYMOON 49
BACK IN THE USA 67
A BABY IS BORN 71
RETURNING TO SAUDI ARABIA 77
MEETING THE FAMILY 81

Part Two: Back in the USA

THE FIRST HIT 107
INFIDELITY AND ABUSE 111
WOMEN'S SHELTER 119
MIDNIGHT ESCAPE 123

Part Three: The Kidnapping

LOSING AISHA 131

Part Four: Life after the Abduction

BEFORE RETURNING TO SAUDI ARABIA, JULY–SEPTEMBER 1987 139
REUNION IN JEDDAH 145
WHAT NOW? 157

SEEING AISHA IN JEDDAH	161
SETTLING IN WITH MY FAMILY	169
LEAVING AGAIN	175
NOT RECOGNIZING MY DAUGHTER	181
SHARIA COURT	185

Part Five: Seeing Aisha

SEEING AISHA	195
LIFE IN JEDDAH	207
MY CONTRACT IN JEDDAH ENDS	211
MOVING TO RIYADH	215
GOING BACK TO COURT	219

Part Six: Visitation with Aisha

FIRST VISIT	225
MY PARENTS' VISIT	231
NEW HOUSING	235
LIFE IN RIYADH	237
LAWYER'S VISIT	245
DO YOU WANT TO PLAY A GAME?	247

Part Seven: First Attempts to Leave

FINDING A WAY	253
FIRST ATTEMPT: TURKEY, 1994	259
SECOND ATTEMPT: TURKEY	269
EGYPT, SUMMER 1994	273

Part Eight: Third Time's a Charm?

FAILED OUTCOMES 279
PREPARATION FOR A THIRD ATTEMPT 283
SMUGGLED INTO BAHRAIN.. 287
MEETING IN BAHRAIN.. 293
THE INVESTIGATION IN RIYADH 299
BACK IN BAHRAIN... 303
THE AMERICAN EMBASSY IN BAHRAIN... 307
LEAVING BAHRAIN 311

Part Nine: Success: America

AMERICA, VALENTINE'S DAY 315

Preface

My story is true. Names of people and places, as well as dates, have been changed to protect the innocent and the guilty. My intent in writing my story is not to wrong anyone, but to share my experience. I have used past letters from friends and family, photos, and journals that I have carted around for many years. I have some heart-wrenching cassette tapes of late-night telephone calls to and from my daughter and ex-husband in Saudi Arabia. I also have tons of photos and videos of my daughter's childhood in Saudi Arabia that are delightful to see.

One thing that is important to me, out of the love I have toward them, is to honor my daughter's paternal grandparents. I know the love they had for their granddaughter, and they knew the love she and I shared, the love we all shared. We became a family. A tight bond was formed in our hearts forever.

I heard rumors that the grandparents supported our efforts to come to America. They told their son to leave us alone and live his own life, but he was intent on keeping my daughter and me from living together in freedom.

Child abduction is common everywhere around the world. Physical, sexual, verbal, and mental abuse occur more often than most people are aware of or want to admit. During the 1980s, the State Department opened a division specializing in international abductions. This story is not unique in and of itself, but it is unique in the idiosyncrasies of the culture and religion in the country where my life has been entangled for over thirty-five years.

Many friends and family have suggested that I tell my story. There is a kind of fear or watchfulness in so doing. Perhaps the fear of any possible retaliation is a concern, whether it is a real danger or not. Am I being paranoid? Maybe. Many people, expats who have worked in Saudi Arabia, understand these feelings. We have experienced a life-changing phenomenon from living there, much the way Saudis experience a life-changing event when they live in or visit the United States.

I mean no harm to anyone. This story is one of many that could be told. I write to reveal what happened from my perspective to the best of my knowledge.

Prologue

Others might say that I am a free spirit, a free thinker, or somewhat of a flower child. Numerous people I knew shared this description, thus not seeming so peculiar to me. Leaving the Midwest, with its conservative environment, to move to Washington, DC, after I graduated from high school in 1969 taught me some valuable lessons in exploring the world of unknowns.

It was an eye-opening experience, living in that big city where my girlfriend Diane worked with the Central Intelligence Agency (CIA). Six of us girls rented a two-bedroom apartment in over-populated Arlington, Virginia. Heavy DC phone books, many inches thick, were piled on top of each other as makeshift chairs. Our new friends, Marines returned from Vietnam, borrowed old, ugly gray metal bunk beds from their base for us to sleep on and use as couches. They brought the beer. We had no money to buy anything else, so we learned to drink this nasty, disgusting beverage, which I enjoy today. Prior to coming to DC, Diane and I had met one of the Marines hitchhiking in Colorado. Coincidentally, he was stationed in DC, where Diane worked for the CIA, and later they married and moved to Alaska.

My work was across the universe from where we lived in apartment row. It took me three city buses and ninety minutes to get to my job in a large toy store. If I wanted to get home a half hour sooner, which always sounded wonderful, I could get off the bus at an earlier stop, but it was known not to be the safest route. Knowing the sketchy neighborhood I chose to enter, I had to psych myself up because of the amount of fear I could experience, especially as the sun set on streets already full of haunting shadows, unfamiliar noises, and frightful stories. I would scramble quickly while I prayed I would get to the other side unharmed.

Selling toys was not my life goal. As a child, I had always wanted to be a stewardess—now called a flight attendant. Unfortunately, I didn't have the correct body proportions, height to weight, and wore contact lenses, which was unacceptable at that time. With hopes dashed, I needed an alternative, so I applied to and was accepted into a one-year licensed practical nurse (LPN/LVN) program, which brought me back to the Midwest from DC. I was twenty-one years old when I graduated in 1972. Little did I know then that being a nurse would give me job security throughout my life, being paid well above the minimum wage and affording me the opportunity to travel.

After obtaining an associate's degree in nursing in May of 1977, my girlfriend Peggy and I loaded my ugly but reliable orange van (with a built-in bed) and headed to the magnificently beautiful state of Alaska for a four-week camping and backpacking road trip with unlimited daylight hours. We raced time while we changed flat tires daily, as we had to utilize the bumpy pot-holed logging roads through British Columbia to get to our northern destination, since the Alaskan highway was still under construction. Things grew bigger than average during Alaska summers, including the armies of enormous, blood-sucking mosquitoes, immune to DEET. We were two girls in the wild, living out our independence, and we did it well.

Exploring other parts of my country helped me spread my wings and whetted my appetite for adventure. It influenced my move to California that August to get my bachelor's degree in nursing. I took a break midway through to travel throughout Europe in 1980. These experiences expanded my horizons and made me less fearful and more willing to take some risks, such as signing on the dotted line to work as a registered nurse in the Kingdom of Saudi Arabia (KSA). In hindsight, it may have been a spur-of-the-moment impulse or another broken relationship that led me to embark on this new escapade. My family and friends didn't discourage me; they were intrigued by my endeavors, though I don't know what they might have said behind my back.

Admittedly, my life has probably had more twists and turns than most. I find pleasure in learning about different cultures. Everybody has some regrets about what he or she did or never did. We could all spend time looking backward. That just may be the impetus that pushes one further.

Is there an innate force that moves us, perhaps one we do not have ultimate control of? Some would call this destiny. For others, their belief and faith in their god defines what happens in their lives. One prays for guidance, and if you listen, your life will be better. My question is, does life work that way? There is a weird twist to that concept. What does it mean when your prayer is answered and your best friend's is not? Does God like you more?

People may say that I was naïve, influenced by the hippie counterculture of San Francisco's Haight-Ashbury. I wore my hip-hugging bell-bottoms and braless tank tops, expressing myself. I smoked pot and experimented with psychedelic drugs as I listened to Peter, Paul and Mary. Eager to learn, I was ready for adventure. I looked at others as equals, but felt experienced in my sense of finding truth and in moving beyond my comfort zone to try something new. Perhaps I lived my life more idealistically than others, not finding it necessary to research all the "ins and outs," as others may have. Living in California in the 1970s and '80s influenced my way of thinking and challenged many of my beliefs. I was no longer feeling so out of place, as I had in the Midwest. Being in a more progressive, liberal environment encouraged me to live outside of the box.

The mentality of people on the West Coast was different from the typical Midwestern mentality. Traveling was part of the norm for my California family, but it was also true for most of my biological family—my mother, father, and six siblings. Though my parents lived within sixty miles of their birthplaces, my mother enjoyed traveling—with or without my dad. They traveled to Europe for a few weeks in 1980 and met up with my youngest brother, who was a foreign exchange student in Germany during his junior year of high school. I joined my parents and brother during the ten weeks I was traveling solo throughout Europe. My mom traveled to Korea and Russia on her own, with the desire to explore more. Later, in the '80s, my parents hit the road in their RV for seven-plus years, touring all the state capitals of the US. According to the story I am told, my mom asked my dad, "Are you going to join me to drive, or should I find someone else?" My parents came to visit me two times while I worked in Saudi Arabia.

My older sister moved to New York with her husband after graduation from college, and traveling became a passion of hers when her children were grown and her marriage ended. My younger sister moved to Las Vegas at an early age with her older African American husband. Later, when single, she relocated to Arizona with her young daughter after she traveled to Spain for the five-hundred-mile pilgrimage, Camino de Santiago, and then toured Peru's jungle by riverboat to various encampments along the Amazon River and went on to Machu Picchu. My oldest brother moved to the wide-open country of the great Northwest in his twenties, where he bought land, felled his own trees, and twice built his own log home. He traveled to Guatemala with my sister and me, but being out of the country was not for him, although he loved to travel south in his van to avoid the cold Washington winters. My oldest sister, by contrast, preferred to stay close to home. She actively helped refugees relocate from Sudan, Somalia, and Bosnia. When I heard she was traveling to Bosnia with one of the refugees, I was quite surprised, actually shocked. My middle brother traveled out of the country while in the military; otherwise, he was a homebody. So, you see, I was not the odd one out in wanting to explore the world.

People are people. That is the biggest identifier I notice wherever I travel. As humans, we are all basically the same. We feel, we love, we hurt, we cry. People are good, and people are bad—in every society. I look beyond the outer attributes of a person's cultural identity without considering what the consequences might be. Perhaps that contributed to the life I am living today, but I wouldn't change this about myself.

My story begins when I was a twenty-seven-year-old farm girl from the Midwest. With nursing certificate in hand, I followed a yearning to further my education and a desire for a new adventure to California, the paradise dreamland. The next five years were great for this single, independent, adventurous young woman.

Years of completing a bachelor's degree, new relationships, broken relationships, and travels to Mexico, Canada, Alaska, Hawaii, and through Europe finally ended when I came to land in Boston, Massachusetts, without a secure place to live and with no job and humongous student debt.

Intrigued by an advertisement for nurses in Saudi Arabia, I signed on the dotted line of a year-long contract with a military hospital in Tabuk, a small desert town in the middle of nowhere in Saudi Arabia, a country I literally knew nothing about. I had nothing to hold me back, and I was ready for yet another quest, thinking it would also get me out of the massive debt I had accumulated.

Do not youth, ignorance, and naïveté sometimes make us bold and fearless? What an incredibly fascinating country I was going to—a land more different from my homeland than I ever expected, a land where a single female has more restrictions than I could have imagined and few of the freedoms that I grew up with. I was so intrigued by the mystery of it all, and I blindly looked forward to whatever this next chapter of my life had in store for me.

Part One

Meeting My Prince

Going to Saudi Arabia

As we neared the Saudi border and the causeway to Bahrain, our driver pulled off the road and stopped. He asked us to get out of the van. Then he pushed a switch and the back seat became a bed. Aisha and I were told to get under the bed. This would be our hiding place for the next thirty minutes. We nervously crawled into this narrow, dark, cramped space. One could discover this hiding place by opening the back door, moving the decoy of pillows, and looking under the bed. We all prayed for our safety and that they would not ask to search the van, as was often done.

My daughter said, in her little giggle of a voice, "Can we sing the song from Sound of Music now?" referring to the scene in the film when the family flees Austria and ascends the mountain.

"No," I said. "We are not singing now. We are going to keep quiet and not move. We have to freeze and not even wiggle. Our lives are in danger." It was too dark to make the gesture of my hand across my neck, but she knew the seriousness of the moment. She understood what could happen if something went wrong.

But our story began twelve years earlier. . .

Working as a nurse in Saudi Arabia was an idea passed around my nursing circle. I had heard of people working overseas making a lot of money with very few out-of-pocket expenses. Housing and health care were provided by one's sponsor/employer. Since women did not drive in Saudi Arabia, car expenses were nonexistent. My hope was to make and save the most money I ever had and to pay off my student loans, or at least put a dent in them.

It was September of 1983 when I flew to Washington, DC, for an eye-opening briefing about living in the Kingdom of Saudi Arabia (KSA), including the dos and don'ts of the country. The thought of going to Saudi Arabia sounded out of the ordinary and fascinating. I found traveling to be a life-altering phenomenon, and I felt blessed to have the opportunities to make this a reality in my life and to be brave enough to take a risk, a risk to leave my comfort zone to see a different horizon.

I freely admit that I didn't do due diligence in terms of becoming more knowledgeable about the culture. Could it be so different? I didn't even know where the KSA was on the map. It didn't bother me, though eventually I would realize that it all should have mattered.

Five other health-care workers going to Saudi Arabia were at the briefing. I was so grateful to meet them, relieved to know I wouldn't be the only American, English-speaking nurse to arrive in the tiny, deserted village of Tabuk, south of the Jordanian border, as my imagination had led me to believe. We were flown to New York City to catch our nine o'clock flight and indulge in our "last" drink before we boarded our plane to Saudi Arabia, where alcohol was illegal. We six women of various ages and lifestyles, all of us properly dressed for our trip to Saudi Arabia, flagged down a taxi at the airport to take us to a nearby bar. I was introduced to a dry martini—my first and last. How could anyone like the bitter, sour taste? I preferred sweeter drinks, margaritas or beer, though I did not drink often. I was happy to know these women were going with me to Saudi Arabia; all of us were about to have our lives changed forever.

A little alcohol in my system helped me board the enormous Saudi Arabian Airlines Boeing 777 double-decker airplane with the capacity to accommodate three hundred passengers. There were twelve seats across in each of three divided sections, with never-ending rows. It was mind-boggling to learn that airplanes were built this large and had two levels for seating. Food, snacks, and drinks (no alcohol on Saudi Airlines flights) were available throughout the lengthy flight, which crossed many time zones. So many emotions coursed through my body; my head was spinning. What had I done? Would I regret going to Saudi Arabia? Perhaps I could have chosen another place to work for my adventure, as I had explored many volunteer and employment opportunities after graduation. Most of my friends and family my age were married and had kids, yet here I was, jaunting around the world.

As we neared Jeddah, an announcement was made that we were flying into Saudi air space. Then a mass transformation took place: the many bathrooms on the plane were suddenly occupied as women changed from Western dress to modest, long and colorful dresses that covered their exposed skin. Many women put on their black abayas, lightweight, loose-fitting robes. These garments wrapped around their bodies to stop any skin from showing. Some women covered their head and hair in a precise manner using a black scarf-like piece of soft, silky material, called a hijab. Several faces were covered with a niqab. Some niqabs covered the whole face, while others had slits in them to show only their eyes. A few women donned black gloves so their bare hands were not exposed for men to see. *Why*, I wondered, *do women wear black to cover? Doesn't it absorb the heat?* Much to my surprise, I learned that black garments of a certain thickness absorb the heat before it reaches the skin, as well as the body heat, keeping the women cooler than white or reflective colors would. Is this the reason women wear black, or is it to disguise them and not draw attention to their appearance?

Men changed into floor-length, loose-fitting white gowns, called *thobes*. Red-and-white-checkered-cloth head coverings, *gutras*, were meticulously centered on each man's head, then wrapped on top of his head, draping down the sides in a precise manner and topped with a thicker black cord, called an *agal*, traditionally made of goat hair, of doubled rings to help hold the gutra in place. I observed the Saudis' attire regress to what it might have been like in Biblical times.

I was no longer able to recognize the passengers sitting next to me who had started the flight with me in NYC; it was quite a bizarre transformation. I would learn that the same theatrical production of changing costumes was acted out when returning to the United States; it just happened in reverse, returning to more revealing Western dress.

Smoking was allowed on the planes, and many men smoked; some chain-smoked. It was truly an impossible feat to keep smoke from the nonsmoking area. Once living in Saudi Arabia, I seldom observed a Saudi woman smoke even the hookahs in public.

After our agonizingly long (fourteen-hour), smoke-ridden flight, our little group of six reunited when we arrived midafternoon in Jeddah at a large metropolitan airport, more modern and abstract than I expected. Our plane was greeted with a transport vehicle, somewhat like a modern subway car, that was raised to the level of the plane for us to board and then lowered to take us to the main terminal for Immigration and Customs Control.

Going through customs at this airport was unlike at any other airport I had experienced. Being in a Muslim country and especially Saudi Arabia, where Arabic seemed to be the only language spoken, I was at a loss. Wasn't someone supposed to be here to help us get through this absurd encounter in this very foreign country?

Many items were confiscated from our luggage. Magazines that showed too much flesh on women were taken, torn up, or blackened with markers. This was also done with mail and gifts coming into the country. Videos brought in were scrutinized for content inappropriate or contradictory to the country's religious ideology. Items deemed not permissible included anything Christmas related, Barbie dolls, and *Playboy* magazines. Bibles were not allowed. While we accompanied our luggage through the long, painfully slow lines, we were told to put undergarments at the top of our suitcases to distract the officials, who were all male.

After customs we were eventually greeted by a male hospital-recruitment representative, who made sure all of our paperwork was in order to enter the Kingdom. It was late afternoon, eight hours later than in NYC, when we boarded a small white shuttle bus that drove us through Jeddah to our hotel. The city of Jeddah was asleep when we arrived, with only a few people on the streets. We were told our experience would have been quite different at another time of the month; usually the city was engaging and full of activity. But we arrived during an important religious holiday celebration during the month of Hajj called Eid al-Adha, which celebrates the ritual pilgrimage to Mecca.

Yearly, hundreds of thousands of Muslims, both male and female, come from all over the world to perform this pilgrimage to Mecca and Medina, the two holy cities. All Muslims try to do it at least once in their lifetime, if financially and physically able. The celebration could be compared to a gift-giving holiday like Christmas. Usually a lamb is sacrificed and given to the poor. Being intrigued and dazed already by this unfamiliar country made me wonder how much more I would experience on this new adventure. Jeddah, a major port city with a very long international trade history dating back before Christ, was another world from the desert town of Tabuk, where I was recruited to work.

Though some women chose to cover themselves with an abaya, it was not the custom in Jeddah, especially for female expats from many countries. Wealth was extravagantly portrayed through the captivating architecture of the modern high-rises of shops, offices, and apartments. To the west, the Red Sea ran the whole length of the desert of Saudi Arabia. Marble or stone statues adorned the corniche in varying themes, colors, and sizes; most tastefully presented. A few families were spotted sitting on top of large, colorful, thick rugs laid in sand or on the paved sidewalks. Women were draped in their abayas, and children played in the sand in their fancy, new, expensive clothes. Girls wore Cinderella dresses like I would have worn to a wedding or on Easter Sunday. Oil money made many entrepreneurs very rich.

It was also the most humid city I had ever experienced. I was accustomed to the humidity of the Midwest, but this did not compare. Once outside, the humidity and heat were so intense it took my breath away; my clothes stuck to my body from perspiration. Air-conditioning was a must, but I would find that not everyone had that luxury.

The sun started to set when we arrived at our hotel, where we were shown to our individual rooms. In our funky hotel in a questionable part of the city, we were offered a buffet meal with a limited selection of food. *Was this an indication of our value in coming here to work?* I wondered. Was it because of the influx of Muslims who had arrived in the country for the pilgrimage and its celebration? Whatever the case, I was relieved to know I was not alone, that my new "family" was only down the hall. We decided to brave the heat and the neighborhood to take a stroll, though there was little to see from our location. The stores were closed, and there were no fancy skyscrapers or seaside to observe—just another glimpse of Jeddah's past. Some buildings were worn down and in need of repair, bearing no comparison to what we had enjoyed on our drive through the unusually calm city.

I would soon learn that every region had its own distinct personality, and that even every family in Saudi had uniquely different religious demands that were influenced by family values or the father/husband's wishes. Some families' beliefs were more liberal than others in regard to religion, dress, drink, and comingling—regardless of where one resided.

Riyadh, the largest city and the capital of the KSA, was known to be extremely religious and conservative, with harsh and stringent rules. It was a ninety-minute flight inland from Jeddah, almost due east, in the middle of the sprawling desert. The strictest areas of all were Mecca and Medina, the holy cities, where only Muslims were allowed, but Riyadh seemed to be in a time warp of its own. Public beheadings were an example of what could happen there if the rules of the country were not respected. Anyone could gather to watch trained men execute the accused in a split second with a sharp sword in "Chop Chop Square." I was grateful for not being assigned to work in that dreadful city.

After a night of sleep in a bed and in a room with air-conditioning, we flew to the small airport in Tabuk for our first overseas work assignment in Saudi Arabia. Strangely enough, I was energized, not scared, as I asked myself, *What the hell am I doing here?* I honestly did not know what to expect. When we arrived in the small airport in Tabuk we were driven to our housing compounds on a company bus, an old school bus painted white and with the Saudi military logo.

Tabuk, a small desert village, was approximately a ninety-minute flight northeast from Jeddah. The presence of wealth was not visible by comparison to Jeddah; Tabuk was older and primitive, not modern. An abandoned group of buildings appeared in the middle of nowhere in a huge, meandering desert. This was my new home—a military base where an older hospital existed. A modern hospital was under construction, soon to be ready for occupancy.

Saudi men were recruited or volunteered to be in the military, but the majority of people from this area lived in the desert. Called Bedouins, they still embraced the nomadic lifestyle, often preferring it to an urban one. The patients we had at the hospital were predominantly Bedouins. Bedouin families had recently become eligible for modern medical care, which was a new and peculiar experience for them. Before the availability of hospitals and medical treatment, it was not uncommon for them to obtain treatment by traditional or Islamic medicine healers.

There was one main street that was paved; the others were dusty, pot-holed dirt roads with no stoplights or sidewalks. It was easy to walk around the town of a few blocks. The side streets branched off from the main street. Shop after shop of gold souks (stores) distinctively decorated the area. I was mesmerized by the quantity of gold jewelry displayed on the mirrored walls and in the glass cabinets that sparkled from the lights of the shops with minimal to no security. It was said a person could leave something of value behind and it would be there when he or she returned. A custom still practiced in Saudi is to cut off the hand of anyone caught stealing, thus deterring theft, which might explain this fact.

There were other markets to peruse. Several fairly well-stocked stores with household items, like pots and pans and plastic containers and toys, took up space on other streets. Chicken Street was well known for delicious spit-fired chicken that filled the air with its tempting aroma from blocks away. The copper store was a favorite. In the meat market huge, unrefrigerated carcasses of meat hung in the open air while flies swarmed around. Only lamb or beef was available in Saudi; pork was not allowed nor to be eaten by Muslims. Halal methods were used in slaughtering animals. A Muslim would slit the throat of an animal using a very sharp knife, letting all the blood drip from its body. There may have been a dead chicken or two for sale beside the other meats on these filthy roads. I tried not to think of what I might be eating in the local restaurants.

We were driven to a large, two-story apartment building consisting of sixty apartments built around two small, grassy common areas.

We were to have our own apartments, but this did not happen at the beginning. There weren't enough apartments to go around, so we shared a tiny apartment of less than three hundred square feet with one bedroom, two twin beds, and one bath.

Shortly after we settled into our apartment, the other women in the compound told us to get ready to go out. I was still jet-lagged—after all, the time was nine hours later than in Kansas. Even so, it seemed it was party time and I would have to adjust quickly. *But what*, I wondered, *do you wear to a party here?* Apparently, you wore whatever you wanted.

An old yellow school bus with the company name painted on it rolled in from another compound, picked us up, and would return us when the party was over. I was told that some women were known to get in the trunks of cars to get into places they were not allowed. Many male expats chose to purchase their own vehicles, providing additional autonomy to get about, go to the Red Sea, and travel with fewer restrictions.

Loud speakers could be heard prior to our arrival at the other compound, blasting songs from groups like the Beatles, the Eagles, and even Bob Marley. Clearly, the party had already begun. Who said there was no alcohol in this country? Many expats had been testing their skills in brewing and distilling their own beer and wine to share or even sell. Another spirit was liquor made from potatoes, called *sidiki*, ironically meaning "friend" in Arabic. It was used in mixed drinks but was quite nasty on its own.

Our party was around the swimming pool, with barbecued hamburgers and hotdogs and an assortment of other side dishes provided by the host compound. It was comparable to any party I might have attended in the States, except for the variation of Western nationalities in one location and stimulating conversations about their countries and why they had come to Saudi Arabia. I talked with Brits, Scots, Irish,

Germans, Australians—people from so many countries I was unaccustomed to encountering.

It was easy to forget that, just one day before, I had departed from my comfort zone in the United States. We danced the night away, flirted with boys, and drank as much as we wanted. Some people got really drunk. Always a lightweight when it came to alcohol, I had only a couple of drinks because I felt unsure and fearful of my surroundings, and I wondered what would happen if we were caught. Some ladies were invited to remain behind as the party continued and were content to do so, despite the rigid laws.

Around midnight, our designated driver drove us to our accommodations, where loneliness overwhelmed me. Nothing was familiar. With no one I knew nearby, I felt barren, like the land I had embarked upon less than twenty-four hours ago, and I was jet-lagged. The reality of where I had come from to where I was at that moment stirred my emotions, and my head was doing jumping jacks. Yet this exploration was just the beginning.

It was easy to understand why expats would gather and party to make this land feel more like home. Throughout my life in Saudi Arabia, most singles partied with mixed company, despite the fact that this was illegal. It was a norm we were accustomed to in our own countries, and so it became a norm living here. People took precautions, however; they didn't flaunt it and were sensible enough not to draw attention to it, so usually no harm followed. It would have taken a lot of *mutaween* to monitor the ongoing mixing off the compounds.

The Mutawa, the Islamic religious police force, monitored most, if not all, activities in the country. They were also called the Committee for the Promotion of Virtue and the Prevention of Vice—and interesting title. They were easy to spot by their shorter "high water"-length thobes and black shoes and socks. They usually sported long, thick, sometimes pointed or henna-stained beards, with their gutras haphazardly placed on their heads. They would often carry wooden sticks to be used to hit people if they deemed it necessary. Living in Saudi Arabia, one learned to walk away from them, to avoid any interaction.

Susan, one of the women from my recruitment group, and I shared an apartment for a couple of months until it was possible to get our own apartments. We were charged sixty dollars a month for them, but it was worth it for us. One Saudi riyal was valued at approximately $3.75. A nurse who lived in an older female compound told me that they were each paid two hundred dollars monthly to share an apartment. My own apartment was on the ground floor. The view from my bedroom window was a large red-and-white-checkered water tower just outside of the housing compound; I tired of it quickly. Our compounds were "Little Americas." Our housing was on the military base not so far from town, but far enough that transportation was necessary. We were within walking distance of the other compounds, the new hospital, the hospital recreation facility, and the female-only swimming pool.

A six-foot plain gray cement wall with only one entrance and exit surrounded our newer single-female compound. Around the circumference of our apartment buildings was a large sandy area with many bright and colorful bougainvillea that would survive the extreme temperatures and provide some color to this drab, arid climate. Our guards were Bedouins who provided twenty-four-hour protection to keep men out of our living quarters. Their makeshift guardhouse was falling apart. The guards wore loose-fitting, often grungy white thobes with thin cotton trousers underneath as they sat or lay on pieces of cardboard placed on the ground. They played games in the dirt with rocks and drank hot, sugary tea, displaying a missing tooth or two, and were cheerful. Laughter was shared as we attempted to communicate with each other.

Married couples and single men had compounds that were less guarded. The guards at their compounds were there to keep the single women out, with some exceptions for visiting married friends or couples.

Frequently, from all the mosques throughout Saudi Arabia, a piercing sound startled my soul with its volume and force. The obtrusive noise sounded like a yell over a loudspeaker or even a megaphone by muezzins. It occurred five times throughout the day for the call to prayer (*adhan*) and for the Friday sermons (Jumu'ah). I never quite got used to that disturbingly loud sound. The muezzin is responsible for maintaining an accurate prayer schedule and is often chosen to serve the mosque based on both his character and the power of his voice. It is a much honored position.

The sounds varied by location of the mosque and by the announcer. The broadcasts could be heard from miles away and often overlapped each other. It was not entertaining if your bedroom window was near a mosque. The first morning prayer was often around four o'clock, quite an annoying and unwanted early-morning alarm clock. I did eventually discover that some mosques had a calmer, more soothing sound, a sweet, song-like voice or melodious chant that was quite pleasant to listen to. This pure sound was considered an art form. In addition to all of the varied announcements that rang from the sky, the *souks* (markets) also sold prayer clocks that would sound an alarm when it was time for prayer. It was a commonly bought Saudi souvenir.

Outside our compound, the guards laid their individual prayer rugs with printed designs on the ground, facing Mecca, the holy city, to perform the obligatory ritual prayer (salat). Prior to prayer, it was customary to perform a certain ritual purification to clean the body (*wudū*). When water was unavailable, using sand or dust to "wash" with was acceptable. Certain activities, such as using the bathroom, passing gas, sleeping, or sex, would invalidate the ablution. Culturally, the beliefs of Islam were remarkably different from my Christian upbringing, the only religion I had been exposed to as a child.

Religions like Islam interested me, seeing what and how others believed. In all religions, there are different interpretations. Whom do you believe? I wondered which restrictions were rooted in culture as opposed to the religion. Was the practice of women covering more cultural than religious? What bothered me most in Saudi Arabia was the lack of freedom to believe or practice another religion, as well as the lack of freedom of speech.

Some members of the royal family seemed to live by a different set of standards from other Saudis and expats. This was a concept I could not understand. If you are a Muslim, a Christian, or whatever religion you embrace, you honor your religion, regardless of if you are being watched or told what to do. Religious hypocrisy is present wherever you live, but this was such a different place and a different set of standards, such a contrast to my other life.

There was little in the way of Western entertainment to be found. There were no public movie theaters in KSA, though I am told there were in the late 1970s, prior to the sizeable influx of Westerners, when life seemingly got stricter, not only for the expats but also the Saudis. Some compounds may have had a movie theater, but they were no longer in use where I worked.

No place overtly existed where people of opposite sex comingled unless married, with the exception of the hospital and its recreation center. Some restaurant owners were prepared to take chances, sometimes allowing unmarried couples to join each other in the "family" section, but that was the extent of it.

The Western embassies and military bases had different standards of freedom. They were permitted to hold mixed gatherings and had the privilege of holding church services, and alcohol was not taboo. They had the liberty to come and go without being guarded and with little scrutiny.

Needless to say, life in Saudi Arabia was an awakening adventure for me. It was an unbelievably unique, often duplicitous way to live. In Tabuk, we went everywhere in my community without covering if dressed appropriately. I wore shorts and short sleeves around my home. My abaya would be utilized depending on my wardrobe off the compound. Muumuus—long, loose-fitting dresses in many colors and patterns—were frequently worn and could be purchased throughout the country. With the temperature being so hot, it was an awkward, uncomfortable adjustment to wear a lot of clothes. Unlike the larger cities, we were very relaxed in Tabuk and not bothered by our clothes and coverings as long as we were considerate about what was appropriate.

Usually British employees, often known to party more, staffed the hospital's incredible recreation and activity department. I soon learned there were certain freedoms and liberties outside of the compound I had not anticipated. In time, I was busier in Tabuk than I had been back at home. I was utterly amazed and excited by all that was offered to help us feel less restricted in a country I thought would be more like a prison.

Perhaps the recent introduction of expats in this small community was why it had not caught up with the larger cities in terms of restrictions. Though all events needed approval by some government office, little was denied except during Ramadan, the holy month, when there was a higher awareness in the country as a whole. We were not closely monitored, allowing us to comingle openly while remaining on the military compound. Swimming pools in the married compounds, tennis courts, exercise and weight-lifting rooms, and a snack bar were available for coed use. Hospital buses provided frequent runs into town to shop or to dine out at excellent Pakistani or Indian restaurants. A diverse choice of activities was conveniently arranged, from scuba diving, snorkeling, and fishing in the Red Sea to desert expeditions for hiking and exploration.

There was one camping trip to the Red Sea I will always remember. The scuba divers did night dives for lobster. More lobsters than

I had ever seen or eaten, along with copious amounts of homebrew, contributed to a delightful starlit night at a camp in the wide-open desert with the sea lopping in the background. (That magical atmosphere aside, there were no bathrooms in the desert, and finding privacy could be challenging.)

For New Year's Eve in 1983, a group from the hospital went to Amman, Jordan, and Petra. In Amman we partied the night away with hotel guests from all over the world. My new lifestyle prompted me to buy my first bottle of expensive champagne, Dom Pérignon. I learned the Chicken Dance; little did I know it was popular all around the world and danced on occasions of all kinds.

After we celebrated the New Year in style we ventured on to Petra, a historical and archaeological city in southern Jordan which is a UNESCO World Heritage Site. To reach Petra, "the Rose City," we rode horses for close to an hour, not quite a mile, through the long, very narrow gorge called the Siq, through mountains of sandstone, until right before my eyes were elaborately carved rock pillars, towers, and tombs—the most ornate rose-colored structures I had ever seen. Al-Khazneh, the "Treasury," was one of many formations that were remarkably preserved. Believed to have been founded as early as 9,000 BC, Petra had once been lost, but was rediscovered in 1812. This area had a spiritual feeling.

It was a very fulfilling weekend, getting back in touch with my normalcy, even if I was in another country.

The reality of returning to Saudi Arabia was often unbelievable, as there were so many peculiar ways about my newly discovered land. At this time, the telephone system was still a work in progress. Calls from outside could be transferred to our compound phones, but we could not make long-distance calls, except at the "phone office" in town. Outgoing long-distance calls were made in town from a small stone building with a room that housed a few telephones. You waited your turn, often outside in the brutal heat, in the long, slow lines. When it was your turn, you gave one of the attendants the number you wanted to call. The number of minutes used, in addition to the time of day and the destination of the call, determined the cost. Numerous languages were being spoken in the room simultaneously. It was often difficult to hear, even though small dividers were provided in an attempt to block the distracting noise. In some larger cities, telephone booths were available on the streets for making local and long-distance calls, but many coins were required.

Outgoing mail was often collected by someone leaving the country who would post from the States or another Western country. We gave them postage stamps or money for postage. Incoming mail would be mailed to our hospital and delivered to our nursing units. It was wonderful to receive mail from home, often a competition to see who got the most letters. Packages sent from other countries didn't always arrive, or were confiscated by customs for being "inappropriate," or because someone wanted what was mailed. During the major Muslim holidays, we did not expect our mail to get delivered. Everything stopped, even mail delivery. Bags of mail would sit idle for days outside of the post offices without being processed or even acknowledged.

I was slowly becoming accustomed to the reality that everything needed to be planned and organized around the prayer calls, as all businesses closed for prayer. If we were able to get inside a restaurant before prayer, we were able to remain, as people were concealed and segregated behind dark curtained windows with dimmed lights. It was much nicer to wait inside in the fan-cooled or air-conditioned restaurants, where we could wait to order or to get our food when prayer was over, after fifteen to thirty minutes. Prayers on Friday afternoons were the longest, usually a half hour or more.

I enjoyed this fabulous opportunity to live in Saudi Arabia, though not all expats felt the same. Many were easily frustrated at being on "Saudi time," meaning often things would take longer than we were accustomed to, or a job may have been done half-assed or not finished at all. I would learn how time was monitored differently by the *inshallah* mentality. Once one caught on to the Saudi *inshallah*, "God willing," lifestyle, it would help one in acclimating to a different reference to time. "Inshallah" would be said after anything that pertained to the future. It was a word used often, not only among the Arabs but also expats.

Hospital Life

What was I to do? How could I communicate without knowing Arabic?

For many years an American company had a lucrative contract with the Saudi government to set up, manage, and staff the military hospitals throughout Saudi Arabia. I had been more apprehensive than I needed to be, as I was just a number among many thousands of people, expatriates (expats), who came from all over the world to work in and help develop Saudi Arabia. Our hospital was staffed with Western doctors, nurses, administrators, and other ancillary staff. A few Saudis had also studied or been trained to assist in these roles. Nurses and doctors were recruited from America, Great Britain, Ireland, Canada, Australia, and New Zealand. Only the Western group of nurses provided registered nursing (RN) care in this American-run military hospital. English was the language of the hospital, though it was not spoken or understood by the majority of the patients.

What was I to do, not knowing the Arabic language? How would I take care of patients who spoke only Arabic? English-speaking nurses, both male and female, from Egypt, Jordan, Palestine, Lebanon, and Syria, were hired as translators, although their nursing education was not equivalent to Western standards. Finding a male translator was not always an easy task, as they might be off the unit to pray, smoke, get tea, or chat with friends. In Tabuk, a few Saudis knew English, as did some of the merchants, which was helpful. The hospital staff and some educated military men were well versed in English, especially higher-ranking officers from Pakistan that came to help train the Saudi military. Another language challenge for me on my unit was having to translate the strong Scottish accent of a nurse who gave me nursing reports in difficult-to-comprehend English when her shift ended.

The hospital provided our nursing uniforms, white pants and tops for registered nurses. Thick, foldable paper nursing caps were part of the uniform; a colored stripe designated your title. When I asked an Egyptian nurse I worked with why she did not cover her head, she replied, "I do not feel that it is necessary." She went on to say, "When I die, I will go to a lower number in heaven. I will have to work to gain higher levels in heaven." It is the Islamic belief that there are seven heavens one must pass through when they die. Not all Muslims felt it necessary to cover their heads in Saudi Arabia or in their own countries.

Fatimah, one of my first patients, was in the hospital to get her diabetes under control, which was often difficult to do when living in the desert. She was not tall, about the same height as me and maybe fifteen years older. (Many Saudis did not know their date of birth, as it was often not recorded, so they would give a date close to what was familiar.) Instead of a hospital gown, Fatimah wore a long, light-blue chiffon dress. It was customary for our female patients to wear their own clothes. Her long, straight, thick, dark hair was pulled back behind her head, and her large brown eyes were beautifully accented with kohl, a type of charcoal women put on their eyelids. I will always remember Fatimah. She taught me my first Arabic words—*marhabaan* (hello), *moya haar* (hot water), *moya barid* (cold water), *min fadlik* (please), *shukran* (thanks), and *ma'a s-salāma* (goodbye)—passing me her water pitcher every time I went past her room. We laughed as I stumbled through the words, repeating them over and over until I grasped them. She mentioned her son to me a number of times, thinking I might be a good wife for him; he had just returned from studying in the States. Because of Fatimah and my interest in communicating with her and my other patients, I started a conversational Arabic class shortly after arriving in Tabuk.

I didn't know the characters of the Arabic alphabet consisted of lines and dots, beautifully written to resemble calligraphy and extremely different from mine. There are twenty-eight characters in the alphabet, twenty-five consonants and three vowels, which are not always used. Arabic is written and read from right to left, numbers are written from left to right, and their books open from back to front. It is amazing to me how people learn to read, write, and speak English and Arabic, two extremely opposite languages and writing styles. Muslims from around the world may not know how to speak Arabic, but they learn how to read the Quran in Arabic at an early age.

An employee of the hospital taught Arabic classes for non-Arabic-speaking employees. Employees signed up for six weeks of evening classes, meeting two times a week. Our work schedules often conflicted with the classes. Many lost interest or got frustrated learning the language and dropped out. Not all employees wanted to learn Arabic.

Though a slow learner, I valued learning how to communicate with my patients, and they enjoyed helping me become skilled at their complicated language. I wished for a wider knowledge of Arabic, though I learned enough to give patient care. I became especially at ease with medical terms. I could perform most of my job without a translator by the time I left Tabuk. As I learned more medical terms and basic conversation, I could ask patients if they had pain, if they had urinated, had they pooped . . . When I was with a group of people speaking Arabic, I could often get the gist of the conversation; but they, like most native speakers, spoke faster and in more detail than I was able to comprehend. I usually followed what was being said well enough to converse with them, though at times I was too shy or frustrated to bother.

Another common feature of the Saudi culture that I had to adapt to was the Islamic Hijri calendar, also known as the lunar calendar. Unlike our Gregorian calendar, the twelve months of the Hijri calendar were based on the cycle of the moon, and there were ten or eleven fewer days per year. The Hijri calendar began when Mohammed became a prophet in the year 622 AD.

Our hospital was far ahead of its time. We had a computerized charting system and order entry for the doctors, unheard of in the early '80s and incongruous in this small desert town. It was quite efficient and easy to use, though it met its demise as the technology was not maintained when hospital contracts changed. It was much later that hospitals in the States started using computers for patient care.

My first position as a charge nurse for an all-female floor in the old hospital was enlightening. As an American, I took so much for granted, thinking that we all did things the same way, our way. There were no coed floors, and only females worked with the female patients. On the women's floor, English was not understood. We were very thankful for our Egyptian translators and for other Western nurses who had worked long enough to be able to speak limited Arabic. Being in the hospital was a new experience for our female patients. It was such a lighthearted unit. Most of our patients gathered in the waiting areas during the day to talk among themselves while sipping hot tea in tiny ceramic cups that fit in one hand, sweetened with three or four cubes of sugar. Often, family members would bring our patients a thermos of tea, already sweetened, and some sort of snack to eat, like date cookies or pistachios, which were shared with others throughout the day. Our patients would laugh as we showed them how to use modern conveniences, like a toothbrush. This was an odd new concept to them. They were familiar with using a tiny light-brown twig, called *miswak or siwak*, from an *arāk* tree, used in the Middle East to clean teeth. Known for its antibacterial and plaque-inhibiting properties, this stick, about six inches long, was often seen sticking out of the pockets of men's thobes.

Running water was an unknown invention for some, and a shower could be an intimidating new occurrence. Some women had not seen toilets, and if they had, they would most likely have been holes in the ground. Occasionally, a patient might be seen squatting on the toilet seat instead of sitting on it. Being pampered was a new voyage for the women, and for me it was a treat to indulge them. The bathroom floors would have water splashed all over during prayer time (salat), as it was customary to wash prior to a Muslim's intention to pray (*niyya*).

In our older hospital, in order to get fresh air, patients would jam the outside doors open, letting flies in. Because there were complaints of headaches, nurses had to remind our patients that it was unhealthy to spray Raid around their faces to keep the bugs away.

Visiting time, when men were present, drastically transformed our unit. Women returned to their rooms and covered themselves with their abayas and head coverings to keep men from seeing them.

Life was easier in the hospital. Our female patients didn't want to go home when it was time to be discharged. Living in the desert was hard work for Bedouin women. The nurses had so much fun with them; it was like a girls' social club. I discovered that, regardless of a person's language, there was a common nonverbal communication through gestures, facial expressions, and tone of voice that could be understood around the world.

A male doctor I worked with took care of one our patients, Miriam, who came in with a compound fracture of her arm. Miriam was a Bedouin from the desert, with a tattoo of lines in bluish-black under her lip and plainly dressed. Being out of the desert was very unfamiliar and a difficult adjustment for her. She didn't like sleeping in a bed nor sitting in chairs, preferring to lie on the floor instead. It was difficult to get a clear answer from her of how she fractured her arm. Had she fallen, or was it an abusive encounter? After weeks of being in the hospital to let her bones repair—difficult to do living in the desert—it was time for an X-ray before removing her cast, so I escorted her to radiology. Upon looking at the X-ray of her arm, I was shocked to see that it had not set properly and hadn't healed as it should have. When the patient accidentally spotted her X-ray on the screen as we passed by, she was surprisingly aware that it was still broken. She became hysterical and started yelling about the outcome. The radiology technician explained that she was upset with our "modern" medicine. She said she should have seen their traditional healers, who were common practice in Saudi Arabia. Often, patients would have scars on their bodies from burns made by healers. I reported my concern to her physician, showing him the X-ray. I was taken aback when he said, "It is fine, and it really does not matter. She lives in the desert, anyway. She can go home now."

My code of ethics as a nurse stabbed me in my heart. Could this be how these hospitals operated in this foreign country? Did Western doctors come over to make excellent money, then go home, regardless of the outcomes? I went to my head nurse, a Canadian Filipino, who consoled me, telling me most doctors were not like this. She said it would be my decision as to whether I felt I would be able to work in such disreputable situations. Still, I really did not want to go home, as I had just arrived. With time, I found this type of practice to be atypical and health care was generally excellent in our hospital. The public hospitals lacked the medical supplies and often used third-world health-care practices and staff. The outcomes were often monstrous because of this.

On our military base, an older hospital housed handicapped and mentally challenged children and adults. It was a sad unit to work on, not just because of the type of patients but also because of the ethics surrounding why the patients may have been there. Some patients had physical disabilities or severe deformities, and others mental challenges. The children who were in this facility could have been from interfamily marriages, cousins who married cousins, or incest.

Some of the patients in this unit were left and forgotten. Girls were abandoned just because they were girls. It was said that before medicine was available family members would take children who had abnormalities out in the desert to die. Some would even do so just because the infant was a girl. There were now laws to prevent this. I was happy to not work on this unit very long. It tugged at my heart and my soul, and I had to remind myself that the concept of modern health care was quite new for this country.

When the new hospital was completed and opened, I was assigned to the male surgical floor, where work was easier. Men in the military were more fluent in English, were often educated, and required less care. Older male members of the military families were quite the opposite: no English, no education, and very unfamiliar with their environment (e.g., beds, chairs, toilets, etc.). I enjoyed talking to the patients and learning more about their lives. Male and female staff worked together on this unit.

One of our patients, Mohammed, a thirteen-year-old boy dying from cancer, had a challenging time with his treatment. Our unit fell in love with him. The country was quite obsessed with drug abuse and had strict rules because of this. When this boy used up his prescribed doses of narcotic pain medication, he would have to go without; a boy who was dying would have to suffer needlessly. As nurses, we successfully rallied to get this changed.

Meeting My Prince

The front door opened. A dark, handsome man entered the apartment.

May and I lived in the same housing compound and worked together in Tabuk. She and her boyfriend John were both intensive care unit (ICU) nurses from New Zealand. He worked in the military hospital in Jeddah with a friend they wanted me to meet, so we planned a trip to Jeddah one weekend in October.

John had purchased his own car. He surprised me when he picked us up at the airport wearing shorts, which seemed unusually casual, perhaps inappropriate. Jeddah was not the quiet city I had observed upon my arrival in Saudi Arabia a few months earlier. Quite the opposite: it had become a thriving metropolis with heavy traffic and endlessly honking horns and seldom-honored stop signs and lights. I had not previously noticed the numerous fast-food chains, like McDonald's and Kentucky Fried Chicken, decorating many corners of the city.

We were invited to stay at John's friend Abdul's apartment, though we were not really "allowed" to stay there. For that matter, a couple could not stay in a hotel together unless they were married. Through his work at the hospital, Abdul was assigned an apartment in the "married" apartment building, even though he was not married. It gave him and others who might use his apartment more freedom to come and go without being watched. The hospital leased apartment buildings for their employees, and this unsecured apartment building had four floors with twenty two-bedroom apartments on each floor. It was quite drab, with a plain brick front and neutral interior. Most apartments were completely furnished by the hospital, including dishes, pots, and pans. Abdul's décor was anything but fancy. He was still getting on his feet after his recent return to Saudi Arabia from the States.

Because his apartment was on the ground floor, the front curtains were kept closed so that no one could glance in. This was a bit difficult for me, as I liked natural light. A lightbulb was on, and little light filtered through the thin beige curtains.

The front door opened, and a dark, handsome man in his soccer uniform entered the apartment. *What a great smile and very good-looking man*, I thought to myself. Noticing his muscular legs, I was somewhat embarrassed to be checking him out. He confidently walked over and offered his right hand to me, while he cautiously put his other hand gently on my shoulder as a friendly gesture. "Hi, I'm Abdul, the man whose apartment you are in," he said, with a chuckle in his voice and that adorable smile again. This was the man my friends had wanted me to meet.

Abdul had recently returned from living seven years in Washington State. He had graduated from college with a degree in health care. Our governments had reciprocal contracts that allowed many Saudi men, and some women, to study at various universities throughout the United States, as their universities were not yet up to par for higher education. Abdul's first job upon his return was as an intern in hospital administration, where he rotated through a variety of departments for a few months to learn and train.

Abdul welcomed us. "Make yourselves at home while I go shower." We laughed since we had already made ourselves at home, sharing a bottle of red wine. Soon Abdul joined us in blue jeans and a T-shirt, casual attire he was familiar with and comfortable wearing. He was five feet ten with short, curly dark-brown hair and brown eyes, and was clean-shaven. He was fit, with a petite, small frame in contrast to my inherited five-foot-six larger-framed German body. I had short dishwater-blonde hair that was soft and fluffy, and very blue eyes that often attracted a lot of attention because they were not a common sight in a country of brown-eyed people.

The four of us had an astonishing evening together, talking and laughing. Abdul baked a chicken-and-rice dish (biryani) with cardamom and allspice that was superb. May and I made a green salad that was to die for and paired it with tasty homemade white wine (although it didn't compare to a good white from anywhere else). I love a man who can cook, and Abdul loved to cook, which was rare for a Saudi man. He told us he'd learned from his mother before he went to the States at seventeen.

Over this fantastic weekend the four of us listened to music, watched videos, went out to eat, and drove to the sea. Westernized music was not on the radio yet, but cassette tapes were easy to buy and quite inexpensive. Counterfeit tapes were recorded and sold. Videos, VHS or Betamax, were easily available and could be checked out from the hospital, or rented or bought from video shops, sometimes censored and other times not. At times, while watching a counterfeit video of a movie that had been recorded in a theater out of country, we would actually hear people laughing on the video, and sometimes a person's head would appear when he stood up in front of the camera recording it.

After that weekend, Abdul and I decided to keep in touch and see each other again. We genuinely enjoyed each other's company. He called me regularly at home or at work, a little more often than I had anticipated. We talked and laughed for hours, getting to know more about each other's family, religious beliefs, and lifestyle.

It seemed there was a certain status in having a Western girlfriend. Abdul was familiar with having Western girlfriends, as was true for some Saudi men when they lived in the States. There were American women (and other nationalities) who dated and married their Saudi boyfriends and then followed them back to live in Saudi Arabia, only to find they were already married! Often, American or Western women who were married to Saudis or other Arabs socialized together, bonded by their shared backgrounds.

As I discovered, courtship in Saudi wasn't all that different than it was back home. Young teenage Saudi girls and boys, until the boys could drive, would have their drivers drop them off at the mall. What did the young boys and girls do? What we did growing up: flirt with the opposite sex and pass notes to each other without getting caught.

Some Western women met younger princes and partied with them, not necessarily interested in getting married. These relationships could go on for years, as they enjoyed the fruits of the country. People found ways to connect when they wanted to, regardless of religion, cultural background, or ethnicity, and many traveled around the world to do so.

Abdul, like me, enjoyed traveling. He was easy to talk with. We both wanted similar things in life. Our beliefs in God or a higher power were similar, and we both felt there was not only one way to believe. We both wanted to marry and have two or three children. Upon Abdul's return from the States, he was expected to learn how to be on his own, to become independent. He was not in a hurry to marry.

Abdul did not believe it was necessary for a woman to cover herself. His family had traveled to the United States and went to Egypt in the summers. His two older brothers had graduated from universities in the US, and one younger brother was in the state of Washington for college. His three other younger brothers and one sister learned English in school. His father learned English in the States while in the military.

Abdul and I wanted to spend more time together, not just talk on the phone until the early hours of the morning. The logistics wouldn't be easy, but we would learn to manage it. The roads and highways in Saudi Arabia were not ready for regular long-distance travel, however. Cars were flown from one city to the next or transported on large trucks if needed at one's destination, an odd concept. There were rental cars available, but the younger boys liked to show off their fancy BMWs or Mercedes, acquired from the nascent oil wealth in this once-forgotten nomadic country. The luxuries of a modern world were anachronistic to the religious values of the kingdom.

Jeddah became our preferred city. It was a beautiful city on the sea, and we had his place to stay at. As a nurse, my schedule allowed more days off in a row than Abdul's, but he had the weekends off (Thursdays and Fridays in Saudi Arabia), even if he was often on call by pager for the hospital as backup administrator. There were more things to do in Jeddah than in Tabuk, and with fewer restrictions. This gave us more freedom to be together, though that did not mean we were not conscious and on alert.

Abdul would drive us to the seaside on the western coast to get away from the scorching heat. A cool breeze would caress our bodies, far enough out in the desert that no one bothered us. The hospital also had its own beach compound, which we frequented. On extremely hot days, the salty sea beckoned women in their abayas. The cool, refreshing water massaged their covered bodies. We would swim, dive, and picnic while we caught up with friends, and then later gathered for a shared meal out or a barbecue at someone's home.

There were beautiful outdoor venues for evenings together in Jeddah. At the sea we sat on raised, covered wooden platforms padded with deep green brocade cushions to smoke hookahs and sip on hot, sugary tea or freshly squeezed juice. A cool wind often joined us as the sea performed a romantic dance in the background. The curtains swayed in the breeze and modestly wrapped us as we snuggled, sneaking a kiss or two.

Restaurants were in abundance in Jeddah, featuring a variety of ethnic cuisines. Major hotels put on delightfully fancy buffets on the weekends. Roadside shops dotted the city streets and sold falafel, hummus, and shawarma (a pita-bread sandwich, like a gyro, with lamb or chicken) that were mouthwateringly delicious and inexpensive. Juice shops frequently decorated the streets. Colorful fruits, such as mangoes and papayas, were delicately displayed in wire baskets or tastefully stacked by shape and color on a tiered stand, artistically presenting an abundant selection.

The culture frowned upon men and women showing signs of affection in public, even holding hands, but it seemed only natural for us to hug at the airport when going back and forth. Trying to be inconspicuous, we would sneak a quick hug or two. In restaurants, we would be seated in the family or the couples section, though this was not within the country's guidelines, but no one seemed concerned. Single or unaccompanied married women had their own section in the restaurants.

The airports had separate waiting areas for women unless they were traveling with a man. Women often preferred the female waiting area because it was more private, and some felt that they could let their guard down and uncover a bit. At this time in history, as was not always so, Saudi women were not to travel unaccompanied by a man, a *mahram* or *walī*. This could be her husband, father, uncle, or son, but not a boyfriend or fiancé. My comfort level was dependent on where I waited at the airports I traveled, always with an abaya, not always worn.

I was so grateful to have met such a wonderful teacher, understanding friend, and lover to share my time with in this far-off country. Abdul was unlike most men I had dated, and he did not display the chauvinistic attitudes that were typical in Saudi Arabia. He helped fill my spare time, and it flew by. How could a woman not like a romantic man who brought her flowers and chocolate? I still chuckle when I see a package of Hershey's Kisses; Abdul liked to bring me the chocolate "pisses," as he always called them. He continued to increase his knowledge of the English language and his vocabulary, but there was the occasional amusing and endearing slip.

Early in our relationship, he did something extraordinarily sentimental: he bought us beautiful matching wristwatches with nice gray leather bands, gold around the glass, and our names sweetly engraved on the back. Until then I had never owned a watch that cost over fifty dollars. These watches were very expensive. I melted, thinking about his thoughtfulness and generosity.

Being privileged in comparison to my meager upbringing, Abdul liked to spend money freely. He didn't have a real concept of money, as it had always been provided to him—unlike me. Now he had to work for it, and that didn't seem to bother him. He took pride in his job. I had little extra money when I was raised. I worked and paid for all my advanced education; there was no money for that in my family. We wore hand-me-down clothing from girls from our church for most of our lives; and by the time I got them, my two older sisters had already worn them. I learned while growing up that it was necessary to earn money if I wanted anything extra in my life.

To have money to spend, I started to babysit at age ten. The average pay was ten, twenty-five, or fifty cents an hour, dependent on the number of kids and the families I babysat for. There was no money for an allowance in our home, and I don't think we even knew the meaning of the word. We shoveled snow or raked leaves before and after school. My older sister cleaned our neighbor's home. I worked at Kmart throughout high school and saved enough money to buy my own car. When I graduated from high school, I chose to move out from my parents' home, as I was not willing to pay rent of forty dollars a month to live at home and still have to abide by my mother's silly rules. I got my own apartment for sixty dollars a month and the freedom I craved. I continued to pay my way through life.

Abdul was raised the opposite. He was given everything. He never needed to learn how to manage money. This was a new experience in his life, to work and earn his own money at twenty-seven years old.

The nature of the culture in Saudi Arabia made women more dependent, and Abdul seemed to understand this concept. He shared that his mother had her own driver to take her wherever she wanted to go. Abdul enjoyed putting me first in his life, and he had extra time to do so. I didn't get that type of attention growing up, and I loved it. Abdul showed me I was important to him and was always helpful. He understood what it was like to be in a strange new country. Speaking English and Arabic, and being Saudi, he knew how his country operated.

Not one to pay much attention to age, Abdul was mature, even though he was five years younger than my "young" thirty-three years. I robbed him from the cradle, but we shared many things in common. Neither of us had been married, we had no children, and we didn't own a home. We were college educated with bachelor's degrees, and we both enjoyed traveling.

Abdul and I had been seeing each other regularly for a few months when we learned that May and John had planned a February wedding in Cyprus. We were asked to join them and excitedly accepted their request. The idea of time out of Saudi Arabia together put a smile in our romance. We would have the freedom to be who we were without constraints.

We were granted the time off work that we requested. I applied for visas to get out of and back into the country and needed them stamped on my passport. I had to return my work visa, my *iqama*, in exchange for my passport from the company's safekeeping. Upon originally arriving in Saudi Arabia and receiving our official work permits, my coworkers and I had relinquished our passports to our sponsor, which was a common practice. Abdul and I purchased our tickets to Cyprus and arranged a place to stay the first few days. We were ready for time out of the Kingdom together and to share in the marriage of our friends.

We were lighthearted as we impatiently waited for our vacation to Cyprus. At the last minute, May and John's wedding was postponed. John was ill and hospitalized. He was unable to fly. Our friends later did get married, but not in Cyprus. Even so, Abdul and I decided we would go to Cyprus as planned for our two-week vacation. Sometimes you do not realize how restrictive life is in Saudi Arabia until you leave.

Vacation

Love was in the air.
With no mutaween to be concerned with, our time together was
unrestrained.

Cyprus, a very small country surrounded by the beautiful Mediterranean Sea, northwest of Jeddah, was cold in February. Coming from Saudi Arabia's winter, which was in the seventies during the day and cooler at night, I was unaccustomed to the cold and rain that met us in Cyprus. I was frozen to the bone. I had not thought it through; Cyprus does have a winter. Did I think love would keep me warm?

We rented a car and both learned to drive on the "wrong" side of the street. We toured the country, almost from corner to corner of the small, quaint island, each corner with its own assortment of charms.

Our fondness for each other continued to grow. Love was in the air. With no mutaween to be concerned with, our time together was unrestrained in our chilly, damp hotel room. We slept late, wrapped in each other's arms, not wanting to get out of the small, cozy, warm bed we shared. There was a chill in our room, but not in our hearts.

The weather was equally cold and damp on the coast, but our love and affection continued to keep us warm. We wrapped up together in our beach towels at the sea as the nearly unbearable wind blew through us. We laughed until we cried; we were having such a fantastic time, enjoying our freedom. We prayed for warmer weather or another blanket, but with neither appearing, we walked briskly back to our car holding hands, stopping for a kiss or two. We vowed to come again when the sun would caress our bodies and the gentle, warm breeze would play symphonies.

Inclined to try a winter activity, we had a different image of the ski resort we were looking for as we stumbled upon Mt. Olympus, at an elevation around six thousand feet. The small, plain sign read Ski Resort. It was attached to a tiny tin building with faded, blotchy green paint. The chairlift did not appear sturdy to us, though it was still operational. We played in the snow and had snowball fights. We were crazy in love, creating snow angels in the powder. Afterward, not having the proper winter clothing, we were grateful to have a heater in the car to warm our cold bodies as we snuggled together.

We went to the "Green Line," a buffer zone controlled by the United Nations for many years dividing northern Cyprus and recognized by both Greece and Turkey. We were not allowed into the Turkish section. There were old sandbags piled on top of each other, opened by the weather and years of use, that divided the area. These dilapidated piles, along with the adjacent rundown buildings and homes, created a strange, eerie feeling.

In the larger coastal cities of Limassol and Larnaca, arm in arm we danced the night away. Wearing all the clothes we'd brought to keep warm, we seemingly floated on the beach, a light breeze teasing our cheeks as we kissed.

We casually drove along the winding country roads and mountainsides, occasionally moving over for cows, sheep, or even a tiny horse-drawn cart. The local folks were always smiling. Short, stocky, older women with rosy cheeks walked in their long, dark wool skirts and light-colored blouses, black scarves pulled back and tied behind their heads. The colorful embroidered shawls around their shoulders were tied together in a knot at their chests. Men walked with their black top hats propped on their heads; wore loose-fitting, long wool pants and big boots; and carried walking sticks. Depending on our location, the men might have had a smoke in their mouth or a beer in their hand, but mostly sat around bullshitting and laughing on the benches in the small towns.

There were many courtyard restaurants, with hanging baskets of dried-up flowers, dormant for winter. Women took pride in their charming garden areas and gave us friendly, intimate service. We were the only customers during this cold winter season.

We braved the beautiful, calm water of different hues of blue and turquoise, but it was too cold for comfort. We strolled through many parks in hibernation, waiting for warmer weather to show their beauty. Our days were heavenly, and we acted like foolish school children, wanting to forget how different our lives would be in just a short while.

Abdul and I had so much fun as we explored the small island of Cyprus. We were not prepared to return to the restrictions of Saudi Arabia and being separated again. We were in our own thoughts as we flew back to Jeddah together. How quickly the freedom to express our affection was taken away when we said our goodbyes at the airport! Unfortunately, I was obliged to continue on to Tabuk to work the next day. How I desired to spend another night in Jeddah in the arms of the man who was capturing my heart.

Abdul and I weren't able to get together for a long stretch after we returned from Cyprus, as my work schedule didn't offer me enough time off to get to Jeddah after my vacation. We missed each other, not wanting to say goodbye when we talked. We tried to hold each other through our words of endearment, especially heartfelt after we had shared two nonstop weeks together.

During this time of absence, I started to feel sick, not quite right. I didn't seem to have the energy to play tennis or get together with friends. I equated it to a lack of sleep while on vacation and missing my new love. It was not until a month after returning from vacation that I realized I was pregnant. How could this be? I got out my calendar to check the dates, and they did not add up correctly. I had just finished my period while in Cyprus, so I shouldn't have ovulated yet.

Not prepared for the trauma and disillusionment of being pregnant in Saudi Arabia, or even in the States, with this new man in my life, I doubted it was possible. I was angry with myself for being irresponsible. It was not my intent to get pregnant, though I knew I wanted children, just not at this time of my life. I was still getting to know this man. I was shocked, single, and pregnant in Saudi Arabia, where it was illegal, even if you were not Saudi. Hypothetically, I could be arrested if the "wrong" person knew I was pregnant. The mutaween could arrest me and put me in jail. I'd heard jails in Saudi were horrible—dirty, crowded, no English spoken . . . I knew of Americans who'd spent a few nights in jail. If you were lucky, once your embassy knew you were in jail, they would try to intervene to get you deported as soon as possible. I worked with a young Saudi man who said his father was "a *mutawa*, but a nice one, the way they are supposed to be," whatever that meant. I was unaware of any nice mutaween.

I trusted a couple of my closer girlfriends in Tabuk to keep this secret of mine. I was restless, not knowing what to do; my bad dream would not go away. I prayed that my period would arrive soon and checked frequently for signs that it had started. It did not happen. I had butterflies in my stomach about what others might say when they knew I had been dating a Saudi. Overall, it was taboo. It was not really accepted by many expats, and a couple of my friends had already tried to talk me out of dating Abdul. I confided in an American female doctor friend, who, behind closed doors, confirmed my condition. I rationalized that my contract was ending in a few months; I could finish and leave. Once out of the Kingdom, my thinking would be clearer, more normal. Nothing was normal in KSA. Weird things happened to the psyche when in this absurd country. It was like being on an alien planet.

My pregnancy would need to be hidden for three months. An abortion was not an option for me, and definitely not in Saudi Arabia. I would have this baby, and I could do it alone. I was sad and uneasy that these were the circumstances. I should have been happy to be having a baby. My head was whirling and troubled, my heart heavy, wondering whether to even tell Abdul. He was young and could have a different life ahead of him. He was not ready to be a father or get married; we had already talked about this. I could not get my head straight as to what to tell him.

After a week of hiding my secret, Abdul knew something was bothering me. I did not react as before to his frequent calls and tried to distance myself. He was not one to pry. He said, "I love you. When you want to share what is bothering you, I'm here for you." Bluffing or lying was something I was never good at; I wore my heart on my sleeve, as they say. Was I as different and distant with him as he perceived me to be? He kept joking with me that we should get married. I ignored him and thought it was not funny.

I decided that discussing my dilemma with Abdul was not a conversation for the telephone. I would wait until I went to Jeddah in a week. Regrettably, by this time I was experiencing morning, noon, and night sickness from the pregnancy. I felt dismal and had difficulty sleeping because I did not want to believe this was happening to me, and in Saudi Arabia.

My flight to Jeddah in the late afternoon was not as much fun as it usually was. I felt distant, nervous, and timid about telling Abdul my shocking news and about what he might say. I would have to orchestrate the right time to let this man I cared so much about know what was happening and why I was acting strangely toward him.

Only one bathroom in his apartment and my being sick made it difficult to hide my pregnancy. It was time to let Abdul know "we" were pregnant. I asked him to wait for me in the living room as I cleaned up. I came out of the bathroom with a sheepish smile on my face; still, I wondered how I would let him know. He started to laugh at my being so ill at ease, at the clumsy way I behaved, as it was so not me. It helped to lighten the suspenseful moment.

We had not seen each other for weeks, since returning from our fantastic trip to Cyprus. I sat down next to my sweet, gentle Abdul and put my arms around him so I did not have to look him in the eye. I felt comforted, feeling his presence again and the love we shared. My tongue flirted ever so gently with his ear as I whispered, "I'm pregnant."

He moved away from me so he could look me in the eye, which was difficult for me to do; I was ashamed. I knew this was not what we wanted at this time in our lives. I started to cry and shared that I was not sure if I wanted him to know I was pregnant. He embraced me with his strong, muscular arms as I sobbed, letting go of all my pent-up emotions from the past month. He kissed my neck, my face, and my lips, and softly said, "Honey, I love you, and I want to marry the woman who is going to be the mother of our child."

After hiding my pregnancy for so long, his acceptance calmed my heart and consoled my edgy spirit, which had been racked with unknowns. To get married because I was pregnant did not sit right, but I would cross that bridge another day.

As the sun set, I went to shower. Abdul got us chocolate ice cream. I prayed I would not get sick again. We lay in bed and felt the warmth of our bodies as we ate ice cream and talked about the possible names for our child. We gently made love and fell asleep in each other's arms. I felt at peace and loved.

I slept in the next morning. I had worked so much and was so emotionally stressed and drained. Abdul needed to work while I was in Jeddah. This was our routine. He arrived home from work that evening with food from my favorite Lebanese restaurant. As I opened the box of warm Arabic bread, my heart skipped a beat when I saw a tiny, colorful, hard plastic box from a jewelry store.

Of course Abdul acted surprised and prompted me to pick it up. I touched it gingerly, as if it were on fire. My anxiety and excitement about what lay ahead were suspended as he opened the box and presented me with a beautiful, sparkling, two-diamond gold ring. Ever so lovingly, Abdul got down on one knee—he must have seen this in the movies—and proposed to me. "Leah, you have brought sunshine and inspiration into my life. I know we have only known each other for a few months, but I love you and want you to be my wife." It took no time for me to accept his proposal. My heart beamed with love. I knew my prince had come.

As the days rolled by, my uniforms got tighter. I was afraid that if someone looked closely, they would see my little belly forming. Being so nauseous, I did not gain a lot of weight, which helped keep my disguise. With morning, noon, and night sickness, I worked hard to conceal my nausea from my coworkers. They questioned why I would walk, almost run, to the farthest bathroom on the unit, where I could not be heard. My diet consisted of Perrier water, mashed potatoes, fresh juice, and chocolate.

When I let May know I was pregnant, she cheerfully informed me she was pregnant, too. We were both excited about being pregnant at the same time. I confided in two of my close girlfriends in the United States. The first questions out of their mouths were, "Are you sure you are doing the right thing? Pay attention to what you are doing here. Is this really what you want to do with your life?" They were not talking about my having a baby. They were questioning me about marrying a Saudi who was raised so differently from the way I was.

Abdul and I started to plan the next chapter of our lives. He wanted to get his master's degree back in the States. It had been a more traumatic transition back into Saudi than he'd thought it would be. My work contract could be over soon if I added my remaining days of vacation. My mother planned to meet me in Egypt on her way to a tour of the Holy Lands. Mom and I would travel for ten days; my future husband would meet us in Cairo, the city of his birth.

Abdul was born and had lived in Egypt for a few years while his father worked in Cairo. He was raised in Riyadh, where his family now lived. Abdul needed to take care of some loose ends with his job and his life. He would leave ten days after me and meet my mother and me in Egypt, *inshallah*.

He was excited to be returning to the US. We both had difficulty keeping our secret. I had started to show if I wore my usual clothes. Abdul confided in one of his brothers who had once lived in Texas. His brother was happy for us and wished us well, as did his best friend. We started to plan our wedding and our exit from the KSA to the US. We both wanted to go back to the States to start our family together.

The idea of meeting Abdul's family excited me. I had heard so much about them. I asked him when I was going to meet them. Abdul looked at me with a bewildered look. I knew they visited Jeddah often. In fact, they had an apartment there. His softly spoken response was, "That will not be possible."

My heart sank as many questions swirled rapidly in my head. I did not know what to say. Why would he not want me to meet his parents? I thought he loved me. Was he ashamed of me? Would they not want him to marry me? Was there more about him and his family that he had not shared? We had planned our lives together, and a child was part of this equation. I sat in silence; my sadness overwhelmed me. I suddenly felt so alone, stranded on an island with no one to turn to. I realized it was not the right time to push with this request. I withdrew into my loneliness until I could better understand. Perhaps he would change his mind.

Married in Cyprus, and Our Honeymoon

In Jeddah, we had been two young people in love, hanging out and having a good time, with few worries in our fairy-tale world. We both started to secretly wonder what the hell we had done.

Our checklist was prepared for leaving Saudi Arabia. As planned, I would depart in a week and Abdul would follow ten days later. Meeting my future husband's large Arab family was on my list of what I wanted to do before we got married, but this was not going to happen. I had heard so much about them, and if they were anything like Abdul, how could I go wrong? We were both from large families. Abdul had six brothers and one sister, the youngest. He was number three in the birth order, same as me out of seven children in my family. When I had asked Abdul about meeting his family, he did not seem to ponder the question; his mind was already made up. Was there so much more to the picture, underlying mysteries I was not privy to? Maybe this should have been my first clue of what lay ahead.

My year-long contract officially ended in September, but I was able to take vacation time, which started at the end June. The flexibility of being a nurse and being able to manipulate my schedule without needing to use vacation time was beneficial. A year had passed so quickly. My world spun around me like a kaleidoscope. My round belly grew before me, and I was still sick three months in. Abdul and I considered getting married and returning to Jeddah to live until our child was due, saving a few more dollars, then returning to the States where Abdul could begin his master's program, but we chose to leave right away. In reality, we were both ready to return to the openness of the US. Had I not gotten pregnant, I would have asked to transfer to the hospital in Jeddah where Abdul worked. It was bittersweet to prepare to leave; but destiny, whether chance or choice, had other plans for me.

It was customary for coworkers and friends to host going-away, or ma'a s-salāma, parties, and my coworkers threw a *ma'a s-salāma* party for me in our break room at the hospital between the day and evening shifts so that more staff could attend.

The general practice when someone left the country was to take up a collection of riyals, the Saudi currency, to buy a gift of gold. In Saudi Arabia, this was quite an endeavor, as there was so much gold to choose from. Shop after shop, wall after wall, in cabinets and hanging in clusters from the ceilings—everywhere you looked there was the luster and sparkle of gold, shining with blinding brightness and brilliancy, so surreal and vivid beyond belief. This was the gold souk.

The going-away present I received was a lovely eighteen-karat gold chain with an attractive rectangular gold pendant that had a small heart-shaped opening in the corner. It was so beautiful, intricate, and thoughtfully selected, a perfect gift for me.

For Saudi and other Muslim women, wearing gold was a customary and predictable adornment, symbolic of wealth, status, and beauty. The only gold sold in Saudi Arabia was eighteen karat up to twenty-four karat. The price we paid was market driven, higher or lower day by day.

In Saudi Arabia and in many other countries in the region, the amount of gold received was symbolic of the worth of the bride. As a gift from her husband or her husband's family, it was often equated to love. On their wedding day, brides would often wear elaborate gold jewelry covering their head, face, hands, arms, and even their chest. Babies also received gold as their first gifts.

Before coming to Saudi Arabia, I had not been interested in gold jewelry, nor did I have the money to be interested. However, gold was the "in" thing to buy in the KSA, as the prices were remarkably inexpensive and the quality was superior. Many people working in Saudi Arabia also liked precious stones. They could buy rubies, sapphires, and emeralds, whatever quality, size, or shape they wanted. It was like a show-and-tell after payday, seeing the gold or other jewelry people had bought with their paychecks.

Touched by the sweet and beautiful parting gift and grateful for my time with my colleagues and the memories we'd created together, I said goodbye to my friends. It had been an incredibly eye-opening and life-changing year.

Abdul's visa to the States was confirmed, and tickets to the US were purchased. In June of '84, I departed from Saudi Arabia and flew into Cairo, Egypt, one of the largest, craziest, most crowded, and dirtiest airports in the world, where I planned to meet my mother. The restrictive nature of Saudi Arabia could be quite taxing on most expats, and add to that being single and concealing a pregnancy now going into the fourth month.

I met a nice gentleman at the airport who worked as a travel agent. He helped me get through customs and immigration, later helping my mother speed through all the paperwork when she arrived, taking the stress out of the whole ordeal.

Having required the basic Arabic communication skills was a valuable asset as I traveled through Egypt. I felt most people appreciated an honest attempt to speak their language, and I enjoyed practicing my skills, especially in Cairo.

Cairo was a huge, ancient, dirty, polluted city with constant traffic and horn honking. The temperature was hot and stifling in the summer. It was an odd time of the year to travel, with this excruciating weather, but we survived. We rested during the hottest hours of the day. We hailed a rundown taxi with faded, worn-out seats and no air-conditioning to take us to our hotel, located fairly close to the airport. I knew my mother would be jet-lagged from flying from Kansas, across one continent into another. We settled into the comfortable but not fancy air-conditioned hotel room that Abdul had booked, and discussed dinner options. Did we want American food or local food? There were shawarma sandwiches; kebabs of lamb, chicken, or beef; falafel; hummus; baba ghanoush; cheeses; and pita-like bread, *aish baladi*, fresh out of wood-burning ovens.

The numerous travel guides I collected had captivating photos and stimulating information about sights that could take days to see. My mom was now fifty-one years young and not intimidated by travel, and I got reacquainted with what was happening in her life. I asked how my dad and family were doing, but did not go into the details of my own life. I saved that for an unmarked new day after a refreshing night of sleep in a hot, muggy, overcrowded, noisy city.

It took little time for my mom to realize I was pregnant; my being sick was her first clue. I had started my second trimester. My loose-fitting clothes, which I had become accustomed to in Saudi Arabia, hid the few pounds I had gained and gave me extra room to grow—the looser the better. I was energized about this tiny, precious being growing inside me. No need to hide my secret any more.

My mom is a matter-of-fact woman, not one to talk about feelings and emotions. My mother's German father was strict and overpowering. Mom was determined to block out my grandpa's stern, hurtful personality that she saw bestowed on her brothers. Because of this, I often felt my mom's inability to "feel" significantly, and it influenced my life and our relationship. She had blocked emotions for so long that she was unable to be empathetic. We talked about my being pregnant, what my plans were, and when the baby was due. She wished me well; she wished *us* well. That was about it. No jumping up and down with excitement. No hugs and kisses. My child would be her eighth grandchild. This is not to imply she would not enjoy or show love to her future kin. Can I say her reactions were hurtful? Naturally, they were. Did I expect anything else? No, not really. This was what my life was like: "Don't dwell on things," and, "Don't cry over spilled milk." You just moved on. Because of this, my mother was not the person I sought out for emotional (or even financial) support throughout my young-adult life. I had found solace with my California "family," people who knew how to feel and how to comfort and support me. "I love you" were not words I knew growing up.

Sharing a love of travel with my mom was a commonality we enjoyed; feelings did not need to be a part of it. We had a fantastic time as we embarked on another journey, traveling together. My dad, mom, and I had traveled in Europe for a couple of weeks in 1980. On that trip, I learned more about my mother than I had ever known.

My mother had had a daunting task to raise seven children. My father's eighth-grade education provided only a minimum-wage income, requiring a second or third job to make ends meet. I felt I was just a number, one of the seven. Mom had her hands full. It was not my purpose to be different.

My birth cycle was the start of a new seven-year generational cycle. Out with tradition and in with women's lib. Perhaps I was born under a different moon sign or with Venus rising. Maybe that was why I was different. I had not followed the traditional path, as my two older sisters had, getting married shortly out of high school and having children. Now my younger siblings were also getting married and having children. I was born to participate in the late sixties' and seventies' values that society doubted and explored. Politics were questioned. The Vietnam War raged on, killing our friends and relatives. Demonstrations exploded everywhere. *Stop the war. End the draft. Stop nuclear power plants. Protest homosexuality . . .* Communes developed. I have friends who still live on the original communes in California.

My college art history class studied the Egyptian pyramids, the Great Sphinx, and most of the ancient tombs scattered throughout Egypt. I had dreamt of the day I might be able to walk on the same land, and now I was seeing it in person with my mom. It was more grandiose and moving than I had imagined. I pondered what life was like during this time in history. In Aswan, after we visited the temples and tombs of Ramses the Great and Nefertiti in Abu Simbel, we enjoyed a relaxing traditional Egyptian sailboat ride on a felucca that drifted with the wind on the calm Nile River, which flows south to north, as the sun vividly set, painting its golden hues along our ancient path. We envisioned Cleopatra or Nefertiti living in the world we witnessed with our own senses. It was an unforgettable memory etched in our minds, and it took our breath away.

The oldest of the Seven Wonders of the Ancient World, the Great Pyramids of Giza boldly stood before us. The three pyramids took twenty years to build, with the oldest built in 2550 BC and the largest 482 feet tall. We saw the Great Sphinx, with the body of a lion and the head of a pharaoh, magnificently carved from a single piece of limestone. It guards the pyramid tombs of Giza. Near Luxor, we walked among the many ancient tombs and temples, including the Karnak Temple and Tutankhamen, which were built for multiple pharaohs from the 16th to 11th centuries, BC, and were scattered throughout the

Valley of the Kings. What a spectacular architectural work of pillars, walkways, hidden gates, and colorfully painted walls of petroglyphs and hieroglyphs, remarkably preserved. Because of the heat, only a few people frequented the sights at that time of year, which gave us all the time we wanted to marvel at these amazing antiquities. Numerous mind-boggling museums and ornate churches were also part of our journey through time while in Egypt.

I regularly called Abdul to see how he was doing, wondering if he missed our baby and me and curious to hear how his plans were moving forward to meet us in a few days. We were eager to see each other and to be together soon. He seemed upbeat and enthusiastic.

After a few days in Egypt, Mom and I flew to Turkey, a more open, colorful, and diverse atmosphere, not as primitive as Egypt. Istanbul, "the City on Seven Hills," was more elevated and cooler. A beautiful city, it was historically known as Constantinople or Byzantium. Its place in history spans many religions and governments. It remains the country's economic, cultural, and historic center. One of the most magnificent buildings in Turkey was the Blue Mosque. It stood so prominently with its magnetic blue color that shined so boldly for all to see. Within the walled city was the Grand Bazaar, one of the largest and oldest covered bazaars in the world. The old city reflected the cultural influences of the different empires that ruled the region. The open-air Hippodrome of the Roman era was for centuries a popular venue, and the Egyptian obelisks remained for us to admire.

Also on our list was Ephesus, a coastal city discovered between 1500 and 1000 BC that was once an influential place of market and spirituality. Ephesus was considered one of the largest and most important centers of the old Mediterranean world. Knowing this region was written about in the Bible was inspirational to us. Mom was sentimental when she explored Ephesus, as it bore witness to the origins of her Christian faith. We were like disciples treading on holy ground that Noah, Jesus, and Mohammed had walked. The spiritual awareness was indescribable and powerful, regardless of one's faith.

Numerous owners of carpet shops coaxed us to share a hot cup of tea, hopeful we would buy a carpet or two. We enjoyed two days of cooler weather at a charming, quiet seaside in Izmir. We observed the beautiful setting sun while we lazily sipped beverages in an open-air courtyard.

Moving on to Greece, I took my mother to places I had traveled to in 1980. The tropical weather appealed to me. We slept on rooftops, listened to traditional Greek music featuring the lyre and lute. We explored the Parthenon and the Acropolis in Athens.

Enjoying the great foods of many cultures was a highlight, as unique culinary tastes flirted with our palates. We tried the exceptional gastronomical delights of Greek foods: baklava, stuffed grape leaves, Greek salads, gyros, moussaka, and skewers of chicken and pork, called souvlaki. We enjoyed the pleasures of sidewalk cafes, visited street vendors, and dined in fancy restaurants, in dark alleyways, and on mountaintops.

Mom and I did so much in ten days, but it was time to return to Cairo to meet up with my fiancé. I was anxious to see him and introduce him to my mother. My mother and I established a different bond after spending this rewarding time together, without the power struggles of my past.

It was the end of June. Abdul had finished his business in Jeddah and joined us in Cairo. It was great to see my handsome man and introduce him to my mother. I was raised to be open to all people, regardless of their ethnicities and their beliefs. My mom liked Abdul and said approvingly, "He is a very charming, likeable guy. He is kind of like your dad." I thought, *Really? What do you see of my dad in him?* I did not see any similarities.

After Abdul and Mom shared a couple of days together, my mother continued her travels to the Holy Land. Mom never discouraged me from getting married. She thought either I was old enough to make my own decision or that this was the right thing to do, since I was pregnant, regardless of Abdul's nationality and religion.

Abdul rented a car, and we traveled west of Cairo to the beach city of Alexandria for two days. As it was once one of the most powerful trade centers in the world, I had envisioned a more magnificent, stunning, and impressive seaside than what was presented.

We flew on to Cyprus to take care of all the paperwork necessary to marry. We wanted to get married right away so we could get an early start on processing the documents we would need for Abdul to obtain a green card and come to the States with me. While we were going to be officially married in Cyprus, a wedding ceremony was being arranged by my two best girlfriends back home, on the gorgeous coast of California in August, upon our return to United States. They designed and mailed out the wedding announcements and invitations with the date and the venue for our celebration.

Generally, weddings in Saudi Arabia were elaborate celebrations that started late in the evening. The bride and groom and their male witnesses came together to sign the official paperwork, then departed to separate rooms to celebrate with members of the same sex. Women, including the bride, arrived all decked out. It reminded me of Cinderella's ball, with long, formal dresses—some more beautiful, colorful, or tasteful than others. All would be adorned in jewelry of gold and other showy jewels, often gaudy to my tastes. Arabian-style dancing was performed among the female guests. Sudanese or Somali women played drums and chanted/sang while making guttural calls and yells. Food was served in abundance, but at a much later point in the night. The women feasted and partied until after midnight. When the new husband was ready to be presented with his new bride, an announcement was made that he would join the women. Promptly, before the groom entered the party, a collective makeover occurred. The women, with the exception of the family of the groom, became black as night by covering with their abayas in an already-darkened room. The newlyweds often sat displayed on large decorated chairs on a stage so they could be admired before they went on their married way.

When a couple in Saudi Arabia want to be together, either by choice or by arrangement, there may be an engagement party during which paperwork is signed, signifying that they are "married," so they can lawfully be together and not be detained. If the couple later choose not to marry, the wedding contract is annulled.

Back in Cypress, on my marriage application it was typed that I was a "spinster." I was not fond of being called a spinster—a label I wasn't accustomed to hearing, let alone seeing written—instead of "single" or "never married." Also, when I was asked for my religion, I preferred leaving it blank, as I could not say I practiced one specific religion over another at that time. Christianity was my religion by birth, but I had been learning about Islam and other religions. I believed in a broader concept of religion/spirituality or God. Abdul got perturbed with me. "Just put down Christian," he said impatiently.

Afterward, we wished we had invited our friends to be witnesses at our wedding. Having strangers who just happened to be in the same room be our witnesses was disheartening. No romantic, dreamy kisses at a flower-decorated altar. No altar, for that matter, nor the traditional "It's my honor to introduce you to Mr. and Mrs. . . . ."

Instead, we hugged and kissed on the ancient, cold stone stairwell as we left the old brick building in Nicosia. The ceremony may have been a disappointment, but we were now happily husband and wife. We had two celebration dinners, one before we married and one after, in two big, beautiful restaurants. We were the only customers in each of them, and we enjoyed being pampered with exceptional, undivided attention. We were presented with an amount of food that could have fed us for days.

The bar we patronized the last time we were in Cyprus was the venue of our wedding party. Everyone in the bar joined in our merriment. In our travels, we met many people who did not seem to care or were unaware of Abdul's nationality. If he didn't have his Saudi clothes on, he looked Italian, his skin paler than many Arabs'.

Getting married in Cyprus was like getting married in Las Vegas: it was fairly easy to do with little fuss. The Saudi government acknowledged marriages performed in Cyprus. In Saudi Arabia, relationships evolved faster because of the need to abide by the stringent rules of separation before being married. Often, a couple married out of convenience if they cared for each other. They could then be together without the risk of getting in trouble or being arrested. The percentage of marriages that lasted between expats and Saudis was low, although some of my closer American friends who met their spouses in Saudi Arabia remain happily married.

Our honeymoon was a lengthy one. In order for me to be eligible for a significant tax break because I worked out of country, I had to be out of the US for 330 days. I used vacation time to leave earlier because of being pregnant, so we took a two-month honeymoon/holiday. I had not considered what my tax deductions would have been for three people. I had a husband and a baby on the way before the tax year was up, which meant, in hindsight, traveling might not have been necessary.

Our hard-earned money dwindled quickly because of our long, extensive vacation. It started to concern me, knowing how much it cost to live in the States and especially in California. Still, I knew how to live on a budget. I learned that early in my life, when I left home at eighteen. Abdul and I each had five thousand dollars when we left Saudi Arabia. To me, it was as if I were a millionaire; it was the most money I'd ever had. And part of my student loans were paid off. Not being a materialistic person, I could live on very little without extra spending. A dollar is a dollar. But Abdul did not know what it was like not to have money at his disposal, as it had come freely to him up until this time. When Abdul attended college, money had been put into his bank account monthly or as needed. The way he boasted about money led me to believe he had easier access to it than he really had. Was it because he was Saudi that I was blinded to his resource pool? We were frugal in where we went and how we spent our money, more at my insistence than his, in the countries we traveled.

Early in our honeymoon, we thought we had food poisoning, though it lasted a few days with high fevers. My being sick from pregnancy had finally subsided. We recovered from our illness, but a disturbing tension started to build in our relationship. The information Abdul shared started to not add up; not all the dots were connecting.

Apparently, only one of his brothers and two of his close friends knew that Abdul was going to America and having a baby. He did not tell his parents or his employer with the government. Now I knew why he didn't want me to meet his parents: he didn't want them to know he was leaving the country. I asked him, "Why did I just now discover you walked out of your job without giving notice?" Abdul was not comfortable when I questioned him about his dealings. He chastised me for overhearing some "mistruths."

To add to the stress Abdul experienced when he left Saudi Arabia, my sister had trouble getting the briefcase he had mailed to her before leaving that held at least twenty expensive watches, including a few Rolexes, along with my recently purchased gold jewelry. We had mailed it because we had not wanted to travel for two months with these valuables. The United States Customs office in Kansas City held his briefcase. Abdul had not thought to send the keys to my sister so customs could perform their inspection prior to her claiming our belongings. Customs had no choice but to hold the briefcase until someone was able to open it for their inspection, but he did not want them to break the lock.

A big warning light flashed before me when Abdul got angry with my family, when in reality this matter was out of their control. He raised his voice and called me names. What was happening? I had never experienced being talked to like this by anyone. It was unusual for him. He had always been so caring, polite, and accommodating. My husband was incensed, and I was unable to calm him.

By now, we both started to secretly wonder what the hell we had done. In Jeddah, we had been two young people in love, hanging out, and having a good time with few worries in our fairy-tale world. In spite of the growing strain, our honeymoon continued; and we made peace after we gave each other time to reflect on our new, mysterious life of unknowns.

On to Delhi, India, to sightsee. We traveled in tut-tuts, which are small, covered carts or rickshaws pedaled by a driver amid the busy, congested traffic. Sacred cows roamed freely, often impeding the traffic in the street, along with cars, motorcycles, bicycles, people, pollution, poverty, and constant horn honking. There were beautiful temples, mosques, and shrines to see as we strolled hand in hand, drinking fresh coconut milk out of coconut shells. We watched the organ grinder with his monkey, and the snake charmer play hypnotic music from a wooden instrument to the coiled cobra that rested in front of him.

Our next destination was Kashmir, in the village of Srinagar, India. We stayed in our own small, rustic houseboat, which was in need of a few repairs. This was a dream of mine; it was extremely romantic. We were in love again, and together, we could surely survive the unknown challenges to our marriage.

Our primitive, century-old houseboat had lights strung up by single cords through its rooms. The inside was indicative of another lifetime, one that was once more colorful and brilliantly decorated but was now dreamily faded, as the Indian tapestries showed their age and wear. We were served three meals a day of deliciously prepared curries and other tastes and flavors of India. Gondolas flowed gently between the pink and white lotus and water lilies along the beautiful Dal Lake. Vendors sold their goods or offered rides. We purchased gorgeous fresh flowers from one boat, exotic fruit from another; whatever we wanted, we could get from the river vendors.

We bought chocolate, in which I had a difficult time not indulging. Abdul's chocolate disappeared, and I was accused of eating it. I joked that the mice ate it. Later we heard mice crawling behind the wall covering of our humble little houseboat at night, and we laughed at actually having caught them in the act. While the mice didn't bother us, we did have one concern about our boat experience: we did not want to know where the contents of our toilet went when it was flushed.

A gondola ride took us to see Kashmir rugs being made on large looms, as talented women and men sat to weave these intricate pieces of art. We bought and shipped three rugs of silk and wool blends in varying sizes, colors, and designs to California to pick up at a later date, as well as papier-mâché ornaments, which were light to carry, for gifts.

Nice and cozy on our houseboat, we were enjoying this magical time together, when a government coup halted travel for a few days. The protest was over an unfair election, and no one seemed too alarmed. Our flights were changed, which was not a problem as we had purchased open-ended tickets, winging it as we traveled.

Our time on the boat was wonderful, but Abdul's shifting and unpredictable moods would return as our journey continued. I started to compare our lives together to a carousel ride: you go up and you go down, for varying moments at a time. I surmised I needed to learn how to adapt to the changing, irregular, lopsided moods of my new husband. An unfamiliar personality I had not witnessed came forward as we traveled. It gave rise to apprehension in me, and I found myself questioning the life decisions I had made.

The city of Agra, India, and the Taj Mahal were our next stops. An absolutely breathtaking white marble mausoleum was built in the 1600s by Shah Jahan for the love of his third wife, who died giving birth to her fourteenth child. The brilliant marble illuminated the colors of its symmetrically arrayed fountains and gardens. The sunset's reflection of the Taj Mahal appeared on the water of the Yamuna River, upon which this enchanting piece of Mughal architecture was built. Sadly, its magnificence and serenity shamefully departed when we explored the surrounding neighborhoods, where slums and poverty appeared.

On to Katmandu, Nepal, where we filed papers at the American embassy for Abdul's entry visa and applied for a green card. We would have to stay there as long as it took to get the paperwork finished. It was a busy, noisy, dirty, big city that was crumbling and in need of a major facelift.

Outside of the hustle and bustle of the city, we stumbled upon an older, delightfully charming white wooden two-story hotel with a balcony. Its quaint rooms surrounded a beautifully lush English flower garden where numerous tables and benches were placed to sit and sip an afternoon cup of tea. Wonderful people from around the world stayed there, and we met a woman named Pauline who lived outside of San Diego, which we planned to call home. She invited us to stay with her until we could find a place to rent when we arrived in the States, a nice option.

Places to eat were plentiful and within walking distance from our hotel. The fresh, sweet papaya smoothies in the morning and hot fruit pies right out of the oven in the afternoon were our favorites. How American.

My belly grew, and I felt good—no further prenatal care needed. Everything was going well for my being close to six months pregnant, a condition that was unnoticeable until I stood up. We enjoyed having tourists around us guess the gender by the way I carried our growing baby and laughing at their predictions.

There was no more news from Saudi Arabia to dishearten us. We enjoyed intimate, secluded lovemaking amid the sweet aroma of jasmine and the colorful assortment of flowers. Birds sang beautiful melodies outside the window of our perfect accommodations. Our carousel was up again.

We took side trips to small villages on local buses while we enjoyed the nuances of cultures that neither of us had experienced. Yes, there were chickens and even goats on the rickety old buses of many colors and washed-out hues. Our luggage was abruptly thrown on top of the already-crowded roofs along with everyone else's; there was no room to keep it with us.

We visited spiritual temples and sacred places. We stayed in a tiny village in hopes of getting a glimpse of Mt. Everest, the tallest mountain in the world. The sun warmed us during our day hikes, but it did not move the fog and clouds that tainted our view. Our tiny, dark-skinned Nepalese hostess told us daily, "Tomorrow will be the day you will see our majestic mountain." Adding to our disillusionment, the compact guestroom in which we stayed was so humid that the bed linen was damp and cold. As it was built into the rocks, it had no heat aside from the warmth of my pregnant body once the sun went down. After four nights, it was time to leave. It seemed that it was not our destiny to see Mt. Everest.

After a three-week wait, we received the paperwork and went on our way to Pakistan. In Pakistan, we took a beautiful tram ride up into the fresh, crisp air of the distant snow-capped mountains of Tilla

Charouni. We shopped at large, old open-air markets and enjoyed evening buffets with varying temperatures of incredible curry dishes that took no time to leave my system once I returned to the hotel room. While we were told that the brown water in our room was "all right" to drink, we chose to drink our own bottled water.

Our next destination was Hong Kong, which was still under British occupancy. On one of our tours in China, I was told there were so many people that there were not enough places to bury their dead. Because of this, after so many years, a body might need to be removed. How morbid it sounded! Whether that would happen depended on one's wealth. In this busy, lively city, Abdul bought me a stunning pair of dazzling half-carat diamond solitaire earrings as a wedding gift, and I bought him lenses for his camera. We ate at a McDonald's with a slightly different menu, including noodles and rice. It seemed there was no place in the world without a McDonald's.

Tokyo was next on our map. In Tokyo, Abdul wanted to get a fancy hotel. He had been incredibly flexible as to where we stayed on our travels for over a month. A fancy hotel was not my desire, however, being that you just slept in them, spending little time to really enjoy the expensive, decadent ambience. This was one area where Abdul and I differed—in where to stay. If we had an extra three hundred dollars to do this, I would have welcomed the treat. Still, this was what he was accustomed to; his family would never have traveled like we did or explored the places we had. Though we both traveled first class when someone else footed the bill, that was never my lifestyle. We could stay in a comfortable hotel for far less, and we had many nights left of our honeymoon. My preference would have been to use the extra money for a nice dinner, to buy something, or even to save it. Though uneasy about the hotel idea, I gave in and compromised. It was, admittedly, superbly fantastic having a fancy, expensive five-star hotel to hang out in and get a good night of sleep in for my weary, pregnant, protruding body. Don't get me wrong: the idea of having the ability to afford a nice hotel, to buy nice things, and to do things that cost money was something I loved. In fact, one thing that attracted me to Abdul was his sense of taste and style.

As I treated myself to a luxurious, hot bubble bath, I wondered how we were going to afford his lifestyle. My background and knowing what life costs made me a more practical and cautious person in relation to spending money. I didn't have my parents or family to fall back on, and living paycheck to paycheck was familiar to me until I could earn the money I needed. Even so, I kept telling myself to stay in the moment and enjoy this time together. It would all work out, as my mom would have said. Once we returned to the States, there would be two incomes and we would be fine.

A new Disneyland had recently opened in Tokyo, and we wanted to have fun, so we went to the Magic Kingdom, seeing it from a Japanese slant. Everything was the same, no different from the States, with the same layout and attractions, except that the foods served catered to the country's desires. The signs were in Japanese, and we saw only Japanese park visitors walking around, conversing in their language. We were the odd ones and felt out of place.

Abdul commented on the fact that I enjoyed seeing older cities and communities, which was true. I did not grow up experiencing older cultures and the lifestyles of desert cities and villages. I was intrigued; it was a different way of living. Conversely, Abdul had grown up with it, and it did not interest him to see it over and over. He made a good point. His country was still establishing a modern world, while I'd grown up in one. It was more my norm.

Back in the USA

Our lovely, unforgettable wedding night was spent
overlooking the ocean.
We were back in America, the Land of the Free.
A new life awaited us.

The end of my required time out of the US arrived. It was August of 1984. Hawaii was our last stop, and we decided to visit friends there before we headed to the mainland. Abdul had not been to Hawaii; I had been there one other time, shortly before going to Saudi Arabia. It was my kind of weather. The palm trees swayed, the temperate and gentle ocean waves warmed my soul. It was my favorite tropical paradise. We went sightseeing in Honolulu, visited Pearl Harbor, snorkeled, hiked a rain forest, and ate fresh pineapple and shaved-ice snow cones with neon-colored sugary toppings. Hawaii was a place I could live, but California was calling our names.

In California at last, I was ready to nest with my family. I was small for being six and a half months along in my pregnancy; and, other than the almost four months of pregnancy-induced sickness I'd experienced, traveling pregnant had not deterred us from doing all we'd wanted to do. Abdul was extremely supportive of my condition, and I loved the hormonal metabolic high of being pregnant. Other than a few crazy, emotional, scary hiccups at the beginning of our honeymoon, we had had a wonderful time bonding. Our love had grown, and we were learning to work out our differences through talking and compromising. We were extremely ready to get settled into our new home and have our baby.

A nurse friend of mine, Ginny, did my prenatal check. I had not had any prenatal care since leaving Saudi Arabia. As a nurse, I felt comfortable in knowing I would have sought medical attention if something had not felt right. Everything was going well, except, for the first time in my life, I was told to gain more weight. I had only gained twelve pounds.

Our wedding day in California was August 9, 1984, the same day as my oldest brother's birthday. My father and four of my siblings joined us to celebrate our blissful union. My mother chose not to come, as she had just vacationed with us. This disappointed and saddened me. Why would she not want to come see her daughter get married? Wounded, I accepted this and tried not to let it overshadow our joy and happiness. My family chose to camp at a local state park in the Redwoods. Camping was something we had enjoyed as kids; it was not too expensive, and it gave us something fun to do. Abdul and I joined my family in camping for a couple of nights before our wedding. He camped in his nice pants and shirt and wore one of his fancy watches. We had not traveled with camping clothes, but I noticed the irony. What a drastic difference: I was raised with only one inexpensive Timex watch, not a whole briefcase full of valuable ones.

The weather on the northern Pacific coast can be quite unpredictable, but our wedding day was gorgeous—warm and sunny with not a cloud in the sky. The ocean, many shades of blue-green, glittered like diamonds, with the powerful sounds of roaring waves spitting puffs of white sea mist through the large holes in the boulders of our picturesque backdrop.

There was instant affection when Abdul and our officiant, my friend Tom, were introduced. They were opposites of each other. Tom was taller, with broad shoulders, and his rugged blue jeans and T-shirt were hidden under the long, royal-blue velvet robe he wore. He had long, wavy, graying hair tied in a ponytail down his back; very wild, bushy, untamed eyebrows; and an untrimmed beard to his chest. His appearance was in stark contrast to Abdul's more manicured style and smaller stature. He was a very handsome man, my prince.

About thirty close friends and family were present to celebrate our union on this incredible summer day at the seaside, my favorite place in the world. One close girlfriend and her husband played their guitars and sang a love song they wrote for our special day. My sister read a passage from "The Prophet," written in 1923 by Kahlil Gibran, an American Lebanese poet.

"On Marriage"

You were born together, and together you shall be forevermore.
You shall be together when the white wings of death scatter
your days.
Ay, you shall be together even in the silent memory of God.
But let there be spaces in your togetherness,
And let the winds of the heavens dance between you.

Love one another, but make not a bond of love:
Let it rather be a moving sea between the shores of your souls.
Fill each other's cup but drink not from one cup.
Give one another of your bread but eat not from the same loaf.

*Sing and dance together and be joyous, but let each one of
 you be alone,
Even as the strings of a lute are alone though they quiver with
 the same music.*

*Give your hearts, but not into each other's keeping.
For only the hand of Life can contain your hearts.
And stand together yet not too near together:
For the pillars of the temple stand apart,
And the oak tree and the cypress grow not in each
 other's shadow.*

Tom performed an uplifting nontraditional ceremony uniting our love and gave a blessing to our baby. The moment we longed for in Cypress had finally come to fruition: *You may now kiss your bride. I'm honored to pronounce you husband and wife, Mr. and Mrs. . . .*

In a small town near the Pacific Ocean our reception followed, with a potluck dinner and live music. We laughed and danced the night away. Abdul had suggested that everyone wear nametags at the reception. I laughed at what seemed quite strange to me, but I understood this request much later, when the tables were turned and I could not remember Arabic names.

The wedding celebration was fabulous; we could not have asked for anything greater and could not have been happier than at this moment of our lives. Our lovely, unforgettable wedding night was spent overlooking the ocean at a beautiful bed-and-breakfast outside the city of Bodega Bay. We were back in America, the land of the free. A new life awaited us.

A Baby Is Born

Call the midwives!
Thanks to amazing teamwork, our beautiful, precious daughter
Aisha was born.

The honeymoon was over. I was having a baby in two months. Were we ready? We flew to Kansas to retrieve my ugly orange van and my items from storage before driving to San Diego, where we had decided to set up our first home. We recovered our briefcase of valuables from customs in Kansas City, and on our way west, the van broke down in Las Vegas, with all of our stuff inside. We needed to decide whether to buy a new engine or look for a new vehicle. We chose a new engine. My cousin lived in Las Vegas, though I had not seen her for years. We were happy to see each other, and she put us up for a few days.

We contacted Pauline, whom we had met in Katmandu, to accept her invitation for us to stay at her beautiful home outside of San Diego until we found a home. It worked out perfectly, as we had limited time to get settled and little money left to our names. Since I had a California nursing license, I was able to work immediately upon arriving in San Diego, regardless of being pregnant. I was grateful for my rewarding new job as a nurse in hospice, which would bring money in for my family.

Abdul's male ego was on the line, especially as a Saudi man who could not support his pregnant new American wife. He thought he would find employment easily, but this did not go as planned. He applied for job after job, yet nothing came through. To occupy his time, he volunteered to help coach a girls' soccer team and looked for a place for us to live.

We found a sweet two-bedroom duplex to rent outside of San Diego, down the hill from Pauline. Our new home was in a quiet neighborhood and had a nice, sunny patio and a private backyard. We had views of breathtaking sunsets and were close to the beautiful ocean and its warm, gentle breezes—just what we wanted.

We set up our home with thrift-shop finds, as what had seemed like a lot of money when we'd left Saudi Arabia had dwindled rapidly. We had a couple thousand dollars between us by this time, after we paid for the new van engine, accounted for travel costs, deducted the deposit and rent for our new home, and set aside a thousand dollars for the certified nurse midwife (CNM) for our home birth.

Home births were quite common from the 1960s to the '80s in parts of California and were performed by lay midwives or certified nurse midwives, who were registered nurses with specialized education and training in obstetrics. At one time in my life, I considered going to England to attend midwifery school. Giving birth at home had always been my wish; I was too familiar with hospitals and wanted to be in the comfort of my home. I also wanted my close friends with me, which was not generally permitted in hospitals in the '80s.

Abdul earnestly continued to apply for jobs, but sadly no bites came. With only four weeks until our baby was due, we decided it best to postpone the job search. Someone would need to watch our baby when I returned to work. I wondered if Abdul would be comfortable approaching his family to help us out financially if needed. Contacting my own parents was not a concept I would consider. When I had first moved to California and was getting on my feet, I asked my mother to help pay my car insurance. Her reply was enough to make me choose not to borrow money from her or ever ask again. Abdul's parents still did not know where he was, and they did not know about me. Overall, things fell in place between us, though we did face the usual adjustments inherent with starting a newly married life, with the complications of pregnancy and the expectation of a baby added to the mix.

Four weeks before my due date, I started having contractions. My CNM ordered me to spend the weekend in bed drinking red wine, as something in the wine was thought to help stop contractions. On the following Monday, I returned to my job with no contractions and was told I would work from the office. No more home visits with the chance of having a baby while out on the road.

Two weeks later, around four in the afternoon, while Abdul and I picked up raspberry tea leaves at a health-food store in San Diego to help ease labor, fluid started dripping down my legs. My water had broken. It was time—our baby was on the way. We needed to get home and let our midwife and birthing team of friends know of the imminent delivery. My mind swirled, and an uncontainable smile appeared on my face. Could this be the day?

Three close friends joined us for the birth. My friend Marci was a labor-and-delivery nurse. Her partner Ron, a respiratory therapist who traveled with his oxygen tank, drove south for three hours through the rush-hour traffic of Los Angeles. Abdul picked up my friend Sally at midnight at the airport in San Diego. She was an ICU and ER nurse. An urgent-care facility was down the street if needed. Everyone arrived and we were prepared. It was two in the morning. I needed to get some sleep; I was going to have a baby. Predictions had been made whether we would have a boy or a girl. My premonition was that we would have a boy who would be just like his wonderful dad, the joy of my life.

Once in bed, the contractions started, and I remember saying to my coworkers, "How will I know I'm in labor?" Their reply was, "You'll know." My contractions quickly got more regular, closer together, and stronger. We could not get to sleep as we started timing the contractions; they did not subside and only got more intense. After thirty minutes, Marci came in and did a cervical check and pleasantly announced, "Call the midwives!" Thanks to the amazing teamwork from everyone, our beautiful, precious daughter, Aisha, was born at 3:23 a.m., December 10, 1984. I asked my midwife to check the gender again; I had always thought I would have a boy, though I was not disappointed.

Other than the intense pain of my natural delivery, it was a totally awesome experience. I was told it was a very quick birth for a first child, with only a few minor post-delivery problems. Abdul was amazing throughout this wonderful phenomenon. We toasted to "birth, a miraculous celebration of a life" with chilled champagne and freshly baked pumpkin pie filling topped with whipped cream, which I'd made the evening before. It was great to get pampered after an incredible spiritual awakening about what the union of a man and woman could create—truly an amazing gift from God. When this tiny little spirit, a bundle of pure love and innocence, was gently placed against my soft, awaiting breast, I was overwhelmed with feelings that floated through all my chakras, and quiet tears warmed my cheeks. I had always wanted to be a mom.

A book our midwife had recommended Abdul read about home births went unheeded. When he looked at the book after labor, he laughed. "You never followed any of the steps." I had an hour-and-twenty-three-minute birth. Abdul's reaction to the birth was so touching. I realized that day that you have to experience birth to understand the feeling, as is true with many life experiences. My husband could not have been more supportive through my pregnancy, my labor, and afterward. The smile on his face and tears down his cheeks said it all when he held his daughter for the first time, and it connected us once again.

Disappointed, sad, and hurt that Abdul's parents were still unaware of his wife and now his beautiful newborn daughter, we called my parents.

"Congratulations, glad everything is all right, talk to you later," my mother groggily answered. Again, why had I expected her to be more excited? It was early in the morning, was my only rationalization.

Aisha was the name we chose for our girl, meaning "life, vivacious, living prosperous." Khalil would have been our choice for a boy's name. In Saudi Arabia and most Arab countries, it is customary for the father's first name to be the middle name of a son or daughter. I was unaware of this and was disappointed at having our girl take a man's middle name. I was told this is how families kept track of each other's clans/tribes and their children throughout generations.

On the seventh day after birth, Abdul did an Islamic blessing (*aqīqah*) in Arabic, which he whispered into the ears of our daughter, a custom in his culture, family, and religion. While many Saudis regard a male child as more acceptable than a girl, I felt no pressure to have a boy. Abdul never said anything about that. In some cultures, it is grounds for divorce if a woman can't produce a baby, and particularly a boy, even if the fertility problem is with the man.

A few days after Aisha's birth, her skin became too yellow; she was jaundiced. When the ER doctor looked at our baby, he teased us about her resembling a pumpkin; her color was bright orange in their light. She cried as blood was taken from her tiny little vein to test her bilirubin. This was a difficult sight to experience as new parents. If the bilirubin got too high, it could adversely affect our child's development and be quite dangerous. We were afraid she might have to stay in the hospital for special treatment. Nervously, we sat while we waited for the verdict.

With good news, we prepared to go home. I secretly wondered if the pumpkin pie filling I had eaten had affected my first breast milk. My milk was in, and the more Aisha nursed, the more the milk flushed the color out of her system. A remedy thought to reduce the bilirubin was time in the sun, so Aisha enjoyed time on the lounge chair with a sock over her eyes for the first few days of her life.

Aisha was registered into the system to obtain MediCal, government health insurance for low-income families, for her medical treatment. We applied for her birth certificate, since she was born at home, and did the paperwork for a social security number. A passport would come later. Our new family adjusted well, considering how we, like most new families, were deprived of sleep for days.

Returning to Saudi Arabia

I began to wonder who this man was that I had married.

After a few months of peace, the past started to preoccupy Abdul along with the present. I was told, "Things heated up in Saudi." I realized I did not hear the entire story. The mistrust of my husband started to stir my conscious awareness. It sounded like going back to Saudi Arabia would happen in the very near future.

Abdul continued to have a tough time when he applied for jobs. He had graduated from college with a bachelor's degree in social science, but to get work based on his experience was difficult. One of the job applications Abdul filled out was left on the table, and it shocked me to see how incomplete and haphazard it appeared, how messy and difficult to read it was. I offered to help him fill out the job applications.

We had planned for Abdul to get his master's degree in social work. This plan soon became improbable. His grade point average was 2.0, not 4.0 as I had been informed. It was often mentioned that many foreigners "hired" people to do their schoolwork for them in order to pass or graduate. Could this have been true with Abdul? He thought that special consideration should be given to him, since English was not his native language. I told him that was not how it worked. It was not what he wanted to hear.

As the days passed, Abdul became increasingly upset. This did not help the already delicate dance of our relationship. Our world did not work out as we had predicted, and our perfect goal was slowly dissolving.

After Aisha's birth, we flew to Kansas to spend Christmas. The holiday visit was a way for Aisha and Abdul to be welcomed into the family. We had a great Christmas, for the most part. Abdul fit in well with my curious family. He wore his Saudi wardrobe and was very accommodating, charming, and friendly. During this visit, though, a new behavior surfaced: jealousy. My sister and I had lunch out, and Abdul got jealous; he thought I had looked up old boyfriends. We had a heated argument, and he threatened to leave right then, even if he had to walk in the snow to get to the airport.

Where was this coming from? I wondered. We had talked about previous relationships. Did being back in the States bring up new feelings for Abdul about his independent, friendly wife? I had heard that Saudi men could get jealous, but many men get jealous. Was there something I had said that triggered his reaction? It upset me, and I felt he was being quite immature. Perhaps our age difference and the maturity gap was becoming more obvious in America.

After two weeks in Kansas we returned to San Diego so I could work, while Abdul watched our daughter. This worked out well for us for a while. Abdul was quite comfortable watching a newborn. He cooked and helped with the household chores. How wonderful was that? Because of the flexibility of my job, I continued to breastfeed Aisha, an experience I was blessed to have and enjoyed. It created a close connection with my baby, one that, sadly, not all moms experience. Aisha's warm, soft, sweet body snuggled against mine; her loving eyes looked up at me as she gently tugged at my breast and cooed with delight. Being able to feed my own offspring was an incredible miracle. Belief in a higher power—God, angels, a universal spirit— was easy to fathom as I held my daughter.

At the end of January 1985, many more private phone calls were made to Saudi Arabia. Abdul said he had to return or his father would be arrested. Abdul had not fulfilled his four-year work obligation to repay the Saudi government for his college education. Secret phone calls had occurred between Abdul, his brother, and one of his uncles who had some influence. Abdul needed to return to Saudi Arabia.

We packed the belongings we had recently unpacked. I quit my job and said goodbye to the friends we had met. Aisha was two months old when we headed to my girlfriend's house in Sacramento to stay while Abdul went ahead to Saudi Arabia. He did not want us to stay alone in San Diego.

Before Abdul left, he asked if I would consider becoming a Muslim. He said it was not important to him, but it would make it easier for us to return to Saudi Arabia. I did not have any problem with this if it was important for Abdul. I could become a Muslim. I didn't have any real allegiance in regard to religion. It was the same God, as far as I was concerned. I had been reading and learning about Islam, a very beautiful religion, as are many religions, when practiced as intended. We went to the imam in Sacramento. After I recited the *shahada*, a testimony of faith ("I believe there is no God but God, and I believe that Mohammed was a profit of God . . ."), I became a Muslim, and a simple Islamic marriage ceremony was performed to assist with the process of my return to Saudi Arabia.

I had developed a very open belief system about religion. I was raised Christian; and at one time in my life, I became very intertwined in Christianity—being born again, speaking in tongues, and living my life giving testimonials to convert others to Jesus. Now I had become a Muslim. After living in Saudi Arabia and among people of so many different religions, my views had continued to evolve, leading me to conclude that God is a good God, and as long as one strives to be a good person, one is blessed.

I would have to learn how to pray as a Muslim. It was important to know how to pray and what script to say in Arabic during the prayer ritual. Certain movements had to be performed: one would bend down, stand up, and then prostrate oneself again. I was raised with another way to pray to God, who was one and the same God. I did not see delineations by religion, but by how one lived her life. For me, to take time out of my life to thank God for all my blessings was a wonderful way to live, however it was done.

Initially, I respected my husband for being a "good" Muslim. It was something I liked about him. Gradually, I discovered he did not really follow the religion; he merely practiced it to accommodate his family and friends. This may have played a part in my eventually becoming disillusioned with organized religion, the hypocrisy and duality of it.

My impression of my husband had slowly changed, something I did not want to admit. I began to wonder who this man was that I had married. Did he say things just to please me? At one point, Abdul began to say things to me that I knew not to be true, and I confronted him. Still, to this day, I remember my shock and disappointment, the stab in my heart, when he replied, "I did not lie to you. I just did not tell you the truth!" I had been raised to tell the truth. It was my way, part of my soul. My carousel was down.

Meeting the Family

Our minds can draw a picture in our head that is so very different than what's real, whether good or bad.

Abdul returned to Saudi Arabia in February 1985. After staying with my girlfriend for a while, I flew with Aisha to my parents' home to wait for Abdul to resolve his work/education contract with the Saudi government. I got the appropriate paperwork and photos for Aisha's US passport. Abdul would apply for her Saudi passport. In the Middle East, the father's passport would often include a photo and documentation of the child's birth, without the need for two passports. Since we would likely travel separately, we thought it easier for Aisha to have her own Saudi passport. Abdul got the paperwork together in case it was decided that Aisha and I should join him. Visas were required for traveling in or out of the country. There were no tourist visas. When I was recruited to work in Saudi Arabia, the company had been my sponsor. Now that I was married and didn't have employment in the country, my husband would be my sponsor.

Since it had been more complicated than anticipated for Abdul to find work in the United States, we decided that if he could find work in Saudi Arabia, we would return. I was comfortable with this decision. Of course, there were many things about the country that drove me crazy at times; but there were also things I really missed, like the delicious food—authentic Arabic, Greek, and Middle Eastern—that I looked forward to enjoying again. Being married would give us more freedom. We would both be able to find jobs and save money moving forward in our lives.

My life seemed to be lived more in the present than many people's were, often driving my friends and family crazy. Abdul and I planned long-term goals for our lives, contrary to others' beliefs, but our present often influenced the outcome, and not always as I may have wished. If I put too much emphasis on the future and it didn't happen as planned, my bubble burst, which could be so self-defeating.

Abdul had been gone for four weeks to resolve his job abandonment and get the document required for us to return to Saudi Arabia. Aisha and I were prepared to travel there on our own, as I had saved a couple thousand dollars. Even so, Abdul, or perhaps his parents, felt it necessary for him to return to accompany us. I felt perturbed by this decision, as I was quite capable of getting us to Saudi Arabia. We had no money for additional airfare, so his parents paid for our tickets. Having others contribute to my personal finances was not part of my upbringing, nor had I learned to be comfortable letting others assist.

My life rapidly transformed in a matter of months. I went from being "me," an independent, free woman, to being a new wife, a very new mother, and now a woman married into a Saudi family with another unfamiliar journey ahead. Traveling alone was no longer the proper thing for a woman to do, a woman with a new baby, a Saudi wife. As my independence quietly slipped away, I wondered if maybe I was making more out of the whole ordeal than was necessary, but I felt the slippage.

It was never in my nature to be subservient. When I moved to California in 1977, it was the first time I had lived with a guy. The issue of inequality between men and women in the home glaringly presented itself. I felt an internal conflict about why women did so much; they cooked, cleaned, shopped, did laundry, took care of the children. I would wake up at six in the morning to get my boyfriend's breakfast, pack his lunch, and get him out the door. Then I got ready for my day. He enjoyed the dinner that I had cooked when he got home from work; then, as most men did, he relaxed while I cleaned up, washed the dishes, did laundry, and so forth. I worked part-time as a nurse and went to school full-time and needed to study.

Financially, I contributed as much as he did. This imbalance did not make sense, but I was playing the role I was raised to follow. My inner being was in turmoil, and I realized I could not play this role any longer, nor did I want to. I recall reflecting on this as the sun started to fade beyond the horizon, as I sat behind the fence of our rented house on the outskirts of that California town. I stared into an empty field, feeling barren and empty, too. My flood of tears flowed onto the dry soil and made tiny puddles. It was not the life I wanted.

No wonder "Prince" Abdul had stolen my heart, with his apparent openness about gender roles and his willingness to help out around the home. It was who he was, without the need to be asked. Once, when my cousin had visited us in Kansas, he asked where my "Arab husband" was and was shocked when I told him he was hanging clothes out on the clothesline.

Although I had concerns about what my role would become in Saudi Arabia, Abdul and I talked on the phone nearly every night while he was away. It was great to laugh with him about life in and out of Saudi Arabia. He was not stressed out and anxious, as he had been before he returned there, and it was a tremendous relief for both of us. Healing was in the air again, and it got us through yet another hurdle of married life. His government commitment issues were alleviated somewhat with the help of his uncle. His parents now knew about his American wife and child, and they were excited to meet us. We decided we would come to live in Saudi Arabia, and at last I would get to meet my husband's family.

Abdul returned to the States in the evening after a long flight. He took a taxi from the airport directly to our downtown hotel room and into our waiting arms. Aisha had changed so quickly in one month. She cooed, drooled all over, and gave awe-inspiring smiles that warmed me from head to toe. She was now three months old.

We celebrated Abdul's return in style. The hotel room was decorated with fresh, colorful flowers, sweetly softening the room with a calming fragrance. The aroma and flicker of lavender-scented candles danced around the warm, inviting hot tub. Chilled Korbel Brut champagne waited for his arrival, and the CD player played "our" song: Lionel Richie's "All Night Long." "Endless Love" was next. It was a lovely night reuniting in each other's arms, as our daughter angelically slept beside us, waking only to nourish her growing body. Seeing Abdul was fantastic; I had missed him more than I had thought I would. I missed his smile, his kiss, and his affectionate and supportive nature. He assured me everything was going to be all right, and though I had doubts, I wondered if what he shared could be true.

The following morning, Abdul surprised me with an engagement gift from his parents. He gently placed a heavy white-gold necklace with a unique, bold teardrop-shaped pendant with diamonds and rubies around my neck. Though I was grateful for such a warm, welcoming gesture of kindness from my in-laws, I felt uncomfortable, not only with accepting such an expensive gift but also with its design, as it was not of my taste. I was displeased with myself for feeling this way, not meaning to be inconsiderate. I had never been good at hiding my feelings and didn't want to rock the boat, so I pretended I liked it and tried not to look directly at my husband, as he would have known the truth. I knew I would be expected to wear the necklace as a token of their acceptance of me. It may have been an unusual style, but the gesture was lovely in its own way.

    Aisha and I loved having our man back. I felt blessed having someone to walk beside me in this journey called life. After we visited my family for a few days, we were off again to Saudi Arabia.

It was difficult to ignore the laborious fourteen-hour-plus flight this time, traveling with a young baby, though she did amazingly well. Once again we witnessed the mass clothes transformation when we flew from New York to Saudi Arabia. To expedite the immigration-and-customs process at Riyadh's airport, we were greeted by one of Abdul's younger brothers, who worked at the airport. The family's driver waited for us in Abdul's father's roomy, shiny black Cadillac with darkened windows. It was an early four o'clock in the morning, and we were spent. The very spacious, ornate airport with tasteful, inspired architecture was not congested, which saved time. My mind kept repeating, *We are in the city with some of the strictest expectations for women.* Was I ready for this? It was my first time in Riyadh. I had heard a few horror stories. I was nervous, but also anxious and excited about my long-awaited meeting with Abdul's family. I wondered what they were like and if they would like me.

    His parents were well aware of our addition to their family by this time. Abdul had shared numerous photos and told them all about us on his earlier visit. I didn't know what to expect. I felt introverted, unsure; my stomach was upset. Abdul was extremely supportive, excited, and so proud of his beautiful daughter and wife. I knew he loved us very much. I also knew how our minds can draw a picture in our head that is so very different from what's real, whether good or bad.

Abdul had shown me a very different, more modern and open picture of the life he'd lived in Jeddah than what I was prepared for and introduced to at his family's home. How very naïve I was about the depth of the culture and religion. There were certain rules I was unaware of, and I had not experienced this lifestyle when I lived in Saudi Arabia before and with Abdul. I was on unstable ground, far out of my comfort zone.

Abdul's family had waited up for us. There is a certain greeting used in the Middle East that I had witnessed numerous times and was familiar with, but had not performed. The huggy-kissy type of person I was in California would not be appropriate at this moment. While holding the other person's right hand, not really a shake, one would then kiss—but not really kiss—the right side of the other person's face two to three times, then switch to the left side and kiss again at least two times before letting go of their hand. We performed this salutation to the five awaiting members of Abdul's family. Then Abdul took his father's right hand, which was held out, and "kissed" the ring he wore on it; he then kissed his father's forehead as a sign of respect. Much to my relief, Abdul's father was genuinely receptive of me and warmly welcomed us to their home.

We were shown to our bedroom on the second floor, in the family section of the large marble home that occupied a large corner lot. Our unadorned room had a king-sized bed; small, covered windows facing the west that let limited natural light in; and its own bathroom hidden behind a set of doors. The driver/houseman and Abdul's brothers carried our luggage up to our designated room. The three maids busily prepared hot tea and snacks in the outside kitchen prior to bringing them up to the family living room, which was surrounded by five bedrooms. There was so much to be in awe of in his home compared to my own family home, but I was so exhausted, being a new breastfeeding mom, trying to be a doting wife with little time to take care of myself, and too jet-lagged to even care. All I wanted to do was excuse our daughter and myself to our room to breastfeed and go to bed. Instead, we were expected to meet in the living room to share tea, snacks, and light conversation.

Abdul introduced the slowly awakening Aisha to his family. She had done so well on this drawn-out trip. Thank God for the ready food of nursing! No one wanted to hold or cuddle our new baby, as was generally done in my world, which surprised and saddened me. Was it because it was five o'clock in the morning? Because we were all tired? What I did hear was *"Amreki,"* meaning Aisha looked American. She did not have the usual Arab abundance of dark hair; she didn't have *any* hair.

Grandma was standoffish, but attempted a gesture and said hello. It was really not her fault, I consoled myself. Wouldn't I have felt the same in her place if my son had come home with a newly converted Muslim American wife and a new baby with no hair? Perhaps this was not what she had wished for him.

By six o'clock in the morning, we lethargically changed into our nightclothes and plopped into our hard bed in our sterile, colorless, undecorated bedroom. Aisha had a homemade bed of blankets and pillows on the thinly carpeted cement floor next to me. Abdul and I attempted to sleep, but it was not an easy task. I was wound up from the painfully long flight and the time difference, and bothered by the nonverbal, solemn reactions of the family I had so deeply anticipated meeting. I kept telling myself, *Don't take it personally; it's still the hormones of pregnancy talking. Get some sleep, especially while Aisha is sleeping. A few hours of sleep will make it a better, brighter new day.*

For some crazy reason, I was aghast, as I had expected his family to be more like Abdul . . . more family-like. Still, I felt grateful that Abdul's father's English was adequate; he consciously engaged me in conversation and seemed to welcome me. His mother, however, didn't speak English and spoke to everyone but me. His two younger brothers and sister who were present had a loose grasp of English, similar to my Arabic, which would have to slowly return after being away from Saudi Arabia for almost nine months.

We were thankful that the family let us sleep in as long as we wanted in our quiet, dark bedroom. It was late afternoon when we woke. The enclosed bedroom and bathroom, with a separate door to the living room, provided a private space for us. Our room had its own key, as did the other bedrooms, and we could lock it at our discretion.

I was not prepared for what lay ahead. After we woke and cleaned up, we joined the family in the living room for the ritual afternoon hot tea with tons of sugar, and we were told what was planned for us. My mother-in-law informed us that the next evening, at eight o'clock, there would be a wedding party in my honor, and their female family members and friends were invited to celebrate and welcome me.

Before evening on the first day of our arrival, we were encouraged to go shopping for a formal dress for the party. Abdul's two teenaged female "cousins" and their mother, Miriam, who was called "Aunt" and was very close to the family but was not blood related, accompanied me to buy clothes. Miriam was married to an Egyptian man and lived in New Jersey. She was on vacation for a few months to visit her two daughters, who lived in Riyadh with their father and stepmother. Miriam stayed with Abdul's parents when in Saudi Arabia. I was happy for her company and her ability to speak English. Abdul drove us to the shops, while he watched Aisha in the car.

The dressy wardrobe I'd brought with me was just not going to cut it on this trip. A frilly, sky-blue chiffon-like dress was chosen for me. The dress matched my bright blue eyes and made them stand out, though I felt I already stood out enough. And although I would never have worn this dress in my "real" life, I did fit in better with my new frills. I felt overwhelmed; there was a lot for me to learn in this new culture and about my new family that I had not anticipated.

One of the first questions I had asked upon arrival was, "Do I need to cover my head or not?" Abdul's father alleged it was up to my husband to decide. If he said I must, then I must; apparently I had no say. Luckily for me, Abdul saw no need for me to cover. Out of respect for others and the family, however, I would cover to honor the tradition if and when it was deemed necessary. I would gradually become accustomed to people staring at Abdul and me when he was in his Saudi dress; we were an unusual sight.

The next day, when I went downstairs, Abdul's mother and aunt were sitting on the floor in the crowded little kitchen, soaking and rolling grape leaves to make dolmas for my party. This was when Abdul's father encouraged me to learn to cook Arabic food, to sit with the women and learn what they were doing. In his words, it was "the right thing" for me to do. The only reply I could get out of my mouth was that my husband cooked Arabic food and I cooked American food. He chose not to understand what I had said.

The small main kitchen was in a separate building in the courtyard away from the main home to avoid spreading the heat when cooking and using the oven. This was the kitchen where Abdul's mother had taught him to cook. Food was being prepared for the party, including the lamb that would be served on top of a pile of cooked rice on a large, plain metal tray, head and all.

A lot of preparation was going into this big celebration. I was nervous and uneasy being at their home, let alone having a party in my honor with a bunch of strangers who didn't speak my language. I couldn't get comfortable in my new environment and often felt like crying or running away to my room. I was grateful to be able to go to our bedroom to breastfeed Aisha, taking longer each time. It was only my second day at my new family's home; how was I going to survive all the rest?

This was not the ideal time for them to have a party for me. There probably would never have been an ideal time, if it had been my choice. Still, I did my best to cope with the awkward situation. What the hell was I thinking when I married this man? People tried to warn me. Abdul worked so hard to help me to blend in, but I was experiencing an extreme culture shock. Every moment was harder than the one before, and this affected our relationship, which again became fragile. Abdul felt I didn't appreciate what his mother did for me. His patience wore thin with my whining. I hadn't looked beyond the little safe haven we had in Jeddah before we married, and now I had no one to turn to.

Before the party, we were asked to change a few dates. Since it takes nine months to have a baby, we were told we had actually been "engaged" the February before Aisha was conceived. Remember, in Saudi Arabia, when couples got engaged, they signed a marriage agreement under Sharia law, the Islamic governing law based on the Quran. Usually, a nice engagement party accompanied the engagement, and the families would meet. This gave couples and their families the opportunity to get to know each other. It was like a trial period. I was never given a trial period to meet my perspective Saudi family, something I believe would have steered my life in a totally different direction.

My mother-in-law went out of her way to prepare a special feast to celebrate our marriage, though my husband, my safety net, was not welcomed at the women-only event. It was beyond my comprehension that my husband could no longer look at the female childhood friends he had grown up with, even with their heads covered. My mother-in-law was genuinely thoughtful and asked a younger family friend to sit with me to translate Arabic to English. I was so thankful for this kind gesture on her part. Our mutual lack of understanding of one another's languages was a huge barrier for both of us. Even though many guests could have spoken to me in English, they did not choose to do so.

The formal living room and dining room were lined with well-wishers, some I doubt I ever saw again. Some women were more concerned with covering up than others. I was indeed the spectacle, the topic of gossip for the night. Without all the class and style that may have been expected of me, I felt like an orphan child, but I was told the party was a huge success.

    Abdul's parents gave me a stunning wedding gift of gold jewelry. More gold jewelry was given to me by other close relatives, including jewelry for our daughter. The gift I received from his parents was a tasteful set that included a heavy gold choker, a bracelet, earrings, and a ring. The necklace and bracelet were beautifully designed chains of diamonds, emeralds, rubies, and sapphires. I had never seen something so beautiful, nor had I ever owned such an expensive, precious gift. I felt the weight of the expectations that came with it.

After the whirlwind experience of my arrival, I began to get my bearings. Abdul's parents' home was a different kind of beautiful. It was large, but not grandiose. Beige marble slabs covered the three-story house. A stucco wall, over eight feet tall, enclosed a marble courtyard surrounding the house, including the small outdoor kitchen, storage room, and servants' bedroom. The doorman/caretaker would let us in and out of either of two heavy metal gates, utilizing a doorbell or honking a horn at the entrance to announce one's arrival.

    The home had a marble entrance that covered half of the walkway; the other half was left open to the sun. Two sets of three large, six-foot triangular marble slabs, six inches deep, were laid unevenly on top of each other, creating three steps in two directions, leading into the foyer. The light-colored marbled walls sparkled inside the foyer, illuminated by a large crystal chandelier that added to the stunning brightness.

    The entrance was adorned with two dark mahogany cloak stands and numerous decorative golden hooks that were used to hold guests' belongings, such as coats, purses, abayas, and gutras. Long mirrors to each side of the stands waited for the appearance check after abayas or other head coverings were removed. Shoes were taken off upon entering.

On the ground floor, to the right of the entrance, were elaborate living and dining rooms with chandeliers and Persian carpets. Tastefully engraved mahogany furniture with thickly padded chairs from Italy portrayed an aura of wealth, and the couch cushions were covered in a delicate light-blue velvet-like fabric. The living room could seat thirty to forty people, and the ornately carved oval mahogany dining-room table would accommodate fourteen or more. In the center of the ground floor was a TV room with numerous couches and oversized chairs, often used to entertain the children's friends and to watch movies. It was also converted into a dining room when many guests were present.

Off the entrance were two guest rooms and bathrooms, again hidden behind closed doors. One of these rooms was used as a private office and sitting room by Abdul's father. It was also a place used by the boys for a hidden cigarette. The other guest room, seldom used yet ornately designed, would later become a sweet haven for Aisha and me. Past the entranceway was a small, informal kitchen where the majority of the family's three daily meals were shared. Guests who were not considered "family" were entertained on the first floor and used the bathroom by the stairway.

A large marble double stairway with mahogany railings led upstairs to the second floor's informal living area, used by family or close friends. Five bedrooms and four bathrooms occupied this private family area, which surrounded the living area. The furnishings were very plain and modest, consisting of two soft, cozy couches of light-blue fabric and a couple of oversized hassocks that didn't match. All of this centered around three simple glass-and-gold-metallic bookshelves that housed a fairly small television and knick-knacks or gifts given to the family. This room was quite drab in comparison to the elaborate design and décor of the first floor. A built-in mahogany cupboard sat against the east wall of the living room. In the corner of that cupboard, a locked cabinet contained snacks, chocolates, candy, and chips, along with the "blue" movies that Abdul's father had confiscated and locked up from the boys, though the boys had a key unbeknownst to Baba ("father" in Arabic).

Abdul's parents' bedroom was on the east side of the house. It was quite large, with its own sitting area and a large marble bathroom. Seldom did anyone go into this bedroom. It was often locked if not occupied. The boys' bedroom, though plainer, was even larger than their parents' room. There were four single beds and three simple, well-used metal desks lined up against three of the walls. A separate shared bathroom was tucked inside the entrance to that bedroom before entering into the common area. Also at the entrance to this bedroom was a small room that housed the iron and ironing board that was used to iron the gutras of the men of the house, either by the boys themselves or by one of the three maids. There were hooks on the wall for gutras or other clothes. Three of the seven boys still lived at home.

On the south side of the house was Abdul's ten-year-old sister's bedroom and another bedroom now occupied by Miriam, the family guest. A common bathroom was shared. Leading into the living room was a small foyer housing a couple of simple wood cabinets and the water cooler, to which was added rose flavoring—an unusual taste I learned to enjoy and missed when it was unavailable. A sewing machine that I became very familiar with sat on the floor just before the doorway.

Another smaller marble stairway led up to the third story, which housed a huge circulating fan, allowing heat to escape through the roof. Though seldom used because of the scorching dry heat, there was a large, open rooftop area almost the size of the house. It could have provided a great rooftop garden during certain times of the year, though it provided no privacy from neighbors, who could openly look onto it.

In the family area, women did not cover. Life went on as "normal." The conversation was in Arabic; thus I felt lost much of the time. There was a button on the wall that could be pushed to ring a bell to beckon one of the maids. Abdul grew up with maids and nannies. While the maids at his parents' home were Muslims from Indonesia, other families had maids from the Philippines or other countries. The maids would leave their children behind with their parents in order to earn money to provide them with a better life from afar. Some paid enormous amounts of money to a recruitment company to work in Saudi Arabia, often needing to mortgage their homes or borrow the funds. Most of their hard-earned income went back to their families. It was my understanding that they were on two-year contracts, not seeing their families until the contract was fulfilled and often not getting paid all they had earned to prevent them from leaving before their contract ended. There were endless stories throughout Saudi Arabia of how the hired help were mistreated.

Most of the maids knew some Arabic because the Quran was written in Arabic. English was seldom spoken, except for those maids coming from the Philippines, who were paid a little more, especially if expected to speak English to the children of the house.

For mealtimes, we gathered around the long, narrow, rectangular table in the small kitchen located by the back door. Abdul's mother—*omi* ("mother" in Arabic) or *siti* (grandmother)—managed the home and the small outdoor kitchen. Every day, early in the morning, she would speak with the maids about what was expected for the day in the way of cleaning, laundry, and food preparation. She assisted as needed. She was the cook, putting together all of the ingredients that had been prepared and adding the correct amount of seasoning and spices. She returned to the kitchen as needed throughout the day. Recipes were not written down. When it was time to eat, the three maids, Siti, and anybody around carried the food from the outdoor kitchen to the indoor kitchen. Basic condiments were kept in the indoor refrigerator and used for meals. After the meal things were moved back to the outdoor kitchen. The maids would do the majority of the cleanup.

My first evening meal with the family was a memorable humiliation. When I went to grab some bread with my left hand, Baba hit my hand. It startled me. I jumped in my chair, and everyone laughed. My face was red as a beet, which did not take much in those days with post-pregnancy hormones. A dam of embarrassment held back my tears. I knew I could not get up and leave for the comfort of my room. Baba calmly explained to me to not do that again. The left hand was considered "dirty." In Saudi Arabia, it was the hand used for toileting, or wiping oneself. At times, I am taken back to this memory when I use my left hand while eating.

At mealtimes, Siti sat at the head of the table. This made it easier for her to get up to get whatever might be needed throughout the meal. Baba sat to her left. My assigned seat was next to Baba. This made me nervous, though he had been the most welcoming of all. He helped explain things to me; maybe he remembered how intimidating being an outsider had felt when he was in the US many years earlier. My husband sat on the other side of me, and I was grateful for this, as he also helped hold my hand. Aisha sat in the car seat that I had insisted we bring, at the other end of the table. The other siblings sat across the table from us, as did as anyone else who might join us for a meal, which was a common occurrence.

Breakfast staples were a variety of cheeses and olives kept in small, white, rectangular covered glass dishes. A wide assortment of fruits would be set on the table. Sometimes there would be fried eggs, falafel, or *fūl*, a delicious dish made of fava beans, onions, tahini, and tomatoes seasoned with allspice. The beans would be made at home or bought fresh along with hot Khemis bread, which was delicious right out of the fire-pit oven. Khemis bread originated from Yemen and was a large, round flatbread, maybe nine inches in diameter.—

The larger meal of the day was around one in the afternoon. The main entree would vary, though lamb and rice were most common, a dish known as *kabsa*. I tasted many new and unusual dishes and liked most of them. Numerous small bowls of hot sauce made of tomatoes, onions, cilantro, and jalapenos would be strategically placed around the table according to each family member's desired level of spiciness. Fresh vegetables always adorned our table. Lettuce was often served uncut on a tray, which seemed odd. When I asked for some lettuce, the whole head of lettuce would be handed to me; I took what I wanted and passed it on around the table.

The evening meal was more casual. It could be a variety of leftovers or something simple, or someone might bring in food from outside vendors or from a fast-food restaurant. Sometimes dessert would be served, but usually fresh fruit was our dessert.

If there was an extraordinary occasion or special guests were invited to share a meal, the furniture of the downstairs TV room would be moved around. Plastic coverings would be placed on the floor once the large, thick, ornate carpets were rolled out of the way. At least thirty people could sit on the floor where plates were laid, including large platters of served food. Often, our hands and the bread were our only eating utensils. I discovered an array of new dining experiences in a short time, and I began to find this fun, however weird it seemed. Often, when lamb—head and all—was served on top of a bed of rice on a huge, heavy metal platter, guests would fight for the brain. This disturbed me. It became known that my space on the floor was to be farthest away from the head of the lamb.

Overall, mealtimes were more pleasant than not. Abdul's family had a sense of humor, and I now knew why Abdul enjoyed having fun. We laughed a lot around that table, mostly because of me, as my learning curve was steep. We were all different, but the basic nucleus was so similar.

Baba had gray hair, thinning on the top, which seemed quite common for Saudi men, perhaps from covering their heads so much. He often walked around the house with his skullcap on, called a *thagiyah*. He was a bit rotund and had an unusual waddle when he walked. He was a slow, curious man, and often stopped in his path, whether inside or outside, to look at whatever caught his eye, which seemed like many things; he was very observant.

All the boys of the family, except one, were similar in height to Abdul, around five foot ten, and had the fairer Turkish skin color. The boys were of a more petite build and were thin in comparison to my chunkier family. The fifth son inherited his mother's darker skin color and stockier body type. He was often teased for being so different in appearance from the others. His personality was also different from the other children's. He seemed so easygoing, enjoying a more carefree life.

The one and only girl was ten and had long, thick, dark brown hair, always pulled back in a braid; she, too, had a slim physique. I spent much time combing her hair and styling it. Basic English was taught in her school, so she helped me when I spoke with Siti. We enjoyed playing card games or whatever I could do to entertain her. She was an obedient, mellow girl, doing whatever her parents told her to do.

Two of the boys where in private high school and had their own cars, and the other brother worked at the airport, having his freedom to come and go. Their personalities were entertaining. They liked to play jokes on people, which brought humor to the home and to the kitchen table. When the men of the family were at home, it was common for their thobes and gutras to be removed in their bedrooms. They would walk around in their white T-shirts and their *sirwals*, the lightweight, loose-fitting white trousers that were worn under their thobes.

When we were in Abdul's father's house it was expected that we pray with the family. His father banged on everyone's bedroom doors at four a.m., yelling that it was time to wake up for the first prayer of the day. He would continue banging on the door until Abdul joined the family. Sometimes Baba and the boys would go to the mosque down the street to pray. When the family prayed as a group, I excused myself. This was probably not the proper thing to do as a new family member and new Muslim. I found myself taking time to be alone, and the family seemed to accept this about me. I could not get used to the rituals around prayer or the purpose for them. It was a concept I understood but one that didn't align with my belief system.

One day as a child, my dad and I took a walk after Sunday school, and he commented that he didn't think he could pray to God. I asked him why he felt this way. His earnest, simple reply was that he couldn't remember all the steps the Sunday school teacher had told them to take in order to pray. My sincere reply was, "Dad, I do not think God cares how we pray as long as we pray, being grateful for all our many blessings. Being a good person and living a life that is respectful and being the best person we can be is what I believe is important to God." I chose to participate in prayer the way my heart and soul was comfortable. I felt that my God understood this belief system and my way of prayer.

Abdul's father and I shared many hours talking. He told me he had a position with the government in the military, though I didn't learn exactly what he did. His son would say he was "important." King Faisal had supposedly given him land in the KSA for his children. Baba was in his early sixties, based on my best guess (I do not recall ever knowing the true age of Abdul's parents), and he was in the process of retiring. I heard rumors that he was "not wanted" anymore, but with the wealth that had come into the country, his retirement income would be close to his current salary.

One night, at the family table in the little kitchen, Baba and I were the only ones left in the room as Aisha slept in her car seat. We shared many conversations at this table after the rest of the family escaped elsewhere in the house. I enjoyed our conversations and learned so much from him. He had lied about his age to join the military; he was only fifteen and needed to be eighteen. It was uncommon to have a birth certificate in those days, so if you could convince someone you were the age you claimed to be, apparently that was all it took. My understanding was that he was also fifteen when he married his wife, Fatimah, when she was just twelve years old. He said they did not consummate their marriage until she was a couple of years older, when she "came of age." They lived with her parents in Medina.

Baba said they planned to return to Medina when their youngest child finished college. I learned a good deal about his country and also about his experience being in the US. I believe he was there twice, once to learn English while in the military and another time to visit while one of his children was enrolled in college there.

Abdul's mother never worked outside the home. I'm sure she was quite busy raising a family of eight children only a few years after oil was discovered in the previously undeveloped country. Women of this generation voiced concern that their children wouldn't know how to survive without oil money. It had become the country's norm, and many enjoyed flaunting it, often in arrogant ways.

Quite a few of my husband's relatives were educated, including the women, and the majority of them spoke a small amount of English. Therefore, when we were with this group of family members, life didn't seem quite so strange. This was a comforting relief for me. I had some "normal" people to identify with among my new relatives.

Two of Abdul's oldest brothers had graduated from college in the States, and a younger brother had gone to college in Washington, at the same school Abdul had attended. A college education was important in his family, as was learning English, though not all did. The two older brothers had master's degrees. I did eventually meet them and their families.

Abdul's mother seemed to be very distant when it came to my daughter and me. I was uncertain if it was because of our language barrier or her son's choice of wife. She did not interact with Aisha, which was heartbreaking. It made me want to withdraw even more than I already was. Luckily, breastfeeding gave me an easy out, though I was told I didn't need to go to the bedroom to breastfeed, that I could do it in the living area. It was important to cover my head when in public, but it was all right to have a breast out to nurse in the living room, a dichotomy which seemed absurd to me.

Often Abdul would go to other cities to look for work, leaving me home alone with the family. For days and weeks I sat on the couch in the family living room with no one to talk to. The TV shows were all in Arabic. While I did my best to initiate conversation with my new relatives, it was as difficult for them as it was for me. We tried, but it was often excruciatingly uncomfortable. I spent as much time as I could in my bedroom or outside on the patios among the flowers. There were a few potted plants around the yard that gave the wonderful feeling of life, fresh and green, especially the welcoming sweet fragrance of jasmine, whose vines wove throughout the windowless plain and boring compound wall.

Abdul's family attempted to make me feel welcome. I was grateful for his English-speaking "aunt" Miriam when she was around. Her teenaged daughters also spoke English quite well and always added humor when present. One day, as we all sat in the upstairs living room watching TV, one of the girls came out of the boys' bedroom with her bra in hand. She acted stunned, saying that her male cousin, Abdul's handsome youngest brother who was about her age, had taken it off her. Everyone laughed and enjoyed the comedy show.

Another time, a close friend of the family came upstairs; she was totally covered when she arrived. When she disrobed, she wore tight leggings and a miniskirt. No one in the family seemed distracted or disgusted about this. That was it, I started to realize: the abaya was only a cover. It was looked upon differently than how Westerners looked at it. Though it was "required" of them, or so society or religion dictated, it was viewed more as a rite of passage, not as a reflection of their personality, and many young girls looked forward to being old enough to cover. Many children would practice wrapping the scarf on their heads, which reminded me of playing dress-up and wearing my mom's or aunt's high-heeled shoes as a child. Covering was also a sign of a girl's maturity. Tradition was that usually when girls had their first menses, it was time for them to start covering. Some stricter families expected their daughters to cover much earlier than this.

This was not the custom in my new family. In fact, Siti wore her abaya loosely when out and was not vigilant in keeping her head tightly covered. I don't remember her covering her face, except to loosely wrap a corner of her abaya over it if she deemed it necessary when someone was looking at her. Women who grew up in earlier generations were not as restricted in covering and had different freedoms. Times had changed over the course of ten or twenty years, and there was a different norm, dictated by a stricter religious society with influence from other countries such as Iran and Afghanistan.

Aisha started solid food when she was five months old; and when we were downstairs, whether to feed Aisha or to sit in the TV room, some of the brothers' friends would stop and talk with me. I really enjoyed this time with them. They were not shy to practice speaking English with me, and I welcomed fresh conversation. I was open and liberal enough to listen to them talk about their lives. Sadly, one day, it was suddenly no longer suitable for them to talk with me. Was it unacceptable for me to be "alone" with them? I wondered. Where had this come from? Was it because I was a woman and they were young boys in their twenties? I didn't know if it was coming from my husband; he never said anything to me about this, but someone was no longer comfortable with it happening. It created another disappointment in my life as each day slowly crawled by.

I had heard some interesting stories in my special talks with the boys. Some I had difficulty believing. One story I was told was about when one boy's girlfriend was getting married. Apparently, they had been sexually active. He said his girlfriend would be having surgery to "put all her female parts back together" to make her appear to be a virgin to her groom. I asked why he would not marry her. He said he was too young and didn't have the means to support her. It sounded as if they had accepted their fate, knowing this would eventually be the outcome.

Abdul was thoughtful when he returned from his job searches, making a point to get me out of the house as much as possible with our growing baby. We would go out to eat, hang out at the malls, or meet other couples, friends of my husband's. I enjoyed this time because most of his friends spoke English and loved to play with Aisha. My father-in-law would wait up for us and was not happy with us when we got in later than he wanted. I started to observe that Abdul's dad was becoming increasingly upset with his son's actions. I learned this was not the first time, nor the last, that his dad had needed to bail his son out.

After three months of living with my in-laws, my impatience grew. Nothing happened. My husband had yet to find a job. What the hell was the plan? Abdul did not share any concrete information that made sense to me. What was I supposed to be doing? I could easily have gotten a job as a nurse to help bring in some money for us to live on and save, but it was no longer acceptable for me to support my family. I started to panic, realizing that I could not leave with Aisha even if I wanted to. I felt trapped, a new, alien feeling for me.

My knowledge of Arabic was not strong enough to get the essence of the conversation that was going on around me within the home I was attempting to live in. My new mother-in-law was not happy, and unspoken tensions were mounting. Finally, one morning, through the closed doors of my sacred bedroom, I heard screaming. Abdul's mother was upset and started to raise her voice at Abdul. I didn't know what she said in Arabic, nor am I sure I got the real translation.

Later, when I talked to Miriam, I asked what the argument was about. By the way she replied, I knew I wasn't getting a clear answer. The mood of the home changed like a chameleon's skin. I mentioned to Miriam my concerns that I would not be able to leave with Aisha and how scared this made me feel.

Abdul's volatile temperament began to reemerge the longer he went without employment. His male ego had taken a dive. It was said that he had been blacklisted for leaving his job without completing his obligation. No one was willing to hire him.

So what was next? I wondered why we were still there. I was hesitant to ask Abdul about going back to the States, where I could work until he was able to work again in Saudi Arabia. I didn't want to make him angry, but I also didn't want to keep living with a family I didn't understand or fit in with. I had given it my best shot for three months. Aisha and I needed to go back home.

Apparently, though I was not involved in the discussion, something was resolved. Within the month, Aisha and I left without my husband, returning to my parents' home in the States. Abdul would join us if no further employment leads materialized. Relieved to be back in Kansas, my body, heart, and soul started to relax. I hadn't realized how stressful living with Abdul and his family had been for me. I knew my place, the place where the language and people were familiar; it calmed my fears.

My mother encouraged me to get out and have some fun. She sensed that my spirit was weak. When I was invited to go out with some friends, she would take no excuses for not going with them. It was the best medicine for me, to hear live music and dance with friends, letting the cares of my world float away, and she was excited to spend time with her six-month-old granddaughter.

My feelings of lightness and being alive were quickly overcome the following morning, after Abdul heard I had gone out and left Aisha with my parents. He became very upset and started to raise his voice, questioning my parenting and my decision to go out. His jealously was resurfacing, and he was on the next flight to the US. At that moment, I did not look forward to his return and was frightened by his recurring anger, a behavior that was beginning to shake me to my core.

Part Two

Back in the USA

The First Hit

Terrified, broken, and mortified, I cowered back into the safety of the car as the tears flowed.

Aisha and I returned to Kansas in May of 1985. When Abdul joined us less than a month later, my independent ways were already shining through. Jealousy is not a virtue for any man, let alone a Saudi man married to an independent woman who has both female and male friends. I had always considered Abdul to have a liberal mentality akin to mine, which had been part of our attraction to each other. We enjoyed life and laughed easily. When life was good, it was really good. We were both liberal thinkers but influenced by how we were raised, and it became steadily more apparent that we were not on common ground.

With one of his brothers and some of his college friends already living there, we believed a move to Washington State would be an easier adaptation for Abdul. Work might be easier to find, and Abdul could apply to get his master's degree at his alma mater. A flood of Saudi citizens had arrived throughout the country to learn English and obtain higher degrees of education. Major universities had contracts with the Saudi government's Department of Education for its citizens to advance academically and return to Saudi to use their newfound knowledge to educate others and assume jobs performed by expats.

My limited earnings would be needed to support three people. Being responsible for anyone but myself was not part of my life experience, but I was now responsible for a child and also a husband—physically, emotionally, and financially. A new world evolved that I did not know, and it was disconcerting for me. Being financially independent was a lesson Abdul had not yet learned. We had little money in the bank until the next job, and once again I was grateful that being an experienced nurse meant a job was available and that I would be paid above minimum wage.

At the end of summer, we bought an inexpensive, used brown Ford four-door sedan that was in good condition and headed west for a long trip to Washington. It was my understanding that donations of money from Abdul's family and friends provided for our car and trip. As we traveled, we stopped in northwest Nebraska's sand hills and saw the awesome gray-colored "lesser" Sandhill cranes with wingspans of more than five to over seven feet. They migrated annually on the plains along the Platte River. We journeyed on to Mount Rushmore National Memorial in the Black Hills of South Dakota, where we saw the spectacular sixty-foot sculptures of four US presidents' heads carved into granite, perched on a mountainside while wild buffalo still roamed the prairies below. Abdul had not seen this part of the country and enjoyed its vast beauty.

Aisha decided she was no longer interested in the once-loved teat at nine months; I was heartbroken. I would no longer have the honor of holding my precious daughter close to my warm breast to channel those intimate moments of consolation, nourishment, and understanding. It had become a welcomed and needed escape in my life. I felt alien living in Saudi with my in-laws and with her dad during those days of discontent, and it had been "our time." A sippy-cup became Aisha's next best friend, which she enjoyed drinking as she sat in her car seat while sightseeing along the road trip. She was such a good baby, very enjoyable, and all of my time with her was rewarding. But how would this hollowness and loss be refilled as my "old" life passed away, leaving me unsure of my future, which was now *our* future? I loved being a mother and the enormous love it created, but still I felt an emptiness inside. I was not happy with the way my life was going. Something was off.

After hours of driving on the interstates of America, we exited in Portland, Oregon. We were both glad to be off the road. We were to stay the night at the home of my friends, Pam and Jed. Abdul knew them from our wedding and other gatherings. The last hour of our drive had taken place in silence. My soul was heavy; the voice in my head asked, *Who am I?* Happy not to drive anymore, I got out of the car. I was excited to see my girlfriend. Abdul, without saying anything, walked around to the driver's side of the car, put his right hand in the air and slapped my face; my left cheek took the blow. The force of it disrupted my balance and made my cheek burn like frostbite on a chilly, bitterly cold night, which is what this warm summer night became.

Terrified, broken, and mortified, the tears flowed as I cowered back into the safety of the car. I had never been hit like this. *What the hell was that for?* Had I said something he did not like, or *not* said something? How could I go visit my best friends and act jovial with red, puffy eyes and an injured heart? A good faker, I am not. Pam and I had become friends when I moved to California in late '70s, and she knew me well. Abdul gave me ultimatums to follow as to what to say and not to say, expecting me to carry on as if nothing had happened; but seeing Pam and Jed, the atmosphere was disturbing and awkward. The pretense was that all was well and that we were simply exhausted.

We excused ourselves from a long day of traveling and settled into our lifeless bedroom of silence and damaged egos.

With the dawn of a new summer day, we said our good-byes and headed north to Washington. Abdul hoped our excuses had worked so that everything appeared "cool" between us. I could not look at or talk to him; all I wanted to do was cry and curl up in the fetal position while I died of humiliation. How could this be happening to me?

Infidelity and Abuse

Where was the man I had married?

One of Abdul's younger brothers, Faisal, a student at Seattle University, had a two-bedroom apartment and invited us to stay for a few weeks. Once we got jobs, we would look for our own home. Faisal was happy to see his brother again, and I was welcomed into the family. Faisal was taller and more filled out than Abdul by a few pounds. He was handsome, as I tended to find many Arab men. Faisal's live-in American girlfriend, Shelly, greeted us cordially. She appeared younger than Faisal, but I had started to feel older and more mature than most in my immediate company. My five-year age difference with Abdul and the many years I lived on my own had started to produce a broader gap of maturity and responsibility.

Their apartment was modest, a basic student environment, and it was apparent that Shelly adored Faisal even when he was condescending and rude to her. This was painful for me to observe. She did much of his homework, housework, and whatever else he wanted. It was not the easiest place to live. Faisal's arrogance did not impress me then or in later years.

When Abdul had attended college in Washington, he'd had a steady American girlfriend, as many young Saudi college men did. These girlfriends often helped them do their homework, as English was not easy for them. What was life like for these boys? I think of hormonal Muslim males leaving their own strict "covered" society to live in a country where girls wandered freely, without restrictions. These boys often explored a playboy lifestyle when in the United States. I remembered the culture shock I had experienced at the age of eighteen, when I had gone to live in Washington, DC. I could only imagine what it would have been like if had I moved from Saudi Arabia to America. There were stories of Saudi boys in the States who married and returned with a new wife and maybe a child or two, only for the new wife to find out that her husband was already married (of course, his Saudi wife would have to deal with this development, as well). In my case, I had married a man I met in Saudi Arabia who had recently returned from the States, and he had seemed pretty normal to me, whatever *normal* is.

Once again, as a registered nurse, jobs were available, and I immediately got employment at a home-health agency. Abdul watched Aisha while I worked, and his brother watched Aisha while Abdul had job interviews, which were seldom.

Aisha needed more involved care. When she was ten months old, we found an African American family not too far from our home, and they were able to provide day care. Aisha was happy at their home, and we were happy with their care. She learned how to play on a computer and expanded her world at this early age.

Abdul found a nursing home that provided a course to train him as a certified nursing assistant (CNA), and with this skill, he could find work. It was totally unheard of for a Saudi man to do this type of work. Even Saudi women who became nurses would be patient educators and hospital administrators; no bedpans for them. Abdul impressed me when he said he really loved working with the patients. For a brief time, he was becoming the soft, gentle, caring man I had met in Jeddah almost two years earlier. He didn't seem upset or too proud to do this training. He said, "It will feel good to be able to help take care of and support my family."

It had been a long year since returning to the United States. In September, I went to California to attend the birth of the son of my friend Alexa. Aisha stayed with her daddy. Abdul was very comfortable caring for her, and I was comfortable leaving her with him. To my surprise, when I returned to Washington, Abdul told me he had picked out a house for us to rent. It would be great to have our own place again. At times, I had felt like Abdul and his brother teamed up against me, and I did not like women being treated disrespectfully, the way Shelly was being treated by Faisal.

The rental Abdul had found was not at all what I had visualized for our next home. Being a bad pretender, I initially gave what was surely a startled look of disbelief, and then I heard my own vulnerable throat quiver when I replied feebly that I liked the home. Nothing in the tone of my voice would have convinced anyone. There was an intense silence in the room, and I felt Abdul's disappointment in me. With a crescendo of nonverbal tension building, the drum in my head continued to pound as Abdul's angry beat rose. Without a moment to spare, I gathered my composure and reined in my unfulfilled expectations. I expressed my appreciation to Abdul for what he did to find a home for us. I was grateful for the time he had taken care of our daughter so I could help my best friend, so I expressed my gratitude for that, as well. A bad scene was avoided, but that would not always be the case. Too bad we cannot rewind scenes in our lives, especially when they should never have happened as they did.

I adapted to our new home the best I could. It did have a lot of the things I had asked for, even if it didn't fit my preconceived image. Our home became a social place, and when the weather was nice the patio was used to barbecue. Abdul was such a fine cook. We loved having new friends and family visit us in our tiny, cozy suburban home, even as the differences in our upbringing started to become more and more apparent.

At one point, Abdul's older brother and his family came to visit from Saudi Arabia. I adored my sister-in-law and their three daughters, whom I had met when I lived with Abdul's parents. I was stunned when their youngest daughter, six months old, started to cry and his brother took her over to the fireplace and threatened to throw her in. The brothers laughed. They thought this humorous, while my eyes bulged out of my head at their response. I was disgusted, sick to my stomach, at what I witnessed. I had heard this brother did not treat his family respectfully. His wife, raised in an open and very progressive household in Jeddah's liberal society, never covered. Now she felt it to be the woman's duty to Allah to be there for her husband, regardless of what it might manifest. It was her life lesson, she said, a concept I could not embrace. She was the most caring, loving woman. Why would a loving God want anyone to accept abuse?

Once Abdul had attended all of his CNA classes and finished his practical work experience, there was a test to complete the course. He studied with a group of people from his class. I was excited for Abdul. He seemed to enjoy what he learned and seemed to be happier than he had been for a while. Overall, life was going well in our new home. Abdul and I were tight again, sharing intimacy regularly.

Unfortunately, it shifted quickly. Feeling off, I went to the doctor to find out I had symptoms of a sexually transmitted disease (STD)—something not caught on a toilet seat. I didn't want to believe my husband had cheated on me. When I confronted Abdul, he vehemently denied it. I also wanted to deny it. I yelled at myself and wanted to deny that this thing had happened to me. Nevertheless, I had proof: I had the papers that stated I had contracted an STD. I was treated,

Abdul was treated, and hopefully his female "study" partner was treated, as well. My body, heart, and soul were violated. How does one profess his love for you as his has sex with another?

"You bastard, I so trusted you!" I screamed. I was torn apart with mistrust. I had worked so hard to make a happy life for my family. I left for work with a knot in my stomach and wondered where my husband would be that day. I came home from work with the same knot in my gut. How does one live in the same home and sleep in the same bed with someone who has betrayed her love? Something told me it was time to get out, but I did not know how. Thus began the days with my unfaithful husband and more lies. Where was the man I had married?

After Abdul had stayed with his brother for a few days, he pledged his undying love for me and for his family; he cried and asked for forgiveness. "It will never happen again," he promised. I so wanted to believe him. We started couple's therapy through a local church and were told our problems had little to do with our cultural differences, that we were having "normal" couples' issues, that we were good at playing, but that we had yet to learn how to fight safely and make up.

I listened to my body and spirit and withdrew sexually from my husband. This led to a rocky and abusive home environment. Name-calling and physical violence became the norm for Abdul as his frustration escalated. It was not easy to be called names, to be threatened and hit, and then to be intimate with him, which was how he wanted to make up. Being numb became my coping mechanism. I did not know what to say or what not to say. Abdul called me names that tore at my heart, and he started hitting me more frequently, which made me withdraw even more. A vicious cycle had begun. The upbeat person and problem solver I had always been failed to emerge in this dark time. Infidelity introduced another level of dissatisfaction and misery to our relationship.

While working different shifts as a CNA in a nursing home, Abdul was offered a job by a wealthy older gentleman as his private assistant, to help him with daily grooming and dressing needs. He drove and escorted the man to doctor appointments, on errands, and so forth. Soon, this became Abdul's primary employment. For a long time, Abdul carried around a wooden box with a huge, portable black telephone for his car, very unheard of in the US at that time, but very handy.

Because my salary far exceeded Abdul's, my money paid the rent and the bills, including my student loans and a car payment. I didn't know how many hours Abdul worked or how much money he earned; I did not see. I assumed he spent his money on things like gas and groceries, as little carried over to the family funds. One day, I was outside with Abdul as he got something out of the trunk of his car, and in the trunk I spotted expensive bottles of cologne, some new clothes, and other things he had hidden from me. I also heard he continued to borrow money from others. I became increasingly cautious and doubtful. I had lost my voice, and my spirit was broken.

Walking on eggshells became a familiar feeling, despite my attempts to make peace in the family. Abdul's anger increased, and the verbal abuse got worse. Being called degrading names became the norm for me, and now Aisha was being scolded frequently by her father because she was too messy or too noisy. She was not yet one year old. It had been a long, painful few months that never seemed to end.

I had fallen in love with a special, caring man. Where had this anger come from? What had caused it? Moving to Washington had not helped. The constant turmoil behind closed doors got the best of him and of me. I was afraid and beaten down. Not wanting to let others know how miserable my life had become, I started to isolate myself. I had not listened to their warnings. We were falling apart; a villain had invaded the fairy-tale life I had dreamt of.

One of the things I had always loved about Abdul was the way he had treated me in Saudi Arabia. He was great to be with, respectful and gentle. Now he was increasingly aggressive, hitting me, pushing me, pulling my arms back, and threatening me. This was a strange place for me, one I had never visited; and I was paralyzed, both mentally and physically. Seldom was a raised voice or any name-calling heard in my upbringing. We didn't hear it from my parents, and my siblings and I would have gotten our mouths washed out with soap had we tried. One parent hitting another was unthinkable, although we did receive some physical discipline as kids when we were younger, as my mom might spank or swat us for misbehaving with whatever was near at hand, as was common practice in those days.

Abdul was now upset and angry if I took too long to get home from work or talked to someone I shouldn't have, or if I said something he didn't like. I was in trouble all the time. His behavior left me frozen, unable to respond anymore, except to my daughter, who kept me going. I took one step after another, at a snail's pace at times, to get through the day. Caring for Aisha saved my life but caused more jealousy from her father.

On the surface, around others, Abdul was still a charming, attractive, and supportive man. Friends and family liked him, but behind closed doors chaos bubbled, like a volcano about to erupt. Little did anyone else know the hell in which I lived. It was an utter shock to me, and I was too embarrassed to admit to anyone that it was happening. The fighting was getting uglier. One morning, when I was getting ready for work, Abdul threatened me with a hot curling iron. I had to forcibly push him away. I knew my breaking point had come, that it was time to get out of there. He yelled and insisted that I just get the hell out of the house and get to work. He insisted he would take Aisha to day care. I usually did that.

I tried to sort through the morning at work, but I was unable to cope. My employer was supportive of my intensely vulnerable situation. My fear of what would happen next to Aisha and to me was all I could focus on. My immediate thought was that I needed help and a safe place to stay until we had other options. I could not believe how low I was, and I didn't have friends to help me. My closest female friends all lived in California, and my relatives who lived nearby didn't know what my life had become. I felt too guarded to ask for their help. So I looked in the telephone book's social services section to see what was available; a women's shelter seemed to be my only option. I didn't know where else to go. I slowly drove to the day care and picked up Aisha, never to return, and then, in a fog, I drove to the shelter. I could not believe what my life had become.

Women's Shelter

Stereotypical thoughts surfaced in my head: What did you expect? You married a man from a country where some believe that beating is acceptable.

Hidden out of the public eye on a safe, quiet, tree-lined street outside of Seattle proper, an attractive woman, middle aged and very inviting, greeted my daughter and me at the side entrance to the shelter. It was a small, plain white home, like most of the homes in that neighborhood. There were four shared bedrooms and a nice private backyard where I got the needed fresh air from a suffocating life that I was losing control of.

The women's shelter had an open living room and kitchen area that was shared. At the desk, in an out-of-the-way corner of the living room, I signed an agreement to stay there and was taken to our room for that night. My daughter, now one and half years old, adapted effortlessly and seemed to sense my predicament. She was already acclimated to the nontraditional lifestyle we lived. Again I wondered, *Are our lives decided by destiny?* I had reached the point of no return.

I was now fearful of what lay ahead, scared by the unknown of my future, feeling that I wasn't in control.

An obligation of staying at the shelter was to participate in a group support session. Each woman had to share why she was there. After I heard horrendous stories from other women, it was my turn to talk. I had listened to the stories of women with broken bones, bruised faces, and stitches from knife wounds. Nervous, anxious, and embarrassed to talk in front of others, I felt vulnerable. My voice squeaked out that my "stuff" seemed so insignificant compared to what everyone else had shared. I remarked meekly, "I've only gotten hit and threatened a few times."

I will never forget the strong, firm words out of the confident facilitator's mouth, "Don't you for one second think this way. It is not all right for anyone to hit you, no matter what the reason. You have sought help early, before more can happen." I hung my head in shame. I was educated about the phases and cycles of abuse: physical, sexual, verbal, and mental. That it can be an addictive roller coaster, even more complicated when a child is involved. The final phase was hardest: leaving an abusive relationship.

Most people would not have imagined my being in a relationship that was verbally and physically abusive, being the free-willed, assertive, spirited, independent woman I was. With my strong German build, one would have thought I might have been able to overpower Abdul's more petite frame. This is where my adrenaline could have been tested, the fight-or-flight theory. I could not believe that I was in this type of relationship.

More stereotypical thoughts surfaced in my head. *What did you expect? You married a man from a country where some believe that beating is acceptable.* Still, I had known American women married to Saudis who had "normal" lives. The bottom line was this: abuse happens in every country. Still, my naïveté amazed me. *Why did I marry a man from a different culture and religion?* We had been told that our "challenges" were not about culture and religion; they were about the difficulties of two people relating peacefully in a new marriage, with a child, and things had not gone as expected. Many couples went through this—or so we had been told.

Aisha started at another day care that I was able to find for her and enroll her in secretly. During certain times of the day, I avoided locations we had used before. Any possible contact with Abdul did not feel safe.

I was able to get a lawyer through the women's shelter; and by the order of a judge, I got permission to return to our home, while Abdul would live with his brother. Later, a restraining order was needed to keep him away from us, and my employer obtained one to keep Abdul from harassing me at work. Divorce proceedings began.

Abdul hired a lawyer, as well. He was granted supervised visitation rights a couple of times a week at a neighbor's house across the street. He was also ordered to leave his and Aisha's passports with the court. Abdul made a big deal out of my neglecting to grab the passports when I left the house before going to the shelter. Safety had been first on my mind, however—not the passports. Abdul was strongly advised to take an anger management class to see if he could improve his temperament. It was the end of May 1986. My spirit was shattered, and my head was spinning in circles. I needed old friends who knew me; they could help me see. My world had become a fog.

Midnight Escape

*I attempted to bury the constant fear of Abdul taking
Aisha to Saudi Arabia.
He swore on the Quran he would never do this.
I wanted to believe him.*

A midnight escape was planned by my friend Janet. She drove a rented U-Haul truck to move Aisha and me and our limited household belongings to her friend's home in California. I hoped I would feel safer with others who knew me and could help calm my troubled soul.

I house-sat for friends in the golden rolling hills of California and remained hidden in a safe environment. I was told that Abdul tried to find us. After a month of respite, mixed feelings of sadness and guilt surfaced, as I had kept our daughter from seeing her father.

My work as an education instructor at a convalescent hospital kept my mind busy and provided money to support us. After a month back in California, Aisha and I moved into a funky trailer and found a great place for childcare on a woman's farm with only three or four other children of similar ages. Aisha's day-care provider had two children in high school who would play with the kids in the afternoons. Their farm had cows, chickens, and even pigs. Aisha talked about her experiences watching the animals and getting to pet them. We made up songs about them. We enjoyed talking, storytelling, or singing as we drove the thirty-minute commute back and forth to our humble, funky abode.

After moving to California, I changed lawyers. Divorce papers were ready but put on hold, as our lawyers from Seattle had been talking. They encouraged Abdul and me to talk. Abdul told his lawyer he wanted another chance. He had finished his anger management class and learned a great deal. He had learned ways to channel his anger. After much consideration, I knew how much I missed Abdul, the man I fell in love with, and I wanted to talk with him. Maybe he was better, I reasoned, although I was still uneasy. Maybe people can change with the proper tools to use to cope when angry. Aisha missed her daddy, too.

A time was arranged with my Washington lawyer to call Abdul at his brother's home on a Sunday evening at five o'clock. I drifted like a ghost, floating ungrounded with a squeamish feeling in my stomach, unsure how I could make this crazy life of mine work. Still fearful, I was not ready for him to know where I was or to give him a number to reach me. I found a public telephone to use outside of a building by the local park where I could openly talk to him. It had been a month since we last spoke.

Using a calling card, I apprehensively dialed his number, exactly on time. I felt split in two, unsure if I was doing the right thing. Various people had coached me on what to do and what not to do. I held my breath until he answered the phone. Damn, I always liked hearing that sweet voice of his. It seemed as if time stopped, and I did not want to look back. I wanted life to be good again. Could we not begin again?

Of course, he said he was so sorry. He really loved me, *us*, and wanted our family back together. He said he had changed. I know how much I wanted to believe him, as others in abusive relationships do when the abuser professes love. How can someone hurt you while he pledges his love for you? I wanted our marriage to work, despite the high percentage of such marriages that do not succeed. The optimistic person I was, the nurse caregiver, believed I could make this work, that I could heal us.

I forgave again. Abdul knew the right words to woo me. My heart and head were in turmoil over the decision, but I wanted to try.

Our friends in Portland, Pam and Jed, were willing to help us. They liked Abdul and empathetically tried to understand him, whereas many of my friends had given up on him. They let us meet at their home for visits, a halfway point for both. Still uncomfortable being alone with Abdul, I felt safe and protected with my friends nearby.

Reconciliation began. We met monthly for several months. I wanted Abdul nearer, but I was not yet ready for us to live together. He was open to finding his own place and going from there. I embraced strong ideals regarding both of us having the right to be with our child. Abdul, on his best behavior, shared our home until he found a room he rented with a shared kitchen from a single mother. He easily found work as a teller at a bank. Perhaps having a work history in the United States was finally helping help him secure jobs. We planned activities together, but mostly on the weekends due to our busy work schedules and my parenting responsibilities.

For Aisha's second birthday, we celebrated with friends at my home, complete with balloons and banners, party hats and kazoos. Aisha was quite a talker by the age of two. She was fun spirited and laughed easily. She thoroughly enjoyed her party and was comfortable being her own person.

Many of our friends at the party had also been at our wedding, so there seemed to be a spirit of celebration about Abdul and me reuniting. Many wanted our relationship to work. They wanted me to be happy with my life. They wished us the best in rekindling and forgiving and moving beyond the past, though they realized this would not be an easy task.

My belief was strong that a father has as much right to be with his child as the mother does, unless, of course, it is an unsafe situation. Abdul had been upset with me, not with his daughter—that was what I wanted to believe. Was I in denial in believing that she was safe with him? When Abdul got mad, he would threaten to take our daughter away. I learned this was common for many bicultural relationships. Attempting to prevent that from ever happening, I had gone to the Department of Immigration and Passport Office to see what they would do. I pursued many empty avenues and struck out all the way around. The response I received was, "Nothing has happened yet, so nothing can be done." I attempted to bury the constant fear of Abdul taking Aisha to Saudi Arabia. He swore on the Quran he would never do this. I wanted to believe him.

Abdul and I continued to see each other regularly. We worked on our relationship and attended counseling. Abdul wanted us to live together again, but I was more content to not live with his mood swings and jealousy. In March 1987, my parents came to visit, and Abdul joined us. My parents had always liked Abdul but were concerned about his abusive ways and my safety.

In May, on Mother's Day, Abdul, Aisha, and I had a family day together. It was the first time we had done something as a family, just the three of us, for quite some time. We had heard about a kite-flying competition in Santa Cruz, not far from my home. It was an unusually warm day on the coast. We strolled without sweaters as we played in the ocean, racing with the waves, and we watched Aisha laugh. On the boardwalk, we grabbed hotdogs and sodas while we watched the kites soar in and out of the gentle wind currents. The talented people at the end of the strings skillfully wove the colorful kites through the air. They created a surreal effect. We laughed and played throughout the day. We held hands and felt like a happy family again, if only for that moment. I was going to cherish it. Arm in arm, with Aisha on our laps, we watched the brilliant sun set on the peaceful sea. For a day, my gloom lifted. This was my prince. I prayed it could continue.

Earlier that spring, I had started a new nursing job. I also found a day care nearer to my home and more convenient for Abdul and me picking up Aisha. We adjusted to this new pattern.

Over Memorial Day weekend, Abdul visited his brother in Washington and took Aisha with him. She loved time with her daddy. When Aisha and I talked after their trip, I found out that Jennifer, our new babysitter, went with them. That surprised me. At first, Abdul was fidgety and defensive when I inquired. He said she had wanted to come and that she was nice company. He thought it was a good idea, just in case he and his brother wanted to go out for a while and, conveniently, she could watch Aisha.

Of course, Abdul had not been upfront with me about the nature of his relationship with the babysitter. Aisha was now at an age where she could divulge many secrets if a question was asked a certain way. I didn't always get the answer I had hoped for. Should it have surprised me? Probably not. Did it hurt? Yes. I tried to minimize it; I felt it justified my decision not to live with him, then or ever again. We weren't divorced, so I didn't think he would start spending time with the babysitter. Still, I needed to let him go. Maybe this was his way of moving on.

Part Three

The Kidnapping

Losing Aisha

*What do you do when you want to say something
but no words come forth?*

It was the Fourth of July holiday weekend of 1987, and I had agreed to let Abdul take Aisha to Disneyland. Although she seemed rather young, it also sounded like fun. I knew she would love seeing Mickey Mouse and all the other Disneyland characters. Still, I wouldn't be a part of their excursion, and I was jealous that I wouldn't accompany them. I wanted to hear her contagious laughter and see her wide, beaming smiles in the fantasyland of Disney.

By then, Abdul had taken Aisha for a long weekend to Washington, and it had seemed to go well. She also occasionally stayed at his home. A few days without a two-and-a-half-year-old was welcome. I no longer wanted to be a couple. My life was freer without the pressures and oppressive lifestyle that occurred when I lived with Abdul.

Before they started their four-day weekend and their drive south to Los Angeles, the three of us met for pizza early Wednesday evening, right after work. Abdul wasn't hungry and seemed nervous. He said he hadn't been feeling well. Aisha didn't seem right, either—a mother's intuition sensed something was off. Still, I gave my hugs and kisses to Aisha and told her I loved her. I wished her a great trip. Abdul put her in the car seat and closed the door, then hugged me goodbye. I wished them a fun, safe trip. Abdul got in the car, and as they drove away, I threw kisses to my fragile, little, lovable girl, and yelled, "Take a lot of pictures!"

Aisha was not her usual joyful self as they drove away; she had seemed clingier to me. I said my customary prayer, the one I said every time she went anywhere with her father: "Please, God, return my daughter safely." It would be a long trip for her and a very long, apprehensive weekend for her mother. Something didn't feel right, but I consoled myself that I always felt like this when Aisha left with her dad.

My holiday weekend was spent with friends. It included watching fireworks, one of my favorite things to do. I constantly wondered how Aisha was doing, missing her, as always, when she was gone, but I was also grateful for some "me" time. Being a single parent isn't always easy. Her jolly voice would not wake me in the morning; my home was so quiet without her. She was such a happy, content child, though she could be stubborn and feisty. She was in her terrible-twos, so it was par for the course. She could easily aggravate her dad and me, which could also wear on his temper.

On Saturday evening, I was so happy when they called me. I was relieved to hear their cheerful voices. Abdul and I spoke first, and he filled me in. Everything was going well, and Aisha was excited to see all the Disney characters. He then passed the phone to Aisha. She had quite a vocabulary for her age, which allowed our conversation to flow smoothly. Aisha excitedly said, with her dad's help, "Mommy, we are in Disneyland." I asked her a few questions about her trip and what fun they were having. I told her I missed her so much and could hardly wait for her to come home to tell me about her weekend. She sang into the phone, "I love you. I miss you, Mommy." I said, "See you tomorrow, Alligator." She replied, in her squeaky little high-pitched voice, "After while, Crocodile." Then click went the phone, along with my heart.

It was Sunday morning. Their eight-hour-plus journey home should have started. Aisha would be home in just a few more hours. I decided to catch up on long-overdue phone calls to distract myself.

Abdul and I had been spending less time together, which was actually fine with me. After reacquainting ourselves for eight months, I still couldn't seem to do things the way he wanted me to, which continued to deflate my self-esteem. I was happier without him in my life, but he was not content to live without his wife and child. I hoped that maybe dating the babysitter would help him move on. He was not happy with me.

The past couple of years of our life together had been unpleasant and painful for me, for both of us. Abdul easily forgave himself of the past hurts and hits, then overcompensated to charm me back into his arms with gifts, flowers, and kind words. It no longer worked for me. I had lost respect after the first hit, the first affair, and the numerous lies. The scars of the past seemed impossible to heal.

Talking on the phone to friends helped pass the time as I started to count the minutes until my girl would be home. I envisioned Aisha getting out of her dad's car, dressed in a colorful Minnie Mouse hat from Disneyland, her skinny little legs running, with her arms reaching out to my waiting arms. All the tight hugs and warm kisses she would offer would be well worth the wait. It was close to four o'clock in the afternoon, she would be home soon, in just a couple of hours.

Then, while I talked to my girlfriend Penny, she mentioned that her husband had seen Abdul at the bank on Wednesday afternoon, and he had told him he was changing jobs. I almost dropped the phone. My heart stopped. I could hardly breathe as I fumbled to sit down. With a shriek in my voice, I blurted, "My daughter is with Abdul! I knew nothing about him leaving the job he said he loved!"

My heart started to race, and it jumped into my throat with nervous, frightful force. I started to pace back and forth. What did Penny just say? I had seen Abdul on Wednesday, and he hadn't mentioned a thing about a new job. No wonder he hadn't eaten and Aisha had behaved as she had. Something was wrong, very wrong!

As my evening dreadfully and painfully crawled by and the time for Aisha's return passed, I got caught up in my fears. Something must have happened. Maybe they'd had car trouble and Abdul was unable to get to a phone to call me. The later it got past the expected time of arrival, the more I had to face the wild, crazy demons that haunted me. Did they not go to Disneyland? Had they called from New York City prior to boarding the nine p.m. plane to Saudi Arabia, the same flight we had taken to Riyadh when Aisha was only a few months old? "Oh, my God, help me!" I yelled as I sank to my knees, not wanting to believe my worst nightmare had come true. *Please let me be wrong.*

I fumbled with the telephone as I called Abdul's landlady. She confirmed my fear. He had moved out the previous week. I had visited his place a week before, and he'd had a couple of packed boxes in his room. He claimed he had gotten them from his brother and was putting them in storage. How dumb could I be? Now I really knew. He had kidnapped Aisha!

Hysterically, I called my good friend Robin, who came over immediately. She had seen Aisha on Wednesday. She held me as I cried in her arms, shaking uncontrollably. Frantically, I tried hard to convince myself he wouldn't do this. Why had I trusted him again? Had he not told me a few months earlier that I trusted too much? I could not forgive myself for being so careless, stupid, and naïve. Robin encouraged me to call the police, who, through my raging, nonstop flow of tears, took a full report. Mortified, I called my family. This was the first night of many, for months and years to come, that I would not sleep.

I knew where they were. Abdul had taken Aisha out of the country without being questioned. A man with dark hair, taking a blonde child to Saudi Arabia alone, and without my permission. Had the babysitter traveled with them? I was unaware he had gotten their passports back from the court when he had moved to California. I was also unaware that he hadn't completed the anger management class. In fact, he had only attended the class a couple of times before he had dropped out. How could someone be so good at lying and so conniving, and how could I be so damn gullible?

It was eight o'clock in California, which made it around four o'clock in the morning, Saudi time, just before the first prayer of the day. My hands trembled as I dialed the telephone number for the home of my husband's father in Riyadh. His father answered. He lied to me and told me he hadn't seen Abdul and Aisha. I insisted I knew they were there and demanded to talk to his son. His dad finally surrendered and got Abdul to the phone. What do you do when you want to say something but no words come forth?

What I said, I do not remember. I was in shock. I was so overwhelmed with anger and hurt. I cried and yelled at him over the phone. "*Why?*" I yelled, "*Why?* How could you do this?"

"The thought of living in the States, divorced, was more than I could handle," Abdul said. "This was not the life I had imagined." He claimed his motive was to get me back and for his daughter to be raised a Muslim with the help of his family. It was his duty to fulfill, under Islam, he said, regardless of having sworn on the Quran he would never take her from me. I was speechless. How do you reply to those words when your daughter is taken from you, thousands of miles away, and there is little hope of her return? What could I possibly say that would bring her back? I knew that would not happen. I was at his mercy. So I worked hard to appease Abdul, without making more waves. I wanted my daughter.

I insisted he let me talk with Aisha. When the phone was passed to Aisha, she asked me sweetly, sleepily, "Where are you, Mommy? Why aren't you here with me, Mommy?" Then her fragile voice started to break and she began to cry. My heart pounded through my chest while I listened to my baby cry. I wanted to crawl through the phone and grab my precious, tiny girl. How could I make this right? My heart shattered into a thousand pieces, like a delicate china teacup dropped to the floor. Moments froze, time stood still, until I had consoled her all I possibly could and had to hang up the phone. She was not even three, and she was gone. Would I ever see her again? I couldn't focus or think. *What do I do now?* I wanted to die, it hurt so badly.

Part Four

Life after the Abduction

Before Returning to Saudi Arabia
July–September 1987

I am left to a whole new world of grief,
one in which I must make a new life,
keep my heart beating every day,
and find any possible path back to my child.

Just when I thought my life might finally be coming together all hell had broken loose. I thought I could relax again, no longer living in an abusive relationship, and shared custody had seemed to be working. My estranged husband had a nice job at a bank and a girlfriend, and Abdul and I seemed to be getting along well with each other. Now, my world had fallen apart.

Having a child abducted has to be the second-worst tragedy that could happen to a mother, a father, a family. My daughter was not yet three years old; she didn't know what it was like to be without her mother. My only consolation was that at least I knew where she was and that she was safe. I didn't need to worry whether she was dead or alive; not knowing this would have intensified the whole scenario to an emotional trauma beyond belief. It was painful enough *knowing*. How does someone cope *without* knowing this?

How would I get through the nightmare of losing my child? I attempted to minimize my feelings by reminding myself that I could speak with her. Regardless of the humongous phone bills, it was well worth any amount of money to reassure my daughter that I loved her. We would talk by phone, sending hugs and kisses over the many miles. I knew she was not in harm's way; and I knew she would survive, as I knew, one way or another, so would I. I just did not know how.

I was tortured. I was angry with a man I called my husband. I was furious at myself for once again trusting this man who could not be trusted. The silence of my home was unbearable. I missed Aisha's jolly, cheerful voice; her warm, caring hugs; and her sloppy, playful kisses as she ever so gently licked my cheek as I quickly moved away while she laughed. Anywhere I went, hearing children's voices killed me. Watching kids play in the parks made me cry. The reality of knowing I might never have that again tore my heart to pieces. I spent my days obsessed with what to do next. I was a total wreck and couldn't seem to sleep, eat, or breathe. My life was a fog of chilling unknowns, and I could not see a way out.

The day after the kidnapping, I called my lawyer. She was as shocked as I was. She obtained the police report and later called the district attorney. Together, they did what they could to help me. Legal papers were filed, which gave me full custody of Aisha. Felony kidnapping charges were filed. Later, the pros and cons of having the felony charges dropped were debated. Logically, if Abdul tried to return, he would be allowed to enter, but he could then be arrested once in the United States.

At the time of Aisha's kidnapping, the powerful movie *Not Without My Daughter*, based on the book by Betty Mahmoody, was being shown in theaters. The story told of an American woman and her daughter who were trapped in Iran, her husband's country. In the movie, after much terror, they were rescued. Needless to say, I was unable to bring myself to watch the movie nor read the book for years. I had my own drama, my own story to tell, and there was no end in sight.

I needed to solve a puzzle that troubled me. Did Abdul's friends know what he had done? I found out that some of his friends had known he planned on traveling to Saudi Arabia. He had told them he had my approval to take Aisha. Little did they know what his plan really entailed.

Would I ever see my daughter again? He had lied to them, as he had lied to me; he had told his friends that his father was ill and wanted to see Aisha and that I would come later.

I discovered that he had sold our new car to one of his friends. A few months before, Abdul had asked for my signature on documents to refinance the car. Things started to add up, and puzzle pieces were coming together. Was I that naïve and stupid? I just did not want to believe it would happen. "I would never do that to my daughter, or to you. In Islam, a child her age belongs with her mother," he would say to me.

I had pursued many avenues to prevent an abduction from ever happening. I had talked with officials at the United States Department of Immigration office in San Francisco in hopes that they could put a hold on her passport, as I had the same fear many mothers do with children of dual citizenship. All I got was a brick wall. "We can't do a thing. She has to be kidnapped before any action can be taken," they told me.

I wanted to go yell at them, now that it had happened. "What are you going to do?" The indignation and anger I felt were overwhelming. I grabbed at every crumb that fell my way if I thought it would make a difference in the outcome.

I did the best I could to function and get through the day. To help cope, I connected with a network of women in similar situations. While I went through my nightmare, other moms were also living theirs. Talking to others who knew what I was going through helped and was insightful. I had gotten in touch with the US State Department and the Saudi embassy in Washington, DC, pleading for their assistance. During this time, there was congressional intervention. Kidnapping of American children was happening quite frequently and continues to this day. The State Department opened a new department, called the Office of Children's Issues, because of the increased number of children being kidnapped and taken out of the country. In the '80s, many women went on *The Phil Donahue Show* about this experience. Geraldo Rivera did a TV show about American children held hostage. Grief-stricken women from various walks of life marched to the White House and begged for help to free their children. There was a great deal of publicity around American children being kidnapped by a parent and taken to a foreign country. Mostly, women were the victims, but an occasional father would join our struggle.

The Hague Service Convention was signed to facilitate an efficient way for laws of one country to be enforced in another country. Not all countries honored this treaty's policies, Saudi Arabia being one of those that did not. If it had, then under the Hague Treaty, with Abdul being "wanted" in the United States, the KSA would theoretically have respected our laws.

Many other helpless, hopeful, frantic mothers asked their politicians to help them. Many took action into their own hands and did whatever was possible. American Children Held Hostage was an organization started by a woman whose son was taken to another Arab country. She was unable to see him or contact him at that time. Eventually, she went on with her life in the United States but continued to pursue her efforts to be with her son. The Center for Missing and Exploited Children and many other organizations were willing to listen and do what they could, which was little in my situation, as I knew where my daughter was.

After Aisha was kidnapped, I sought out options for rescuing her. My lawyer heard of a man, Randy, who apparently had helped get a child out of some foreign country. She invited me to go with her to meet this charming man who truly thought he could help, and my hopes went wild. We drove through the winding country roads to Randy's small, simple family home on the California coast. As we sat together to talk about my dilemma, he boldly announced, "I can go to Saudi and help get your daughter out. I'm sure I could do that." My mouth hung open at his response when I asked how he planned to do it. Not knowing a thing about Saudi Arabia, he overconfidently said, "I'll just ring the doorbell, burst in, grab her, and run."

"Really?" I asked. "Do you think it's that easy? Don't you think I would have done that by now if it were that easy?" Perturbed, I realized he didn't have a clue. I was sick with disappointment. My hopes were dashed. First of all, how would he get the visas needed? Walls surrounded the majority of homes, and their gates and doors were locked. Someone either honked or rang a bell at the entrance, and a houseman would let that person enter, but only if he knew who the person was. Did he think they were going to just let him in? They wouldn't even open the gate. Of course, I didn't talk to him again. I don't remember if we even talked about the price for his services, but I'm sure it would have exceeded fifty thousand dollars.

After that meeting, I was both disappointed and fuming. He was as clueless as I had been when I'd gone to Saudi Arabia the first time. Was he just out for the money? Well, I didn't have the money, anyway, and he had no knowledge of life in Saudi Arabia.

I was then referred to a private investigator named Bob. We met at a local restaurant in California. He also claimed to have experience in getting others out of a foreign country. Again, he didn't know about Saudi customs. The price he gave was $100,000. How could I possibly afford this amount? I definitely did not have it, nor did my family or friends. Regrettably, I replied, "Sorry, I cannot afford this, and you can provide no guarantees."

Now what was I to do? I could easily find work in Saudi Arabia as a nurse, and I was prepared to work there in order to be with my daughter. I was miserable in the States, anyway, living in a vapor of darkness now that she was gone. I needed to accept that she was in Saudi Arabia now. *What can I do to be closer to her, and how can I be a part of her life?*

The problem was more with Abdul, not his family. Not that I really believed that his family would support me in seeing my daughter. That would be a betrayal to their son, regardless of what he had done. Abdul hadn't been "home" that long, but the longer he was back, the more influenced he seemed by the culture of his past. It wasn't easy for me to keep from hating my husband and his family for their participation in this terrible act. How could someone take a young child away from her mother? My very young daughter was still learning English, and she had been kidnapped and taken to a land where it was rarely spoken.

My insides ached. My time on Earth held little value until I was with her. I knew the kidnapping was mostly an act of revenge by Abdul because I had wanted to escape; I had wanted a divorce to get away from the verbal, physical, and psychological abuse. I did fear my child could be taken; and once it happened, I was left with a whole new world of grief, one in which I knew I'd have to make a new life, keep my heart beating every day, and find any possible path back to my child.

Reunion in Jeddah

I was in a trance;
I could not talk as I lay on the cold marble landing of the stairway.

Once my daughter was kidnapped, I realized that returning to Saudi Arabia could be a very dangerous situation in which I wouldn't have control or protection. When I had first gone to there, an American company had sponsored me, providing some clout if something happened to me. Now I was on the outside looking in, and the only way to see my daughter was to go back in again, alone. What security would I have? From my prior experience in Saudi Arabia, and based on that of others, I didn't really know. I knew it was a very strange and mysterious country. It was, in many ways, an ancient culture with ancient, ingrained beliefs.

Abdul had the freedom to let me into his country or not. He also had the ability to force me out. The State Department gave lip service, but to get a commitment from them was impossible. Their standard response was, "Unfortunately, the frequency of international abductions of children by parents continues to rise every year. Our organization strives to raise public awareness, counsel victims, and works on improving relationships to aid. If we can be of further assistance . . ."

Our country wouldn't risk upsetting the Saudi government, and vice versa.

There were just so many stories, some with horrendous outcomes. What would happen to me if I returned to Saudi Arabia? What consequences would I face? What if I disappeared? Should I just give up? Could a mother really do this? If I was responsible for a family in the States, then maybe I would've had to stay for them. But Aisha was my only child, my blood. I had brought her into the world, and I was not going to let her live her life without her mother's presence. She had been there long enough without me. I couldn't stand to hear her sad, pitiful cries on the phone, sobbing as she tried to catch her breath, yet doing her best to be so brave. Poor little soul. "I am so sorry," I would tell her.

I would have to be brave for her, although I was sick with fear about what could happen to me. I didn't know what to do, what to expect, and who to trust. Was I being too paranoid?

During the months after Aisha was kidnapped, Abdul and I talked many times about our relationship, about how to get back together and make it work again. Placating Abdul, in spite of the abuse I had endured, was the only way I would ever be able to see my daughter again. I taped every phone call with him and my daughter. These tapes are still in my possession and are still painful to listen to. Abdul wanted me to come live in Saudi Arabia with him and Aisha. He "loved" me. Aisha cried so much for her mommy. Bottom line: if I wanted to see her again, I knew what I had to do.

Before I returned to Saudi Arabia, the State Department and the American embassy in the KSA communicated with the Saudi embassy in the United States on my behalf. It was decided that, before I returned to Saudi, I should have Abdul write a letter to confirm his permission for me to leave Saudi Arabia at any time, of my free will—

of course, without our daughter. This letter would only partly ease my fear that he could and would prevent me from leaving. Because he sponsored me, he was responsible for my visa into and out of the country. I worked very closely with the American embassy in Jeddah, and they would, in turn, periodically inform my family in the States that I was all right—a "well-being check."

In September 1987, Abdul sponsored me to come back into Saudi Arabia. He had worked for over a month at a hospital and was provided hospital housing with a day care on-site, one with English as its predominant language. He lined up a nursing job for me in the hospital's outpatient clinic. When I arrived in Jeddah, I would share a simple two-bedroom apartment with him and Aisha.

I was beside myself with anticipation. After the usual grueling flight, I was greeted with a shy embrace by Abdul at the airport. His demeanor seemed to be one of caring and love. He was genuinely happy about our reunion. This helped me get a grip on my ever-changing emotions—from the depths of anger to fear of the unknown. In truth, I longed to hold and comfort my daughter, who was anxiously waiting for me at their home with her nanny. To reunite with Aisha was foremost to me. To hear her angelic voice, receive her smiles, and feel her soft, gentle touch. As hard as I tried, it was difficult for me to hide my resentment about the reason for my return to Saudi Arabia and to my husband. I prayed for divine help to get me through it.

In less than an hour, we arrived at the hospital apartment complex. My heart was jumping out of my chest. I had dreamt of my daughter nightly for what seemed like years, although it had "only" been two long, agonizing months. While getting out of the car, Abdul suddenly and passionately kissed me. "Welcome home," he said. "Aisha is also very excited to see her mommy." If I had known where to go, I would have darted to my destination, but I reluctantly waited for Abdul to get my luggage. Finally Abdul nodded, "Go ahead. Second floor, apartment on the right, number 202. I'm right behind you."

In a flash, I was knocking on the apartment door, saying, "Little girl, little girl, let your mommy come in."

As the maid checked the peephole and unlocked the door, I could hear Aisha's little squeal as she yelled, "Mommy, Mommy, Mommy!" Barely inside the door, I fell to my knees. Tears streaked my cheeks as Aisha jumped into my lap. She cried and laughed at the same time as we rolled onto the floor. I kissed and tickled her sweet little body as she begged for more. We were together. I would do what was possible not to be separated again. Aisha and I shared a bond words could not explain.

My relationship with my husband was another matter, although Abdul and I would work to find ways to repair it. Unfortunately, he quickly made it clear that Aisha would never be allowed to come back to the States, even if we did do well together. What a tough place to be. My one hope would be for Aisha to graduate from high school and be able to go to college in the States. Of course, that would take many years—a haunting thought.

How could I respect and live with someone who took my daughter all the way across the world, cheated on me, lied to me, and was abusive? How was I going to make this relationship work? But the calling of a mother is so deep that she will forfeit her own well-being for the sake of her child.

Thus, my new life with my daughter and her father began. With persistence, I attempted to build this new life. I felt betrayed, small, and too weak to stand tall.

Friends and family who wrote me were told to include Abdul in the letters. They were encouraged to keep the conversation simple and light, as I expected or assumed he would read all of my mail. Outside mail came to the hospital's mailroom, which Abdul would pick up. Eventually, my friends started numbering their letters because they didn't think I received all of them.

The situation was tenuous enough that I felt a need to create a series of codes. I started it with my sister and my friends, and I would do this later with my daughter. We were referred to as birds in cages, as another way to relate to life in Saudi Arabia. My girlfriend would write, "I think of your finches in their cages, and I pray you learn as they do, to at least fly and soar within." We also created a code word: *juniper*. When I replied to letters, I would indicate the general mood by describing how the trees were growing. In a letter, I would write, "The juniper trees seem to be growing faster than I thought they would," meaning things were moving too fast. Alternatively, "The junipers are doing well," or "They are not looking very good today," and so forth, and they would know what was meant.

Shortly after I returned to Saudi Arabia, Abdul disclosed information that few outside of the American embassy knew. There was a leak in the system at the American embassy in Jeddah. Non-American embassy employees could be bribed. From that day forward, I made sure my file was no longer kept with the main records. I asked that it be kept in a safe place in the consulate's office because of the information breach.

The majority of my time away from work was spent with Aisha, who would be three years old in December. We spent all the time together that we could; we did not take it for granted. I would tell Aisha, "Mommy loves you very much, and it makes me sad when you are sad. I do not know what your daddy might do. Mommy might be leaving to go to America for a little while, but I will return. I will always do what I can to be with you and be near you. If I can't be with you, then I will call you, so we will always talk and sing to each other." She, at a young age, had already experienced not being with me. She understood what she could on her level. It had been hard for her, but I saw her fortitude. I spoke straightforwardly with her and prepared her for what might lie ahead. Her resilience was remarkable.

In spite of all that Abdul had done, I endeavored to make the most of this new situation, a reconciliation I'd essentially been blackmailed into, because it meant I got to be with my precious daughter. At times, for moments, it even felt like the life we had dreamed of. As a family, we went to the seaside for nice, cool evenings and enjoyed drinking fresh fruit juice. We went swimming at the compound pool or in the Red Sea. There were many restaurants and many different ethnic cuisines. On the weekends, Thursdays and Fridays, fancy hotels had great buffets with fantastic carved statues made from ice or butter. We would hike in the desert and have picnics. Watching the sunsets along the corniche by the Red Sea was common for many families and one of my favorite activities. We would have parties with friends and co-workers. We would go to *ma'a s-salāmas* (going-away parties). People would come and go in that crazy country. That was a constant. Most people traveled out of Saudi on their off time. One of the benefits of working abroad was the amount of vacation time. Sadly, this was no longer going to happen for us as a family of three again, a thought that would bring me back to my wretched reality.

An American woman and I also shared a lot of time together. Teresa and her Saudi husband had met in the States while going to college, and they were now very comfortable living in Saudi. Her husband said, "My tradition is who I am, and if people do not like it, so be it." Teresa embraced Islam and learned Arabic. They had a beautiful family and lived in a huge compound with different homes for the whole extended family. She was happily immersed in the culture.

That was not my reality. Life was hard during the time I was in Jeddah. Abdul and I were no longer on a carousel; it had become a continuous roller coaster of emotions. One day, Aisha and I were outside on the patio of our second-floor apartment. Aisha said to me, in a whisper, "Mama . . . maybe we could tie sheets together and throw them over the balcony and get down and run away." I was stunned.

Her little mind was already thinking of ways to escape. Where was this coming from?

My pathetic reply was, "Where would we go?"

Already, her little mind strategized options. How aware was an almost-three-year-old? How deep was her understanding of what had happened, that she had been kidnapped and that her life was not the same? I had been the constant in her life until she was taken. Children are so smart. They may not be able to vocalize what is happening, but they are definitely aware of the discord surrounding them.

Aisha was familiar with the anger and abuse that had occurred in the States. It started to happen again. Being with Abdul was quickly becoming unbearable, and I was unable to make the marriage work. It just got worse, and Aisha lived with the escalating violence. She saw her dad literally pick me up and throw me down on the marble landing of the stairway on the second floor of our apartment complex. His plan was to kick me down the stairs, but Aisha cried and screamed so loudly that our neighbor, a female doctor from Egypt, heard the commotion on the stairway and came to see what was happening. In Arabic, she asked what was going on. Whatever she said, Abdul stopped. The whole thing was like a scene from a scary movie, and I was one of the actors, the victim. It was hard to believe how strong Abdul was when he got mad.

I couldn't speak as I lay on the cold marble landing, embarrassed to be seen in that condition, and I didn't know what to do. Never had I been through anything like this. I was caught up in the cycle of domestic abuse, humiliated and weak in body, mind, and spirit.

My demons laughed at me, saying, *You cannot even take care of yourself. How can you help your daughter?* These intimidating, unnerving thoughts and emotions beat me down further. I was unable to move. After the neighbor's confrontation, Abdul yelled in a low, deep voice at a terrified, crying Aisha to get inside the apartment. I stumbled my way into the apartment and flopped onto a chair. As Abdul came inside he mumbled a few words and grabbed Aisha, who was petrified. He told her to quit crying. She knew to obey, and he took her away.

When Abdul came back, she was not with him, and I didn't know where he had taken her. I wouldn't see her for a few days. This wasn't the first time he had done this. When he was angry it could happen. He knew how much it hurt me. She often ended up being left with someone whom she had never met. Though I felt desperate and hopeless about my own life, I felt worse for my daughter and what she must have been going through. I wept blood, it hurt so intensely.

From the depths of my being, I had to find whatever strength I could to appease Abdul. Then Aisha could come home. I became a puppet on his string, and that very thin string held my life together.

When Aisha came back, we would talk when we felt it was safe. I would hold my delicate, vulnerable baby girl in my weak and shaking arms and let her cry while my heart silently wept. She cried because she had been left with people she didn't know. She cried because she had been taken away from her mother again. She cried because she was afraid of her father. During this period of time, I was forever telling Aisha that Mommy might not be with her all the time, but to "know that I am *with* you." I continued to prepare her. I knew the clock was ticking and that soon I would be kicked out of the country without my daughter. The writing was on the wall.

I explained to Aisha that the behavior she witnessed had nothing to do with her. How could I get my three-year-old to understand what was going on with her father and me? I told her how much I loved her and that I knew her daddy loved her, too. I explained that he was having a hard time and that he needed our love. We would try to make him happy.

Aisha and I intuitively knew our time together was limited, and we became inseparable. We did everything together and laughed as much as we could. This created even more jealousy and discord with Abdul.

During a telephone call with Abdul's father, he questioned and scolded me as to why I hadn't told him of the abuse. I replied that I was told by his son that it was no one's business.

Abdul's short temper was increasingly affecting Aisha. He would call me into the room to handle discipline issues with her, saying he was afraid of what he might do. The situation was deteriorating; there was more fighting, screaming, cursing, verbal accusations, and hitting. I had become a person I did not know as I yelled back at him. I didn't understand why Abdul was so upset and angry. I didn't know if or when I should talk. It seemed that it no longer mattered what I did or did not do—nothing seemed to work. My broken, downtrodden spirit wondered why I had ever thought I could keep this together. I was riding rough ocean waters with surf far over my head, crashing down on me; I was drowning.

My own family was aware, to a certain degree, of what was happening in Jeddah. What was difficult to convey was what life was like in Saudi Arabia to someone who hadn't experienced living in the country. There were so many challenges that were difficult to explain.

Mail took weeks to get to or from the States. I could make phone calls through the hospital, but didn't trust the process and who might be listening to my conversations. Because of this, I only used "phone companies" but had to take a limo there or ask my husband to take me. He kept track of everything I did. I was sure he had his spies, too. Computers and e-mail were nonexistent at that time, as was trouble-free international communication.

Finally, the dreaded day arrived. After three months, Abdul's eldest brother sternly informed me that they wouldn't sponsor me on Abdul's visa anymore. He said I needed to return to the States and would have to get a visa through the hospital I currently worked for if I wanted to return. I was essentially forced to leave the country.

In December, after celebrating Aisha's third birthday, I reluctantly left Jeddah and my daughter. I was scared, enraged, and wounded.

Aisha had been conveniently sent to play at her cousins', but we had already said many goodbyes. In a haze so thick I cannot remember the specific details, I was driven to the airport to board a flight to the United States, with no reentry visa stamped on my passport.

Back in the United States, a hollowness consumed my heart. The hospital was supposed to send me a visa to return right away, but nothing happened. I repeatedly called the hospital to get answers regarding the whereabouts of my visa so that I could return. I was soon on a first-name basis with most of the employees in human resources. After one month of my attempts to get answers, someone was finally brave enough to be honest with me. Abdul's family had arranged to have my contract canceled. I was blocked from reentering the country. I would not be able to go back as planned or get the visa I was promised.

I was informed that Abdul had had a nervous breakdown and that it would be better for me not to come back. But what about my daughter? Clearly, she was not their concern.

I had little strength left, but the fight for Aisha was still in me somewhere. When would I get to see my daughter again? Sobbing, I called a woman I had come to know through the organizations I'd reached out to, another mother who also had children abducted and taken to Saudi Arabia. She had been tracking the chain of events. She consoled me and said, "I need you to hang up the phone right now. You need to go be with one of your girlfriends, and then you call me back." She recognized exactly how I felt. She had experienced her own low place, so she identified with my cry for help. It was a familiar place for her. She heard me talk about not being able to live like this anymore. The pain was so deep, I was suicidal. Because she knew this feeling, she saved my life. I did hang up and took my broken, withering body to my friend Robin's home. I then realized what was happening: I could no longer cope. All I did was cry nonstop. This woman had recognized my hopelessness. I didn't know what else I could do. Stunned and frozen, I stayed with friends so that someone was around me for a couple of days.

What Now?

There were times I wanted to slug the next person who said, "Remember, God never gives you more than you can handle," or, "When a window closes, another one opens."

Before I was kicked out of the country, I met an American woman, Kay, who lived in the same compound in Jeddah. She and her husband had jobs at the same hospital as Abdul. Kay secretly kept me informed about what was happening with my daughter. Kay told me that after I left Aisha lived with her uncle's family in Jeddah for a while and then was sent to stay with her grandparents in Riyadh until Abdul recovered from his breakdown and was able to care for her again at his home in Jeddah.

I also learned that after a few months Aisha returned to the same day care while Abdul worked. His parents sent the help of one of their maids, and Kay purposely made herself available to take care of Aisha for Abdul. If Abdul went out, she offered to let Aisha come over to play with her son, who was a couple of years older. Abdul never knew of this secret communication Kay and I shared. They had become "friends," but she was my spy. She would let Aisha, now three years old, call me from her home, or she would let the day care know when I would call. When I talked with Aisha I desperately tried to keep our conversations light and happy. We often sang songs and laughed together on the phone, but we still shared many painful, tearful conversations.

Despite my many attempts, the American embassy in Jeddah wouldn't help me acquire a visa. I searched for ways to get into Saudi Arabia. I requested the help of the State Department. I was in contact with the Saudi embassy. I had contacted Saudi Arabia's American lawyer and my US congressmen for help. I spent hours in my girlfriend's small cottage, where I literally typed, on a typewriter, letter after letter to politicians, to the Saudi embassy, and to Prince Bandar bin Sultan, who was Saudi Arabia's ambassador to the United States, and pleaded for their help to get my daughter back or to get me a visa to return. I was frantic. I was an emotional mess. There were times I wanted to slug the next person who said, "Remember, God never gives you more than you can handle," or, "When a window closes, another one opens." Does anyone who says this even begin to know what he or she is talking about? I wondered how *they* would react in a similar situation. I lived by the poem "Footprints." God carried me when I could not take another step.

> One night a man dreamed he was walking along the beach with the Lord.
> As scenes of his life flashed before him, he noticed that there were two sets of footprints in the sand.
> He also noticed at his saddest, lowest times there was but one set of footprints.
> This bothered the man.
> He asked the Lord, "Did you not promise that if I gave my heart to you, that you'd be with me all the way?

Then why is there but one set of footprints during my most
  troublesome times?
The Lord replied, "My precious child, I love you and would
  never forsake you.
During those times of trial and suffering,
  when you see only one set of footprints,
  it was then I carried you."

I had been encouraged to take a leave of absence from my job in the United States when I had left for Saudi Arabia at the end of September. Back in America, returning to my nursing job kept me busy and engaged, instead of sitting around in my morbid mood.

After a few long, drawn-out, painful, miserable months, I decided to take things into my own hands because nothing was happening. I recognized that they—the politicians, the Saudi embassy, the State Department—might have been "outraged" about the abduction of my daughter, but they weren't going to make anything happen. It was imperative that I return to work in Saudi Arabia and have contact with Aisha. I would do whatever I could to be with my broken daughter. Maybe I could glue the pieces back together again.

Throughout my struggles to obtain a visa, I had mistakenly believed that Abdul or his family had the power to keep me out of the country. This was not so. I would go back.

Kay helped me get contacts for jobs in Jeddah; a new private hospital had opened there, and they were looking for nurses. I faxed my extensive résumé, interviewed over the telephone, and was hired. It would be another month until I got a contract with the new hospital. My employment began at the end of October 1988. Ten months after I had been kicked out of Saudi Arabia, I returned. I was ecstatic and relieved to be back in Jeddah. Abdul had no clue.

Seeing Aisha in Jeddah

I became restless. My daughter and I were in the same city.
The fact that I had not seen her for ten months haunted me.

After ten grueling months, grateful for the emotional support of a wonderful network of friends and family, I finally returned to Saudi Arabia with renewed hope. In October 1988, I boarded that awful fourteen-hour flight to Jeddah with a visa to work at a new private hospital. The job I had been offered as a registered nurse (RN) was Director of Staff Development for nurses, and I was the only person in the department. Companies applied, were approved for, and received a certain number and certain types of visas at a time. A lab tech visa had been available, so my visa claimed I was a lab technician.

I arrived in the country, determined to see my daughter. I had my own apartment and was familiar with Jeddah, and my husband had no knowledge that I had returned to his country. I felt an advantage in that.

After my arrival in Jeddah, I was greeted and driven to my awaiting apartment by a gentleman from India who worked in personnel.

Because I worked for a new hospital, its employees also lived in a nicer, more modern new housing compound two blocks from the hospital. We walked on the newly laid, wide sidewalks in the scorching heat or waited to take a shuttle bus to or from work. The compound consisted of several apartment buildings with balconies. The southern side of the compound held larger apartments for doctors, their families, and some department heads from countries, like Germany and Jordan. No Saudis resided here, and less than a handful worked in the hospital. Wooden gates were present but not used to separate one area from another. A high stucco wall surrounded the guarded compound from a growing new community. A small seven-foot-by-seven-foot guard station was manned by one or two men, usually from India. They were the eyes of the compound.

The compound was inviting, clean, and spruced up with a few short, immature palm trees. When I moved in, the gleaming new hospital had only been occupied for six months and had space to expand. Sadly, within three years, its attractive appearance would be close to nonexistent. Not all have the same standard of cleanliness. Garbage would be thrown everywhere, creating a growing stench, even with garbage cans around. Things were not maintained; it was disappointing to see this deterioration.

My tiny one-bedroom apartment, maybe two hundred square feet, was located on the second floor, on the northwest side of the compound. Here, department heads, both single and married, lived. The hospital could be seen from my bedroom window, separated by several empty (but not for long), sandy lots in one long, desolate block. This part of Jeddah was being developed. An excellent view of the Red Sea could be seen from the upper, unused floors of the new hospital, a place where I found my solace. Soon I discovered that my office also offered a magnificent view of the sunset; my favorite time of the day soothed me and brought me some inner peace. Clouds were not a familiar sight due to the climate, though blinding sandstorms could appear out of nowhere.

Other hospital staff included Filipinos, Indians, Pakistanis, Sri Lankans, and Egyptians, who all lived in dormitory-like units with maybe twenty rooms to a floor. There could be six to eight people in a small room of bunk beds that shared one small window. All tenants on each floor shared one common, dorm-style bathroom area. Complaints had been filed about mixing married with unmarried, men with women, etc. This was changed to married staff together, with single males and single females arranged in separated units. Hospital staff worked a variety of hours, days, and nights; thus sleep was a challenge. Overall, it was a chaotic scene. It never would have been an acceptable standard in the United States.

Three meals a day were provided for the lower-paid staff. The choices of food offered were Middle Eastern, Indian, and Filipino cuisine. I enjoyed all the ethnic varieties and still do. At the beginning of my tenure, I attempted to eat the hot curried Indian flavors, causing tears to run down my cheeks. Eventually, I no longer cried, having grown accustomed to the spices.

The hospital also had a beach house for staff to use if we wanted. Someone would call ahead to let the guard of the beach compound know. At times, a bus would be available to take groups out for the afternoon. For those who had cars, more frequent visits could be made. The beach house was located north of Jeddah in an isolated area in the middle of the desert, about an hour away. It became our spot for snorkeling and diving, and a getaway for more peace and privacy from a busy home compound of people who worked together some grueling sixty hours a week. We didn't worry about the Mutawa so far out.

After I settled into my new home, I became restless. My daughter and I were in the same city now, and the fact that I had not seen her for ten months haunted me. I mustered the courage to pay a surprise visit to her and her dad. Since I had lived in Jeddah before, I knew how to navigate quite well. In some ways, I felt at home. There was a familiarity in being back.

Abdul and Aisha lived in the same apartment, a mere fifteen minutes from my new living accommodations. The public bus was my preferred mode of transportation. The bus stopped right in front of my apartment complex, and then I could take it to a stop that was a short walk to Abdul's apartment. In the past, Aisha and I had loved to ride the bus, though it wasn't customary for Americans to do so. In Saudi Arabia, people would ride the bus and its well-established routes only if they couldn't afford to take limos or hire a driver. The bus was divided by one-inch-thick metal bars that separated the men, who rode in the front of the bus, from the colorfully dressed, dark-skinned women, mostly from Sudan and Somali, who occupied the back of the bus. We had always found the interaction with the women on the bus delightful, and they had loved to talk to Aisha. They loved her blonde hair and blue eyes; and when she spoke to them in perfect Arabic with a Saudi accent, they were stunned and amazed for those words to come out of her tiny little mouth.

On this day, though, the bus was unavailable. I threw an abaya on over my slacks and blouse and hailed a limo to their home. It was late afternoon, and a feeling of exhilaration came over me. My breath caught in my throat as the limo drove closer to the compound. I could not believe I was, in reality, going to see my daughter. I had the necessary money, Saudi riyals, to pay the driver when I arrived. Quickly, I scurried past the guardhouse as if I belonged there. Not wanting to draw attention to myself, I walked to the back unit, my previous home. It didn't appear that anyone was home; the unit was dark, and there wasn't a car parked nearby. I found a quiet, private place near the swimming pool where no one could see me and attempted to calm my frayed nerves. While I waited around the compound, the sun set and the automatic outside lights turned on. My body stood on guard as I waited for signs of life in Aisha's home.

Every ten to fifteen minutes, for an hour, I checked; then I was startled when I saw Abdul's car parked and the apartment lights on. I assumed Abdul and Aisha would be there. I took a deep breath and slowly started to climb the two flights of stairs, bringing back memories of what had happened there before. When I reached the door, I paused long enough to get my breath and say a prayer.

I nervously rang the doorbell while covering the peephole with my finger. I was sure Abdul could hear my apprehensive heart pounding out of control as I stood vulnerably before his door. I can still vividly see the look on his face when he opened it. He went pale, chalky white, as if he had seen a ghost. He was caught off guard to see me standing in his doorway and could barely speak. He faintly asked, "How did you get here?"

Not wanting anyone to see me, he quickly invited me in and gave me a cordial hug. He had thought I would never get back into the country again and that I was out of his and Aisha's lives in Saudi Arabia.

I was proud of my boldness yet uneasy, as I didn't know what to expect from Abdul. As I looked around the room, I began to panic, neither seeing nor hearing any sign of Aisha. I frantically wondered where my child was, while I maintained an outer air of calmness as I explained that I had a work visa at the new private hospital. With all the confidence I could retrieve, I told him I wanted to see Aisha.

Abdul was befuddled but actually seemed glad to see me. Now on his best behavior, he apologized that Aisha wasn't home. She was out with her cousins, the cousins I had enjoyed being with. Relieved, I could breathe again. At least she was in Jeddah and would be home soon. He invited me for a cup of hot tea while I waited. Frightened of the unknown, I flipped out on the inside as I worked hard not to show my hate, which was somehow mixed with a hint of wistful, still-lingering love.

On a handful of occasions over the previous ten months, I had spoken with Abdul on the telephone at select times when I might also talk with Aisha. Abdul and I no longer talked about being together. He had sought the help of a therapist after I left, and we kept the conversations as simple as possible. I had learned through those simple conversations that Abdul was hurting, too. The fact that he had gone through therapy had given me a faint glimmer of hope. The bottom line, as daunting as it was after all the abuse, was that in order to be with Aisha, I had to be with him. Aisha was everything to me, so I emboldened myself for another try.

My own therapist in the States consoled my weary soul and gave me strength to replace that which had waned after I had been kicked out; he was my lifesaver. While I worked with him about my return to Saudi Arabia, I voiced concern at how difficult it would be for me not to get tangled again in Abdul's web.

My therapist asked, "What is your fear?"

After some thought, I said, "If I could only make it work, somehow, but he is such a liar, and I do not trust him."

The gentle, cautious reply of my therapist was, "The good thing is you already know that. It is not as if you are going into this blind, thinking that everything is going to be perfect."

As Abdul and I sat and made awkwardly polite conversation, a knock on the apartment door startled me. It caused me to jump and my heart to gallop. Oh, my God—was Aisha home? My body tingled with anticipation. Abdul apologetically whispered for me to hide in Aisha's bedroom so his relatives wouldn't know I was back in the country.

Aisha greeted her father with a hug when she came home. She had a way of curling her skinny little arms with tightly closed fists around your neck when she hugged. We called them "snugs." They lovingly said their goodbyes to her aunt. The heavy wooden outside door seemed so loud as it closed and locked. Once the door was secured, Abdul told her there was a surprise in her bedroom. "What? What is it, Daddy? What is the surprise?" she asked, wiggling up to him. Abdul walked a step ahead of her into the bedroom and turned on the light.

Slowly and apprehensively, she made her way into the bedroom. As her widened blue eyes caught a glimpse of me, she broke into a huge smile, fell shaking into my long-awaiting arms, and cried uncontrollably. Her grip was tight; she would not let me go. Oh, my God, she had grown so much; she was almost four. Ecstatic to see her, I held Aisha protectively, like a mother lion protecting her cub. She'd had no hope that I might ever be back again; it was not talked about. And Abdul had never had the wildest idea I would get back into the country.

Just to be near Aisha, to feel her sweet, little, warm, lovely, soft body next to me was a dream come true. When I was asked to stay that night and sleep with our daughter, I could not believe what I had heard. She was not going to let me go. She was never going to let me go, she said.

Waking up the next morning in my former home was awkward and unsettling, even though there was a sense of familiarity. Too much had happened in this apartment; the mood was unpredictable. It was Friday, likened to our Sunday in the States. My first workday was Saturday, the next day, as was Abdul's. After Abdul saw how happy Aisha was to have me with her again, he asked if I wanted to have breakfast with them, which progressed to being asked to spend the day with them.

Here was the man I had married. Maybe his therapy had healed him; maybe it had brought him back to being the loving, caring, wonderful man I had fallen in love with, my prince. Could this be happening again? Before the night was over, I was invited to live with my family again. I didn't want to leave the welcoming warmth of it all. I had been asked back with open arms.

So afraid I would be weak and vulnerable and get sucked back into Abdul's vicious, volatile web, I reminded myself of what my therapist had said: "The good thing is you already know he does not tell the truth. You are not going into it blinded, as if everything is going to be perfect. Prepare yourself that this is how life is today. You cannot change him."

On this day, my happy, surprised prayer was, "Help me create a peaceful home. Not everything will be perfect."

And I wondered how long my bliss would last.

Settling In with My Family

*As much as I loved Aisha and wanted her to be with me,
living with Abdul was just too unbearable.*

My wishful bliss didn't last long before the stories unraveled about everything that had happened while I was delayed in the States for ten months. First, I found out that Abdul had divorced me—not once, but three times. Saying three times, with two witnesses before a judge, "I divorce you, I divorce you, I divorce you," was called a "triple *talaq*." I did not need to be present and was unaware that he had divorced me. He was told he needed to move on with his life and get married again. Someone needed to help him raise our daughter.

In fact, Abdul had recently been engaged to be married; and, Aisha told me, there had been a big party to recognize the occasion. Upon my return to Jeddah and our decision to be a family again, Abdul had called off his engagement. Since they had signed papers, Abdul had to legally break the engagement.

Abdul didn't want his family to know I was back in the picture again. They would have been as shocked as Abdul that I had returned—probably more shocked, due to the disruption this had caused. Many people and some of our friends were surprised to see me again and in Abdul's life.

Abdul wanted to appeal the divorce so that we could still be married. It would allow us to be together in accordance with Sharia law. There was a certain condition in which this could be done: a Muslim man cannot divorce his wife while she is on her period or pregnant. I went along with this charade, going to court with him. In the courtroom with Abdul, all covered in black, I listened to the conversation in Arabic with the judge. Abdul presented his case to convince the judge that he should never have been able to divorce me because I was on my period. I went along with the story when I was asked. The judge decided he was unwilling to cancel the divorce, saying, "You are divorced. Had you divorced her one time, that could be different, but you chose to divorce her three times, so you are divorced."

Being unsuccessful in getting our divorce reversed enraged Abdul. I wondered if the same judge had canceled his recent engagement. Under Sharia law, we would actually need to remarry and be divorced, and then we could marry again, an arrangement called *nikah halala* (Quran 2:230).

By the time of our failed court proceeding, Abdul's family knew I was back in Saudi Arabia. Abdul seemed to avoid his family, and they were a blur to me at that point. The last time I had been at their home in Riyadh was when Aisha was a baby, over four years earlier. I would occasionally talk with his father, who spoke English, but more as a common courtesy to acknowledge each other. There was little connection. His mother and I exchanged the basic greetings in Arabic, "How are you? How's your mother? How's your father?" and so on. The situation wasn't perfect, but I counted my blessings while Abdul, Aisha, and I continued to live together like a family, dysfunctional as it was.

Our friends were from many different nationalities, and we did things with Westerners from the compound. We carried on where we had left off with some friends and met new people. We would go out to eat or we would barbecue. Abdul and I took a scuba-diving course, and we spent many weekends diving. Aisha would come with us, and there was always someone to watch her while we played. She had one of those bubbly, laughter-producing personalities that people enjoyed.

Living and working in Saudi Arabia once again had its pros and cons, but I disliked not having the same freedom as in the United States. This was not a place that I wanted to live forever. There was a part of me that would get angry for having to be there to see my daughter. To survive, I needed to find ways to cope or change. Needless to say, I never forgot that Aisha had been kidnapped. Life was challenging.

Then the inevitable happened. The cycle of abuse started to resurface after a few months of us living together again. In his own way, Abdul loved Aisha and me, and he realized my love for him was vanishing. He had kidnapped our daughter as a way to control me in his country of limited freedoms. He knew I wouldn't leave my daughter, although I wanted to leave him. I suppose abuse was one way to react. This was a guy who convinced me he still loved me. I know it can be difficult to understand, but it is an addictive pattern, comparable to drinking or drugs, which is why women (and men) often don't leave abusive relationships. The cycle repeats again and again.

I felt it was important to be aware of the cycle of abuse, to attempt to comprehend its craziness. Often, in our cycle, Abdul would get angry and verbally attack me, building to the point of physical harm. It became difficult for me not to engage, not to yell back. I hated the "me" that responded like that. Abdul would apologize: "I love you. I am sorry; I did not mean to hurt you. I feel so bad. It will never happen again"—perhaps even tears. He would then treat me well, all roses and kisses and love-making, and life was beautiful again. Women get sucked in, in a different hormonal way than men. Everything's "perfect" again.

Yes, he promised over and over he would "not do that again." That is what I hoped. Living in Saudi Arabia, how was I to get help or leave, except without my child?

My thoughts returned to what I could do to get Aisha out. I needed money to make something happen. One advantage of working in Saudi Arabia was the money I could save. I could work toward my goal so that one day, we would be "free" again.

In many Arab countries, babies and children are added to their father's passport for up to two years. A Lebanese male friend from work had a daughter close to Aisha's age. He considered letting me use his daughter's passport. Unfortunately, that would have caused future issues in obtaining the necessary visas in and out for his own child, so it was not a viable option. Not to mention that my daughter had her mother's lighter hair color and blue eyes, unlike most Arab children.

It had been four increasingly long, difficult, desperate months that I had been back in Jeddah with my ex-husband. My job kept me busy, and I liked the experience and the new people I met. Living with Aisha and having my family together was a dream come true, even if it was short-lived. But I was not really living. I was slowly dying.

A life of normalcy was nearly impossible. My world was of one of survival, spinning uncontrollably. I was not doing well. At work, I pretended everything was just fine and thought I was pulling it off, until one day my director looked at me empathetically and said, "You cannot keep doing this. You're killing yourself." She made me look at myself in a mirror. "If you keep doing this, Aisha will no longer have a mother." She saw how broken I was, and she knew Abdul.

I had attempted to have peace. As much as I loved Aisha and wanted her to be with me, living with Abdul had become too unbearable. His physical and verbal abuse escalated daily. I walked on eggshells all the time, never knowing what would occur. Through all of this, I talked with Aisha, again and again, about the possibility of not being able to see her or be with her all the time. I reassured her I would always love her and would do all that I could to be with her. Grief was my enemy; Aisha knew deeply of it. I cannot begin to describe what an exceptional child I had. How could we survive so much pain?

After my horrendous revelation at work, I wanted to scream in desperation. My director had spoken the truth: I was killing myself. But who would want to admit such a thing was true? As usual, Abdul picked me up from work. I could no longer speak. Tears caused my throat to throb as I faced the reality of what my life had become.

With my heart aching profusely, I went back to our shared apartment and packed up my belongings. While Aisha sat on my lap, as bravely and as stoically as I could muster the words, trying to keep my voice from cracking, I whispered into my daughter's ear: "Aisha, the time has come. Mommy has to leave. I'll stay at my apartment by my hospital for now. We can still see each other, just not as often. We can talk on the phone. Your daddy and I are not able to be happy together."

We relived that tearful, sad, and emotionally heart-wrenching situation again; it had been close to a year earlier when I had left her. Abdul just stared at me. I don't remember him making any attempt to restrain me. His repetitive apologies had fallen on deaf ears. As I gently closed the door behind me, I prayed I could get to my apartment without breaking down. I was numb; I could no longer even feel the stabs of pain and misery that shot through my body.

Leaving Again

I had prepared Aisha as much as I could prepare a four-year-old.

Beaten down again, I went back to my apartment in February of 1989. Living with the abuse of my now-ex-husband was intolerable, and our relationship had deteriorated past the point of no return. How could living with him be worse than the hell of not being with Aisha? It was an excruciating choice, but it hurt most to know how painful it was for my daughter.

For a few months afterward, Abdul was cooperative enough to let me see Aisha, and sometimes he let her come over on a weekend. Was he thinking that maybe we could make it work again or that if he was good, I would come back? His motives were unclear, but my only chance at survival was to stay on course toward finding myself again, a course necessary for keeping my sanity. Tomorrow would be another day, and one day, I would get Aisha and myself out.

Was there some sense of relief or calmness when I returned to my apartment? No. The words that came to mind were *failure* and *disappointment*. I had left my child behind to fend for herself because I, as an adult, could no longer appease her father. This part was so hard, and it tore me apart. I had no idea what was going to happen from then on. I had prepared Aisha as much as I could prepare a four-year-old.

We were able to see each other regularly for a few months, and then it stopped, with no explanation as to why. Presumably, it had something to do with the fact that Abdul had gotten a different job, so he and Aisha moved into his family's second-floor apartment in a six-apartment complex that I was told his mother and sister owned. I wasn't allowed to see Aisha again. My plea to Abdul's father fell on deaf ears. He had not assisted earlier in allowing visitation with my daughter; why would he help now?

Most compounds had guards, unarmed staff that were aware of everyone's coming and going. Since Abdul had moved into his family's apartment building, there were no guards at their compound's entrance. People I worked with told me that Abdul had approached the guards at my own compound and asked them to "watch" me. He wanted to know when and where I was going and with whom.

After not seeing Aisha for a few months, I got up the nerve and went to their apartment. I wanted to see my daughter. When I arrived, I saw that the maid had accidentally left the door open when she brought in the groceries, and I happened to catch the moment when the door was open and went in. Aisha was excited, but the maid was very upset and told me I had to leave. She knew the rules and the consequences of not following them. I refused.

In a panic, she called Abdul. Before he arrived, I turned on the VCR to watch a movie with Aisha only to find there was a porn movie in the machine. I confiscated it, hiding it in my abaya that lay on the couch. Abdul rushed home immediately, and he was extremely angry. As I got ready to leave, in my nervousness, I forgot about the video. It fell out of my abaya and clattered onto the hard cement floor. Of course, this made Abdul angrier. He threatened to call the police because I did not want to leave. Instead, he called the CEO of my hospital. He told the CEO to get me out of his apartment or he would call the police.

My boss, the CEO, knew nothing about my domestic life. He convinced me to come back to the compound and said that we would talk the next day. Now the owners at the hospital were aware of my plight. Up until that time, they didn't have a clue about this other life I lived. It was not a subject that I spoke of to many people, and my bosses were no exception.

After this incident, Abdul locked up the telephone at their home. Now Aisha could not call me or answer the phone when I called. She was instructed not to touch it. Now four and a half, she had memorized my telephone number. Determined to talk to me, she took the risk of calling me whenever and from wherever she could if she thought she could get away with it.

The owners of the hospital now knew of my challenges with my ex-husband and visitation with Aisha. In fact, the confrontation at Abdul's apartment had a positive impact. After the incident, I had talked with the owners about my crazy life and why I was in Saudi. I shared a part of my story with them so they could better understand me. I mentioned that I was afraid to leave the country for fear of not getting back in. The CEO said, "Do you think Abdul has the power to do that? He doesn't. You work for us, and we are responsible for you." It actually felt good to unload this heavy burden. Not all men were like my ex; I knew that. My life was all out in the open with them, and I felt supported.

During our discussion, I was asked if I was a Muslim. With a deep, contemplative sigh and a finger to my lip, I responded, "I believe there is a God, and I believe Mohammed is a prophet of God. I believe there are many ways to God and many interpretations of who God is." I further explained I was raised a Christian, so those teachings and doctrine were also part of my life, and who was I to judge what a person should believe? The CEO asked why I did not cover my head. "I could," I replied. "However, I find it hypocritical, as I do not feel it's necessary. God is more interested in the person I am, not whether I am covered or not. I strive to be a good person."

At the end of our conversation, I was quite taken by surprise when one of the owners asked, "Why don't you get your daughter out?"

I gasped, not believing what I had heard. My shocked response was, "Do you know how I might do that?"

Of course, I wanted to know how I might be able to get my daughter out of Saudi Arabia. What an odd suggestion for him to make to me. While he would have the financial means and the influential network of people to accomplish this daunting feat, it was not my reality. Wishfully, I prayed that he might one day shed some light on how I might accomplish this seemingly impossible feat, but it never did manifest itself.

Still not allowed visitation with Aisha, I heard that she took summer vacation with her grandparents in Egypt. She loved being with others and going to Egypt, as it was a much freer country. After her summer vacation with her grandparents, Aisha returned to live with her father in their apartment. Abdul continued to refuse my visits. His father would not intervene to let Aisha see me, and it became impossible to see her at Abdul's home or anywhere else. The reasons were unclear, and the laws offered no support for an American woman. Maybe he was told something by the guards, the spies—it could have been for any reason.

The hospital allowed my parents to come visit in October 1989, after I had been in Jeddah for one year. They wanted to see their grandchild and the country. My mother's visa was for an obstetrics doctor, and my father's was for an ophthalmologist. We laughed a lot about these visas, the only available visas at that time. My parents stayed with me for three weeks in my tiny apartment, and we had a great time. They knew almost everyone in the housing compound before they left. Many people invited us over, and we went to the beach house and took other excursions. The time went so fast. I bought a TV so my parents had something to do when I was at work; and though there were no English programs, there were videos available they could watch.

Abdul still wouldn't let me or my parents see Aisha. One morning, while at work, Abdul called me and angrily told me to tell my mother to stop calling his boss. Under my breath, I laughed when he mentioned this, as I knew nothing about it. Apparently, my brave mother had somehow gotten the telephone number for his hospital and had called Abdul's boss at work numerous times. She told his boss of Abdul's unwillingness to cooperate in letting them see their granddaughter while they were in Saudi Arabia. I didn't know how my mother knew where he worked or how she got his boss's number.

Through her persistence, we eventually did get to see Aisha. Abdul brought her to meet us at a Pizza Hut. It was the first time I had seen Aisha in six months. Seeing her was overwhelming. She was so beautiful and so happy to see me, and I ate up her special hugs and kisses.

As always, I wondered how an almost-five-year-old could understand that she might not be able to see her mommy very often, but that her mother would always be with her. Did Aisha understand, or was she too young? When I did see her, our connection was so powerful, it made the whole ordeal worth it.

My parents and I got to see Aisha only one more time before they left. The visit was at Abdul's parents' apartment in Jeddah. After this visit, I was denied other visits. In spite of the limited time with Aisha, my parents said they had a great time visiting Jeddah.

It was months until I saw Aisha again, though even then it was only by accident. I had done the best I could to keep busy and occupy my time, leaving myself as little room as possible to replay the crazy scenario I had been dealt. Work was so busy; nursing units, policies, and procedures needed to be developed. I trained hospital staff in cardiopulmonary resuscitation (CPR) and other medical-related learning. I continued to make recruitment trips to other countries.

And I continued to call Aisha to no avail. I had started going on outings with German and American couples and other friends just to further occupy my time. I didn't want to think about my life. Often, for something to do, I would go diving with whomever happened to be going. I was in mixed company; I thought this could be the reason I was not allowed to see Aisha. Abdul's spies told him about my comings and goings. Perhaps because of this, I wasn't "decent" enough to spend time with our daughter. I surmised these were his judgments.

Abdul and I had friends in common who lived in a compound close to my apartment. Cindy was an American RN I worked with. She lived with her husband, Tim, and their school-aged child in this Western compound, and we had done many things as couples together. Aisha and I had also visited them the previous year at Christmas, when they had lit up the Christmas tree for an unrestricted holiday celebration. One day, I had gone out to brunch with Cindy and Tim. After brunch we returned to their compound. As we chatted, I mentioned that I was going over to their neighbors', our friends next door, to say hello. Shortly after I mentioned this, Cindy looked out the window and saw that Abdul had just pulled up in his car. My body went tense. I was uneasy that Abdul was around. Was my daughter with him? Cindy said he headed into the home of the common friends I was planning to say hello to. I looked out the window and insisted I would still go over, though my friends questioned my rationale. It was not to talk to Abdul; it was to see Aisha.

Not Recognizing My Daughter

Her spirit was gone; it had been beaten out of her.

I was suffused with a toxic sadness; this was my new normal. What could I do? I had not seen Aisha for over six months. Who could help me? As I walked defiantly to my friends' home, their maid was on the sidewalk with a few kids; they were headed to the park at the end of the block. We greeted each other, and I stopped to speak to the children before going inside. I asked if my daughter was there.

My girlfriend looked surprised and replied, "Your daughter was with the group of kids you just spoke with on their way to the park." I felt faint and my breath stopped as this jagged sword stabbed my already tender, vulnerable heart. I could not believe I hadn't recognized my own daughter!

The recollection of this day still sends chills through my spine. Was it any wonder I hadn't recognized her? Her face had had no color, and she had shown little resemblance to the spunky, upbeat girl I had seen six months earlier. I had looked right into her spiritless eyes and even talked to her and all the other children.

Not waiting a second longer, I flew out of the house and ran down the block as I yelled out to her, "Aisha, it is your mommy! Wait!"

As Aisha heard my voice, she stopped. She meekly replied, "Mommy, why did not you say hi to me, your daughter, Aisha?" I didn't know how to answer her. As we hugged each other, she whispered, "My daddy told me you died." She hadn't thought I was alive and had probably thought I was her mother's ghost, but now she knew I was alive.

I looked intently at my sad and broken daughter who stood in front of me, and I hugged and kissed her. Passionately, I replied, "It is your mommy!"

She said with a sigh of relief, "Oh, Mommy," and as we hugged, her fisted little hands wrapped tightly around my neck.

She was not the jolly little girl I had seen a few months before with my parents. She looked sick and pale, her eyes sunken in. As I squatted down to look at her more closely, I could not believe what I saw. There was a fresh handprint on her face from where her father had clearly slapped her. She had been hit hard enough to leave a reddened imprint on her tender cheek.

Now I understood. Her spirit had vanished. It had been beaten out of her. I knew what it felt like to be hit by her father and now realized that he was treating her as he had treated me. It made me sick to my stomach, and I wanted to vomit. The bubbly, happy girl I once knew had nothing to be happy about. Something had to be done, but what?

My fight-or-flight hormones were raging. I wanted to grab her and run, but where the hell would I run? I was a prisoner in this country of craziness. After what seemed like only a couple of seconds, her father burst out of the neighbors' home and demanded that she come back to him.

She was frightened. "Bye, Mommy . . ." Her voice trailed off as her shaking, fragile body ran away.

"I love you, Aisha," spilled out of my paralyzed mouth. I wanted to die; I was frozen as I knelt on the sidewalk and sobbed. What was I going to do?

After Aisha left with Abdul, I stumbled, blinded by my tears, back into my friends' home and totally lost it. As I shouted, I pounded the couch pillows and asked God to help protect my poor, helpless child. Not knowing what else to do, I called Abdul's oldest brother, prepared with an enraged speech. I was so intensely upset that my voice was shrill as I interrogated his brother and told him what I had seen.

He calmly replied, "Aisha is staying at our home, and I have never seen any handprints on her face."

Angrily, I shouted, "Then you are not looking!"

My rage-addicted ex-husband was single-parenting my daughter. I wasn't allowed to see her or participate in her care. No wonder her spirit was extinguished.

Shortly after this incident, one of the Indonesian maids from his parents' home in Riyadh came to live with them. The maid had taken my place in caring for Aisha, but it was better for Aisha to be with her than her father. Now Abdul could go out and do whatever he wanted to do.

I heard from my American hairdresser, who had clients that worked with my ex, about a woman Abdul worked with who would come to take Aisha out. This Yemeni lady later became his next wife.

Sharia Court

The injustice was unbearable, especially when I, her mother, was in the country, willing to live there to be with my daughter.

The abuse my daughter endured was not something I took lightly. Legal action was needed, but what did that mean in this country?

From my friends' home, still hysterical, I called Hannah, a Saudi girlfriend I worked with. We had become close friends over the past year. She had met my ex-husband and daughter once. Much of my spare time was spent with her and our group of multicultural friends. Her husband was British. They had met when she was in boarding school in London, and he had become Muslim to marry her. Hannah said she would send her driver to pick me up. Her father was a lawyer in Riyadh who had married an American lawyer. She would call her father to see what he suggested I do. I was so thankful for her friendship and support.

Her father referred me to a lawyer in Jeddah, and I also consulted a couple of American lawyers I had picked from the recommendation list provided by the American embassy. How were they going to help me in this country? What was I to do? As it was the weekend, I had to wait a day to call the lawyer recommended by Hannah's father. I was taking a journey into the unknown, and I didn't know what to expect.

The laws in Saudi Arabia are governed by the religion, and Sharia law is supposed to be followed. There are only a few other countries that live under this strict ruling. What knowledge I had of the Sharia laws was that they seemed to be interpreted in different ways. I still didn't know how things worked there. By whom would the law be interpreted? And how?

By the time I met the lawyer, Mohammed, I was frantic and sick with worry about the unknown and about my daughter's safety. Mohammed was a nice-looking, small-framed older man who spoke perfect English. He was very gentle and soft-spoken. He wore a "skull hat" on his head, and his loose white thobe was unbuttoned at his neck. I assumed he was in his early sixties. We had the usual casual exchange at the beginning of our conversation. This custom was wise to learn, as it seemed rude to speak right from the beginning about the subject at hand. After some time, we got down to business.

On this visit, I informed the lawyer about what had been happening in my life and why I had called him. "First of all," he answered, "we will not go to court. This is not the custom of our country. We will work with the family and find a peaceful solution under Islam. I will be your spokesperson, your male voice; I will be your *mahram* to talk to your ex-husband. If he does not cooperate, I will talk with his father. Let's make an appointment for next week." I left his office in a stupor, with mixed feelings of desperation and hope.

On my next visit, after the polite greetings, I was surprised that the first thing out of my lawyer's mouth was, "We are going to court." He had gotten no cooperation from Abdul or his father. He just shook his head in amazement and astonishment at their unwillingness to negotiate a solution. What I heard later was that Abdul had said, "Over my dead body will she get her," and, "I will kill my daughter first," or something to that effect. Understandably, my lawyer had been appalled at Abdul's insane words.

Mohammed was extremely capable, caring, and knowledgeable. He was what I called a "true" Muslim, as he lived his religion and was humble. He knew the Quran and was able to recite it at will. In the past, Mohammed had been in different positions with the government, once as a diplomat to another country. He had valuable life experiences outside of Saudi, which I grew to appreciate greatly.

We developed a rapport that was supportive and sympathetic. I would call him when I was angry and irrational, and he guided me through transcendental meditation to calm my weary, tearful soul. In his soft-spoken, soothing, angelic voice he suggested that I sit or lie down and find an object to look at in my apartment. I was to keep looking at the object. He continued to walk me through the process to ease my emotional thoughts. I would come in roaring like a lion and end our time as a calm, gentle lamb. He would always say, "We will win this with love." I wanted to believe him, but I knew how mean and nasty my ex was capable of being.

At times I would say, "All I want to do is to take my daughter for an ice cream cone." And he would always reply, "You will." I so desperately wanted to believe this.

We prepared for court. The closest I'd come to being in court in the States was to appear for jury duty selection. What would going to court be like in Saudi Arabia? My lawyer would represent me and attempt to get me visitation rights. I hadn't been allowed to see Aisha for over a year, except for the two occasions during my parents' visit in November of '89. It was now March 1990.

The first court hearing was held at the Sharia court building in a busy area of downtown Jeddah. I was not invited to attend. My boss had written a reference/support letter that stated that I was a good

Muslim woman and employee. My lawyer, his assistant (his handsome, fun-loving son), and Abdul and his lawyer were present. Both lawyers presented their cases to the Muslim scribe who would then take his written testimonials to the judge.

A second court appearance was required, and my lawyer asked me to join him. In full cover except for my face, I sat in the same room, fairly close to my lawyer, as he presented my case. Abdul was not present in court that day. I listened to what was said; and though it was all in Arabic, I had a general understanding. When I was questioned in Arabic, it was translated to English so I could appropriately reply to the question at hand. After both sides had debated the case, the scribe presented his written testament to the judge in order for him to consider his written verdict.

My amazing lawyer remained calm and spoke only when asked. He quoted sayings of the Quran to justify his points. Abdul's lawyer presented their concerns as to why Aisha shouldn't be allowed to be with me:

- I lived in a "mixed" compound of married and unmarried men and could not prevent Aisha from being at risk with the men on the compound.
- I was around mixed company in my life.
- I was a new Muslim, so I would not be a good teacher for Aisha. What could I teach her about Islam and prayer?
- I would continue to celebrate Christian holidays with her.
- I would run away with her.

All of these factors were considered.

After two appearances in court, the judgment was made. The Sharia court in Jeddah ordered Aisha to come to my home on the weekends. We had won! As far as I knew, I was the first American woman to have gotten this judgment. Had I not been Muslim, I may have only been given supervised visits, if that.

Abdul was furious with the judgment and had his lawyer file an appeal. Because of this, the judgment was then sent to the highest court in the KSA, in Mecca, for the ruling of religious scholars who would further review and decide how to proceed.

In June 1990, the Sharia court in Mecca approved the judgment as it was. It was determined by the top imam of Saudi Arabia that Aisha was to come to my home on weekends, from Thursday morning until Friday evening, Saudi weekends. I was so elated that I cried my heart out. My lawyer, his son, and I celebrated our victory. I couldn't believe what I had heard. What a wonderful, history-making event.

By this time, Abdul's lawyer had tired of dealing with Abdul's anger and unrealistic expectations. Abdul's nasty attitude bothered him, a devoted Muslim. At one point, Abdul's lawyer mentioned to me he would do anything he could to help me see my daughter. He was unhappy with Abdul's explosive behavior. I couldn't believe his lawyer would say this; it meant so much to me for him to take a stand like that. These lawyers were "good" Muslims, and they believed in Islam and the laws of their ancient religion.

Aisha had a right to be with me, and this was where Abdul's lawyer said he had to follow the law and his heart. Even though the laws were upheld and the ruling was clear, Abdul opposed it. There were certain restrictions laid out by the court as to what steps I was to follow for Aisha to come to my home. Unfortunately, I never got the chance to take those steps.

During the court proceedings, after hearing of their son's physical abuse of Aisha from their oldest son, Abdul's parents came to Jeddah to take Aisha with them to Riyadh. They realized their son was not capable of taking care of her, and I knew she would have a safer and more stable lifestyle in Riyadh. It may not have been a perfect situation, but it was better for her than living with Abdul. But now that the verdict was in, there was a heartbreaking catch. Aisha was in Riyadh. How was I ever going to see her now? Not that a flight from Jeddah to Riyadh was long, it was only an hour and a half, but getting the time off would be a challenge.

At times, the injustice was unbearable, especially when I, her mother, was in the country, willing to live there to be with my daughter. However, Aisha now lived with her paternal grandparents, whose son didn't even come to see her. Still, even after the court ruling, he continued to dictate when and if I could visit her. This was perhaps the craziest thing to me; how could this be?

For months I was refused permission to see my daughter after she was taken to Riyadh to live with her grandparents. She started to sneak an occasional phone call to me when no one was around. She still had the number memorized. "Mommy, I am on the phone," she would whisper in her sweet, tender voice with a British accent. "How are you?" I would barely have the chance to tell her I was okay before she would hurriedly say, "Got to go, Mom, got to go," and then hang up.

She warmed my heart over the telephone, and I hoped it would go well with her grandparents. My experience with Abdul's family was limited. I prayed Aisha would be loved. She was an easy child to love.

Early one morning, I was awakened by a telephone call. Aisha cried on the other end of hundreds of miles of phone line. Her grandmother had let her call me. This was the first time, the first of many. Aisha had had a nightmare about the day her father had tried to push me down the stairs, and she needed comfort and to know I was all right. After this, her calls become more frequent. Aisha's grandparents started to warm to her personality and the love she so readily shared. They became compassionate about the life she had lived since birth, in her father's home and without her mother.

With time, Aisha and I were able to talk on the phone more freely. A cordial dialogue began between her grandparents and me. They were always warm and respectful.

Although I had this solace, I was still not given the mercy of visitations with Aisha. Her grandparents and aunt took her on a summer vacation to Egypt. For that entire period, we had no telephone contact. With my reason for being in Saudi Arabia gone, I left the country for my own vacation during this time. Our initial conversations when she returned to Riyadh were jumbled with Arabic and English words. She had forgotten how to speak English. Even with this challenge, however, most of the time our conversations were upbeat and full of laughter.

My daughter now lived in Riyadh. How could I get my weekly court-ordered visits with her there? What were my options? Upset with having no visitation, I told her grandfather that I needed to come and see my daughter regularly when I wanted. I reminded him of what the judgment said and that this was their law. She was to come to my house. Naturally, Abdul's father, being the spokesperson for their family, said he was unfamiliar with the judgment and asked how I proposed to have visitation. Logistically and financially, leaving work every weekend to visit Aisha was not an option, and I wasn't even invited to do so. Of course, the family wasn't going to fly a five-year-old every weekend alone or bring her to visit me. And who would pay for it?

Time continued to crawl along at a snail's pace, and I started to doubt my belief in Sharia law. Abdul's family wouldn't honor the court order. Was it all a joke? What was I to do? I insisted on seeing her but was denied.

I found the Sharia laws in regard to child custody could be interpreted differently, depending on whom you spoke with. There were certain parameters, guidelines, and interpretations that were to be followed: If a daughter was under twelve and hadn't started her menses, then she should live with the mother until she started her menses. At that point, she would live with the father because he had to protect her. Seven years was often quoted as the minimum age a daughter should remain with her mother. Of course, being an American mother was not a common component in this picture and seemed to change the interpretation.

Part Five

Seeing Aisha

Seeing Aisha

I needed to learn how to play his game of manipulation as long as there was a glimmer of hope that it would encourage him to let me see my daughter again.

In February 1991, Abdul and I started to talk again. Why? I wanted to see my daughter. Aisha had turned six in December and started school in Riyadh in September. Over a year had passed since the day I had last seen Aisha, when I had not recognized her and realized that her father had been abusing her. What was the magical formula to get permission to see my own daughter? The court order hadn't worked. Aisha was supposed to be at my home on the weekends, and it had never happened. I had returned to Saudi Arabia only to be with her, and now we lived in different cities, hundreds of miles apart.

Occasionally, I started to spend time in the evening with Abdul. I was a prisoner in his grip, as he controlled my ability to see Aisha. We would share a meal and watch a video at his nondescript Jeddah apartment, where couches were replaced with cushions on the floor. Either

Abdul would pick up some food or he would occasionally cook. We never went out to eat. We stayed out of the scrutiny of the public eye.

My insides screamed for freedom, but I did the one thing I knew might make a difference: I offered sex. I felt weak, vulnerable, and sleazy for having sex with my ex-husband; but I was tired and exhausted, weary of his conniving ways. My body was limp, nauseated, and repulsed by the thought of his overpowering cologne; his skinny, bony body on top of mine; and his horny, reckless hands as they touched me while I avoided his molesting lips on my mouth. At least I always knew it would be brief. A skilled lover he was not. How had it ever seemed magical?

I needed to learn how to play his game of manipulation as long as there was a glimmer of hope that it would encourage him to let me see my daughter again. I had hit a new low. The sharp edge of the sword of dysfunction had cut me in half. My power was depleted. I was willing to have sex with my daughter's father in order to see her, and it worked. He needed to feel loved by me, but how could I love this man who was so cruel and manipulative?

It was not until March that I finally got to see Aisha. My kind favors of "intimacy" helped with Abdul's decision to allow me to see our daughter in Riyadh. Had he forgotten I had a court order? One morning, a sated Abdul spoke with his parents. The visits would start the next weekend. I had paid my dues.

The logistics had to be set up. It was decided that I would not stay at Abdul's parents' home or have use of their driver to or from the airport, and I would need to be supervised when with my daughter.

Fortunately, my former neighbors from Jeddah now lived in Riyadh. I arranged to stay with them in their compound while in Riyadh. I could easily take a limo from the airport to their home and also to get around Riyadh.

This visit would be the first time I would set foot inside Abdul's parents' home since Aisha was a baby, six years earlier. I was excited beyond measure that I would be seeing her. While Aisha's grandmother had let us talk occasionally on the telephone, Aisha always questioned why I didn't visit her. I explained it was a problem with her father that I was working on solving.

How my daughter survived through all the changes, through all the heartaches, was astounding. Her resiliency kept me going. She provided the strength I needed to take one more step. When I heard her high-pitched singsong voice, a smile would adorn my face. She had started making up silly songs to sing to me when we talked, and as they became more frequent, I had started to write them down.

After I finished my seemingly endless sixty-hour workweek, a male coworker would drop me off at the Jeddah airport. I boarded the ninety-minute Wednesday-evening flight to Riyadh, then hopped in a limo and headed to my friends' home. Traveling in Saudi Arabia was little hassle for me now, as I respected the culture and lightly covered my hair, and my simple black abaya embraced my body. Apprehensive and emotionally spent, I was greeted with a nice glass of homemade red wine when I arrived at my friends' place in their modern Western compound. I felt at home, as if we were in the States, with no restrictions. As the evening progressed, I was able to unwind and even laugh again as I strategized with friends who understood my plight. Seeing my daughter was all I could think about as I counted down the hours.

Unable to sleep, I woke early; my anticipation got the best of me. I had prayed for this day for so long. My friends wished me good luck as I left the comfort and warmth of their friendship to face an unknown milieu of unsolved mysteries.

As agreed, I arrived by limo at Abdul's parents' home promptly at nine in the morning; it was a rarity for me to be somewhere on time. Their home was unrecognizable from my previous visit years before. Swiftly and ungracefully, I paid the driver and jumped out of the limo. I grabbed my suitcase, as well as a bag full of surprises I'd brought for Aisha, and hurried to the entrance gate to ring the doorbell. A tall, locked metal gate, dulled yellow by the brilliant scorching sun, blocked my entry into the courtyard of the large marble home. A handsome, older, gray-haired, bearded man in a thobe and with a gutra loosely draped over his head, Aisha's grandfather, or *jedi* (Baba to me), greeted my call. He warmly welcomed me to his home, as he always had. Very aware of how excited we were to see each other, he motioned to my daughter, who waited on the cold white-and-black-marbled porch for the gesture from her jedi that she could come greet her mother. Words can't describe our jubilation and exhilaration in seeing each other again. Aisha wouldn't let me leave her side. She knew who I was, at that deep level only the two of us could know. Baba had tears in his eyes at our bittersweet reunion. Why had it taken so long?

It was apparent to me that Aisha's grandparents had become quite fond of my daughter, and the love flowed easily between them. Aisha introduced a different generation and a different culture with a twist of American to their regular, well-established lives. She was a contented, very jovial girl, despite her life's misfortunes.

Although I attempted to make light of it, I was taken aback when I heard Aisha call her grandma Mommy, or Omi in Arabic. She didn't seem to know to call her Siti ("grandmother" in Arabic) instead of Mom. It was hurtful, and it stabbed at my already tender, broken heart. Someone had taken over my role as her mother. What a bitter blow this was, even though I knew it wasn't meant to hurt me. She knew who I was in her life, whether I was there in person or not. When Aisha would call her grandmother Mom, she would repeatedly say, "No, no, I am your grandma, your siti. Leah is your mom, your omi."

Clearly, Aisha's grandmother sensed my uncomfortable, wounded spirit when Aisha called her Mom, but it took a while for that to change. It wasn't that Aisha had been asked to call her that; it was simply that she had been in the role of mother for quite a few months, and Aisha had heard the older children who lived at home call her Omi.

While it hurt, I was grateful that Aisha's grandmother had assumed this role in my absence; it gave me comfort. Aisha seemed loved.

After I spent the day with Aisha, she sweet-talked her grandparents so I could stay the night. They prepared the bedroom upstairs for us, the same bedroom we had shared as a family six years before, when she was a baby.

It seemed as if nothing had changed; and, in a sense, that was true. Aisha's grandparents were caught up in their son's destructive behavior once again. To my surprise and humiliation, I was mortified to learn that Aisha and I were under lock and key and that someone had to be with us at all times. We were prisoners in their compound. I was under surveillance per strict orders from their son. The idea that I was being locked in was a blow to me; I was being treated like a criminal. Where was I to go?

My boss didn't know I had left Jeddah for the weekend, which was to be the first of many times I did so. It would be difficult to leave Aisha after such a nice weekend, even if it was spent locked behind bars. We had played with Aisha's twenty-plus illegal Barbie dolls, and I had helped Aisha with her English homework. We colored, played games, watched videos in the first-floor TV room, or went outside on the patio when the weather was cooler. Window air-conditioners in every room provided the necessary cooling, a sound I tired of hearing.

I prayed that my preparation of Aisha throughout the weekend that, "Mommy will be leaving," helped her acceptance at the culmination. As difficult as it was, I knew we had to say our goodbyes.

After my weekend visit, the family acquiesced a bit and offered their driver to take me to the airport so I wouldn't have to take a limo. It was late afternoon on Friday, and I needed to catch my flight so I could be at work bright and early the next day. I hugged and kissed my incredibly sweet, innocent little girl goodbye. I attempted to let go of her to get in the car, but Aisha wouldn't loosen her tight grip. She cried frantically, grabbed at me, and begged me not to leave her. I silently sobbed as I tried to be strong for her. Her grandmother cried and held my daughter back, and two maids who witnessed the scene cried. Only mothers know this pain. As I left, I threw kisses and told Aisha I would be back as soon as I could.

Showing no emotion, the driver pulled out of the driveway. The noisy, clumsy gate clanged as it closed, separating us once again. My remembrance of this scene will never leave my consciousness, remaining just as vivid today as it was then. It was pitifully frustrating and maddening, but I was so grateful for my crumbs, which were better than nothing.

I had been sabotaged by her father, who spent less and less time with Aisha. I had lowered myself to have sex with him so that I could be with my daughter, but she was worth it.

My visit with Aisha gave me hope for future visits; and though I was ecstatic to have been able to spend time with her, I cried all the way back to the airport. I did the best I could to think positively and look toward the future.

After my first visit to Aisha's grandparents' home, it was decided that I could stay with them when I visited Aisha. For the first few months, we were locked in the house and couldn't leave unless someone was with us. As time went on, however, we were given more freedom. It was a hassle for the family to have to chaperone us, and they grew tired of this ridiculous, insane order from their son. Eventually, we were allowed to walk to a small shopping mall close to the family home. About a month after that, we were finally given free range to come and go on our own.

One day, Aisha's uncle took her for an ice cream and brought ice cream to the rest of us. When they returned, he shared the story of how a policeman had stopped him and asked who my daughter was. He replied, "This is my niece." They looked at her, looked at him, and wondered what he was doing. My daughter had blonde hair and blue eyes, with an olive complexion. In stark contrast, this uncle looked more like his mother and was large framed, with dark hair, dark eyes, and a darker skin color.

Apparently suspicious, the officer questioned my daughter. She spoke to the policeman in fluent Arabic with a Saudi accent and laughed, "He is my uncle, and my mommy is an American." Often, children of American women married to Middle Eastern men carried the genetic traits of the father, with dark hair and eyes; not so in Aisha's case. I had been ecstatic when Aisha had been younger and I had seen that blue eyes and blonde hair would prevail. There was no mistaking that Aisha was not only Arab but also mine.

I continued to work at the hospital during the Gulf War. Operation Desert Storm took place from August 1990 to February 1991, as war had exploded when Iraq invaded Kuwait. From the burning oil fields, ash drifted to Riyadh to blur the usual blue sky, along with a Scud missile or two. I felt it wouldn't be right for me to leave others behind, though many American expats did leave at that tumultuous time. My daughter was in Riyadh; how could I leave her?

Regular visits continued every other week, even with war raging around us. The schools handed out gas masks for the children to wear when a blaring warning siren would sound. Women wouldn't bother to cover to run onto the rooftops to see a Scud missile flying through Riyadh's targeted sky. I questioned Baba as to why the family didn't go to Jeddah, a safer city to live in during wartime. He didn't seem concerned about any danger, but I found it scary. I had not experienced war before.

Whatever I could do to accommodate Aisha's grandparents, I did, and it was reciprocated. My ex-husband might be seen occasionally when I was at his parents' home, but I tried to avoid him. He disturbed my psyche, tugged my mood in the wrong direction, and stirred up emotions of rage and resentment.

A recently married son and his new wife began living at the home in order to save money, a common and efficient practice. Aisha and I enjoyed their company, and they were housed in "our" bedroom upstairs. Reem, the wife, became a confidante and knew what it was like to be separated from her mother at a young age. She empathized with both Aisha and me because of this. I had met Reem on my first visit in Riyadh, but she had been a teenager when Aisha was a baby. Reem had dark, beautiful features and an attractive, slim body under her cover, which she opposed wearing. She understood me, more than any American would.

Aisha and I were moved to our own little room on the ground floor, out of the way and off the "family" floor. It became our own precious little haven. A hard, lumpy, oversized cotton mattress was placed on top of a delicately designed, almost-room-sized rug of pinks, gold, and blue that rested on top of a plush beige carpeted floor. The room was dark and dreary, crowded with heavy, intricately designed furniture from Italy. The built-in mahogany cabinets on the north side of the room and the thick floor-length blue velvet curtains on the west did nothing to brighten our room, but we didn't care; we created our own light and warm, healing energy. We were just happy to be together.

Many hours were spent in the comfort and privacy of our room. We played games, read books, did homework, and sewed Barbie clothes by hand with a needle and thread. On one occasion as we played on the floor, I was lying on the mattress with my legs straight up in the air, with Aisha balancing on my legs and her arms flared out, when her grandmother walked into the room. We all started laughing, and I dropped Aisha to the carpeted floor. In Arabic, Aisha's grandmother smiled and chuckled, "What are you doing?"

Aisha explained, "We are just playing circus, Grandma." Her grandma laughed with us and told us it was time to eat.

She knew how much my daughter loved my visits and me. She had become Aisha's confidante. She took my place for the warm, sweet hugs and sad tears of my daughter's hurts when I was missing in action, and I thanked God daily for how much Siti contributed to and inspired my wonderful daughter. Siti was caught between her son's chronic manipulation and the granddaughter she had fallen in love with—this charming, affectionate girl who was so grateful to have someone love her back. Aisha needed not be fearful; her devoted grandma was there for her and protected her.

Aisha became the translator between her grandmother and me, and her grandparents' home became a sanctuary for us. We baked sugar cookies with brightly colored frosting and made banana bread, the family's favorite. Time with the grandparents, though not ideal, had become quite comfortable. We were all bonding, making the proverbial lemonade out of the sour lemons we had been given. We were becoming a family, developing our own healing memories.

On one occasion, while we were in our little haven of a room, Baba came to say hello. When I asked him about something I wanted to do with Aisha, his reply was to speak to her father about it. Frustrated by his answer, my honest reply was, "Sleeping with her father is the only way to get his favor." Nosey and mean-spirited Uncle Faisal walked into our room when I was explaining this detail to Baba. Baba had understood what I said to him, though he pretended not to; his intrusive son thought it was his job to explain my dilemma to him in Arabic.

From that day forward, Baba said, "You can come to me for anything and not Abdul."

A few weeks passed. Aisha wanted me to ask her dad for something and said, "Mommy, if you sleep with Daddy, he will let me have it." I realized she had listened to our earlier conversation.

By this time, Abdul's behavior no longer charmed anyone. One day, Aisha and I played on the patio while her dad was visiting. I preferred being outside in the walled garden area rather than cooped up inside, even when the weather was hot. Aisha was in her swimsuit on this hot summer day; and when she heard her father honk as he arrived at the gate, I watched her transform into a frightened little girl. "My daddy is coming!" she said nervously. "My daddy is coming! Mama, I have to put some clothes on!" I hadn't seen this terrified side of her around her dad for some time. She trembled, she was so afraid. When had this started again?

On one of my visits, I was invited to accompany the grandparents to a family gathering where my ex's uncle lived. This was the uncle who had intervened with the government on Abdul's behalf years before. I loved this wonderful family who lived in a humongous, elaborately decorated home. I had always enjoyed their visits, during which English was easily spoken and I was included as part of their lively family scene. Laughter danced throughout their home. Abdul's extended family knew only too well the hell I was living, being caught between the duality of two worlds. One of the cousins asked me why I had ever gotten involved with Abdul, as his reputation was far from stellar and he could "lie to your face without blinking an eye." Where had they been to warn me before I had married him?

After my first visit to Riyadh, I had started to take every other weekend off. My boss was not happy about this when he realized I was gone, so I tried to cover my tracks. He knew I needed to see my daughter, though he tried to be really tough about it when he found out.

After a few months of visits, I mentioned to a relative that Abdul and I had been spending some time together. She asked why. It was difficult to accept that my daughter lived with other relatives when I was in the same country. I was quite capable of taking care of my own child. My reply to her was, "In hopes that things will work out so that I can keep seeing my daughter."

As I said this, her face turned pale, white as snow, and she replied, "I want you to know that Abdul is engaged to be married, so whatever he's telling you is another lie." This left me speechless. "We had an engagement party for them last week," she went on. I didn't want to believe what I'd heard. I closed my eyes, feeling as though I'd been slapped across the face. Why hadn't he, or someone at the home, said something to me? They lived two lives. Was it unacceptable to discuss when I was around? Was it taboo? Had I understood Arabic more fluently, perhaps I would have understood this, too.

When was I going to get it? My chest tightened as my breath was taken away. The betrayal left me speechless, my tongue too dry to burble the words, "That lying bastard." As I turned and walked away, I mumbled unheard obscenities.

Angry, with a bitter, metallic taste in my mouth, I was determined not to show my emotions. I needed to be strong and above it all, when all I wanted to do was curl up, give up, and die. I couldn't let anyone see the vulnerable me. Was this not what I had learned growing up? My mother had taught me well. As she would say, move on, don't feel, or it will kill you. My insides burned like bright, hot red flames. I couldn't leave their home quickly enough. Another game and another lie. I was steaming as I flew home from Riyadh. I couldn't wait to get to the safety of my tiny Jeddah apartment. It comforted me that it was mine. It was close to midnight as I clumsily hauled my luggage up the two flights of wide cement stairs, and I prayed no one watched me. I was emotionally exhausted.

A peaceful comfort filled me as I reached my apartment and entered into my garden oasis. I had created a private area with lattice partitions around the corner of the end unit to block the views of close neighbors, and I had built a locked entry gate. With time, the flowers grew on the lattice and walled me in, creating my safe haven. I was so tired of people being around all the time. My home was a sacred place to rest in the midst of chaos, and my patio was gorgeous and elegant.

With time, people had come to know me by my garden, and the compound gardener would leave me plants and flowers to add to my palace. My porch allowed me to sit hidden away and listen to whomever walked by in that busy, multicultural Peyton Place. I again thanked God for my little haven, but I had business to attend to.

After settling into my inviting apartment, I called Abdul. When he answered, and before he started his phony sweet talk to ask about my weekend, I stopped him and said, "You are a fucking liar! I am never going to trust you again. You never told me you were getting married!"

He took a deep sigh and irritably said, "If you were a good woman, you would understand and accept that."

My angry reply was, "I'm not a good woman." I hung up and walked away from the phone. He continued to call throughout the night. I didn't need him, not anymore. My visits didn't skip a beat. I had already paid my dues to this devil. His father said I no longer needed to interact with him. A new heaven was unfolding.

Life in Jeddah

After being back in Saudi Arabia for eighteen months with no break, I was breaking.

By this time, the new private hospital was doing quite well. We entertained doctors from around the world, inviting them to speak and to set up clinics for their specialties. Huge buffets were arranged for guests either in the beautiful hospital or at the owners' magnificent family villas on the Red Sea. The hospital continued to grow, which was good news. Recruitment was a favorite task of mine, and leaving the country was part of my job. I created my own team of nurses to work with who shared common values in making the nursing department fantastic and strong.

Due to the limited medical vocabulary of our Saudi female translators, I taught an "anatomy" class for Saudi women—we might call it sex education in the States—and they learned a great deal. They would arrive with a list of questions they felt comfortable enough to ask me about their bodies, male bodies, sex, and so forth. It was amazing to realize how limited full-grown women in their twenties could be in their knowledge about their bodies and about the opposite sex.

The Saudi women I worked with seemed well informed about my ex. They knew of Abdul's engagement and where he worked. For whatever reason, maybe to get "brownie points," they kept me abreast of my ex-husband's whereabouts and mentioned that Abdul had his wife-to-be "checked out" to make sure she was still a virgin. A double standard, I would say, in any country.

During this same period of time, Abdul's car was set on fire on two different occasions in Jeddah. A Saudi coworker's uncle worked at the police department in Jeddah, and he was able to find out more about these incidents. I wanted to know if Abdul had mentioned me as a possible suspect in starting the fires. Apparently, I was listed as a suspect. The first time the car was set on fire, in front of his apartment complex, the car was repairable. The second fire totaled his car.

When I told a girlfriend about these incidents, she laughed. "Don't they know that if you were going to set fire to his car, you would have made sure he was in it?" I was ready for this type of humor by then and found it funny.

Rumor had it that Abdul had had an affair with a Filipino woman whose husband had started the fires. Abdul also lost his job, I was informed, because of inappropriate sexual relations while he was engaged to be married.

My American hair stylist was privy to some of this gossip from Abdul's hospital. She was married to a cool Saudi man who chose to dress in Western garb. He seemed to have the ability to question the culture and religious dogmas, and he had the maturity to live according to his own interpretation and not be hypocritical. I respected that.

Most people in my hospital had a good idea of what had been happening in my life and were quite empathetic. One owner's view of life was more liberal and understanding, perhaps because of his American wife. The CEO—a tougher, rougher man who ruled by fear, though his bark was worse than his bite—said to me, "I am a lot like your husband, a difficult man with a temper." I smiled and agreed with him and said he was lucky that I had some damn good practice and that he was not my husband, so the boundaries were a bit different.

He and I learned to work quite well together, though our working relationship was laden with drama and occasional raised voices, threatening this and that. During one telephone conversation, we argued about my getting a vacation. I *needed* a vacation. After being back in Saudi Arabia for eighteen months with no break, I was breaking. I worked hard, long hours. I was coping with frequent and debilitating migraine headaches. I needed to get out of the country. I needed the sanity break, so I would be leaving soon for six weeks.

Initially, I had managed the whole nursing department, including the clinics, and had a finger on every department because of it. Everything was going well in that regard. On one of my recruitment trips, I hired a woman to be my office assistant, and a nurse who had previous staff-training experience who could take over that part of my job. My lead nurses assumed some of my overladen burden. My core nursing staff was getting stronger, as well, thanks to my selection of nurses at recruitment and ongoing education. Having experienced nurses in more leadership roles and now supervisors for each shift eased my time requirements as I delegated some of my responsibilities. After a few months, the CEO asked about these positions when he became aware that I had hired additional help. I explained that if he wanted a quality hospital, additional help was needed as the hospital grew.

My Contract in Jeddah Ends

The familiarity of my type of saneness comforted my soul.
With every minute in the Kingdom, my view of
normalcy had been tainted.

My contract with the private hospital would end in October 1991, and I wasn't interested in renewing it. I wanted to get a job where my daughter was, in Riyadh. The owners granted me an opportunity to transfer my *iqama* (work permit) from their hospital to another employer, which meant I was given permission to remain in the Kingdom to find a job. This was a rare occurrence. This was also what I had asked for over three years earlier when my husband had kicked me out of Saudi Arabia.

A rumor floated around that someone in the family had said that if I moved to Riyadh, then they would move Aisha back to Jeddah. It was the mean-spirited uncle who said this, Uncle Faisal, the brother we had lived with in Washington. He had always stirred things up, and I did not trust him. Now I wondered, *What do I do? Do I stay in Jeddah? Do I go to Riyadh? Where should I find a job?* I decided it was time for me to stand up to Baba, to ask him myself.

On my next visit, I apprehensively asked to talk with Baba alone. We went into the gigantic, empty formal living room on the ground floor. The room now seemed larger than it had when my marriage celebration had been held in it years before. Baba attentively listened as I nervously inquired about the plan for my daughter. My question was, "Will Aisha be attending school in Riyadh?" Her grandfather adamantly told me that Aisha would not be moving to Jeddah, but would stay in Riyadh. He went on to say he had already paid for her school and that her father had contributed nothing. He was upset about Abdul's lack of responsibility and financial contribution toward his daughter's life.

I asked Baba if he was all right with me finding work in Riyadh. He supported this, and replied, "You are her mother," with a smile on his face. I was relieved and so glad that I'd had the courage to ask him. Something had shifted. With tears in his eyes, Baba shared stories about the numerous times Aisha had consoled him when he wasn't feeling well. She was such a loving, caring girl.

Aisha and her aunt, who was ten years older, went to a private all-girls religious school, for grades 1–12. Lessons were taught in Arabic, but they also had a class in English. The students wore uniforms—long, dark skirts with long-sleeved white blouses and dark vests. Some of the young students had already started to cover when they went to school, but not Aisha. Her family wasn't so strict about this. She was still young, almost seven.

When my contract was completed, Aisha returned from her usual two months in Egypt. This year, our vacations would not coincide. I was more than ready to return to the country of my birth for a few months, but it was bittersweet to leave my girl behind. Sad and disheartened, we took our separate vacations. We no longer questioned the absurdity of this yearly occurrence. I wrapped numerous packages and gave them to Aisha when I left so she could open a package a day. This would help ease the distance between us and our longing for each other. I was now able to talk with Aisha over the phone at her grandparents' home. I called weekly, though I didn't always connect with her. Still, a gentle shift had occurred.

The welcome freedom of my country and reacquainting with friends and family uplifted me and replenished my broken-down soul. Though I did my best to create a life in Saudi Arabia, it would never be my home; no one *really* knew me. While in California, my family from different corners of the country joined me at the home I had been able to buy while I was working in Jeddah. A dream come true. My parents and all six of my siblings, with various members of their families, gathered at my humble hillside dwelling in the redwoods near the Pacific Ocean for Christmas 1991.

Aisha had now turned seven, and I missed the birthday party her grandfather let her have at his home; and, of course, she missed our celebration. I'd brought videos of Aisha for all to see. While on my vacation, I shot videos of America to share with Aisha and her grandparents. Being back in California, near the Pacific, nurtured a warm feeling of elation and joy; I was home. The familiarity of my type of saneness comforted my damaged spirit. I felt I could take a deep breath again—wear whatever I wanted, drive my car, eat pork, and eat with my left hand. With every minute in the Kingdom, my view of normalcy had been tainted.

Moving to Riyadh

*How could beheading, such a barbaric form of punishment,
still be practiced in a country that seemed to want
to emulate a modern world?*

At the beginning of 1992, Aisha was seven years old, my contract was finished in Jeddah, and I headed to Riyadh after a wonderful vacation without work issues or concerns. I was relaxed, ready to conquer the next battle in my insane life: finding a way for my daughter to have visitations at my home. Once in Riyadh, my visits to her grandparents' home became more regular, soon becoming weekly. Little was heard about Aisha's father. I was revitalized, though it would be short-lived.

Fortune presented me with a place to stay, in a funky, somewhat-run-down, old concrete apartment complex with an American woman, Kathy, and her teenaged Saudi American son, while I looked for work that would provide me housing. My housemate's unusual story was yet another of a mother whose children had been taken. There were many such heart-wrenching stories. How does one not get bitter about an unfair system and not become filled with hate? Children were taken and kept away from mothers in some countries for months or for years, despite the many efforts those mothers made to be with them.

Kathy's ex-husband had had her set up and arrested for not leaving the country after her visit to Saudi Arabia, a visit he had arranged for her as a "favor." The police had taken her in handcuffs, in front of her two children; and she was hauled to jail, a horrendous, repulsive, rat-infested place. No one spoke English. Her young son had learned how to live on his own on the streets after his stepmother had kicked him out of his Saudi father's house, but he didn't know what to do to help his jailed mother. He begged the aid of a princess, who helped his mother obtain a visa in exchange for English tutoring. This saga continued for years. I don't know the ending of this story or their whereabouts.

My first-floor room was a storeroom in the front part of their apartment. My dozen cardboard boxes, stuffed to the brim, were added to the two dozen boxes they stored. I covered the boxes with sheets to make my cold, bare room look more like a home. Though we shared an inside door, my room had its own entrance, which was handy, so I wouldn't need to disturb my friends. My toilet was a hole in the floor that actually had a thin raised U-shaped stone where one's feet could be placed for squatting. Daily use of the hole in the floor was a new experience for me, though I had used a hole several times when I traveled.

Being out among the tenants of public housing in Riyadh gave me an appreciation for the safety in the manned compounds and at my daughter's family home, surrounded by a gate, knowing someone was aware I existed. I was now dealing with a different, unfamiliar, and unprotected way of life on the streets that I had been unaware of, though I didn't feel like I was in harm's way.

With my updated résumé in hand, I searched for a nursing job. I rode in limos and took buses around the large capital city, applying for many positions at different hospitals around Riyadh. I was open to anything, any type of job, though I did want to be closer to where Aisha lived, making transportation easier for our visits.

After a few weeks of laboriously pounding the intensely hot pavement, I was offered and gratefully accepted a job with a large government hospital. This American-run hospital became my new sponsor.

My completely furnished one-bedroom apartment on the third floor was quite roomy in comparison to my place in Jeddah. It was in a single-female housing complex on hospital grounds, and we had a nice garden area with a swimming pool on the ground floor. Our individual housing units were not guarded, though there were two main guard stations at the entrances of the large, somewhat-modern hospital, said to be quite progressive, with physicians and nurses from around the world.

My position would be to "reorganize" a large medical clinic and heal a troubled past for the current staff. The difference between this position and my last was like night and day. I now worked in a fully running, very organized specialty hospital with predominately Western staff whose caliber of care and expectations was very different.

The nursing department was comprised of Western nurses and offered camaraderie like I had had in the States. English was the language of the hospital. This large specialty medical clinic wanted my administrative expertise and helped me learn a new area of nursing. As my previous boss, the CEO, had said, "Your knowledge of a discipline does not matter as long as you know how to manage."

We treated up to three hundred patients a day, a large volume for clinics. There were fifteen nationalities working on the floor I managed, and we had awesome and delicious potlucks. Everybody brought their own country's dishes, and I loved that.

During this time, I found out that Abdul had married in Cairo. Being a more liberal country, mixed weddings were more the norm there. Aisha talked about her father's glamorous wedding, saying it was beautiful and that she wanted a wedding like that in Egypt someday. She had worn a beautiful, frilly white lace dress and white patent-leather shoes.

Abdul and his new wife were moving to Riyadh now that they were married. I feared Aisha would move in with them, which was the custom. Concerned about this, I asked Siti, who had been over to visit their new home several times, and she said, "No, I do not like it there." Aisha was not fond of visiting them there, either. She continued to live with her grandparents, which was a great relief and a blessing to me, although she visited her father regularly.

In the fall of 1992, after the family returned from their vacation in Egypt, I resumed my weekly visits with Aisha. I asked Aisha about her vacation, and she described what her family had worn when they were in Egypt, comically demonstrating that she had worn her skirts above the knee, her aunt had worn her skirts at the knee, and her grandmother had worn her skirts to the calf. She said they didn't cover when in Cairo. Aisha's grasp of English was better when she returned, though seldom used when away. She was beginning to better differentiate one language from another. Perhaps translating for her grandmother and me had helped with this.

I was settling in, and life in Riyadh fascinated me, but I can't say it wasn't frustrating and bizarre. Knowing that people were being beheaded in downtown Riyadh every Friday afternoon at "Chop Chop Square" was unsettling. This, to me, was such an archaic way to punish people. People from all walks of life were encouraged to see what would happen to them if they did something wrong, from beheadings to the hands of thieves being chopped off. I chose not to be a spectator of this gruesome weekly event. The thought of it alone made me sick, that such a barbaric form of punishment was still practiced in a country that seemed to want to emulate a modern world.

Going Back to Court

Fully covered, with my abaya and hijab over my head and face, alone in the small, stale female waiting room of the courthouse, I waited under the glow of a single dim lightbulb that dangled from the ceiling. The windows were covered with old newspapers, yellowed and brittle from years of wear.

During my time in Riyadh, I had taken up regular visits with Aisha, staying overnight at her grandparents' home less frequently now that I had my own home and Abdul lived in Riyadh. Aisha was unable to stay with me yet.

I made new friends and connected with a supportive group of women married to Saudis (or other Arabs), just as I had in Jeddah. The children enjoyed playing together. I also met people through such things as hiking clubs, American embassy gatherings, and events at the hospital.

A Saudi woman who worked at the hospital, Noora, and I became friends. In time, I shared my story with her, about having a court order that said Aisha could start coming to my house, and told her that the family wasn't honoring the judgment. She suggested I go back to court to get it reinforced. A Muslim man we worked with was willing to be my *mahram* or *walī*, the male representative for me in court. I didn't need a lawyer and don't remember paying any court fees. It was August 1992 when Mohammed, my mahram, arranged a court date while Aisha and her grandparents were in Egypt.

Mohammed and I would face Abdul in court in Riyadh. My mahram explained the procedure to me. Only speak when asked to, say as little as possible, etc. I was fully covered, with my abaya and hijab over my head and face when we got to court. I was escorted to a small, stale female waiting room where a single dim lightbulb hung from the ceiling. The small room's windows were covered with old newspapers, yellowed as if stained with urine and brittle from years of wear. I couldn't see out of the room, though limited light snuck through.

I waited alone for over an hour as my mahram and Abdul discussed the case with the scribe. It was my turn to come into the courtroom so my comments could be heard and written down. This interaction became a mini private battleground between Abdul and me. Abdul would say something, and I would contradict what he said. He tried to make me look like an unfit mother. He held an American flag, indicating I wanted Aisha to become an American, and I could only wonder where he had gotten the flag. He said I had introduced her to Christmas and Christianity, and he mentioned something about Aisha seeing Santa Claus. I whispered to Abdul and asked if he would like me to show them the picture of him and Aisha sitting on Santa's lap. He knew there was one, but he did *not* know that I didn't actually have it. He then quit harassing me about Santa. Still, Abdul and I kept this private, whispered, argumentative tug-of-war going. He threatened me, and I threatened back. He became cautious of what he said, however, as I had a ready rebuttal up my sleeve. After some time, the scribe indicated he had enough information. I was asked to go back into my archaic little room, and the scribe went to present the information to the judge. We would get the verdict either that day or the next.

After I waited another hour, my mahram retrieved me and we left the court building. My heart was in my throat, beating irregularly in anticipation. He told me the verdict: the previous judgment had to be followed. Aisha would come to my home on the weekends, starting immediately. If the family did not comply, then they would be arrested. I was relieved, though also skeptical based on my past experience with the legal system.

I was so grateful for Mohammed's assistance that I wanted to give him a big hug, though I knew this was not the place for that. I thanked him and cried with joy as we walked to the car. Before getting into the car I gave him a hug of gratitude.

My mahram laughed with a sly grin on his face when he mentioned that his uncle was the judge that day and that he had been willing to hear the case. He was the person who had declared that the judgment must be followed, especially since the highest court in Mecca had determined it months before.

I couldn't have been happier. Aisha would start coming to my home. It was summer, and the family was still in Egypt on vacation. I would have to wait for their return. Again, I felt as though the angels were with me along my path. How had I survived this much? The light and unconditional love from a little girl and my god had gotten me through.

Part Six

Visitation with Aisha

First Visit

"I know I'm half American and half Saudi. Which half is which?"

When my Saudi family returned to Riyadh, I mentioned to Baba that I had returned to court and that Aisha was to start coming to my house. Her grandfather implied that he knew nothing of the ruling and that they would not accept it. Apparently, his son hadn't shared the judgment with them; or if he had, Baba did a great of job covering it up.

The biggest concerns Abdul had brought up at trial were that I would run and escape with Aisha and that I would not be a good role model for her. By now the family knew my character, however, and who was their son to talk? He was no role model at all. Whenever Abdul mentioned me running with Aisha, I would ask him, "How might I be able to do this?"

With the court paperwork that supported Aisha's visits in hand, I went to her grandparents' house. One thing I said to Baba was, "I know that, as a good Muslim, you will do what is right." The highest court in Mecca had determined this to be the right thing. Ultimately, he followed the order, not necessarily because he wanted to, but because he wanted to be a good Muslim.

He determined that I would have to come and pick up Aisha, so I would take a limo from my home and arrive at her home at nine o'clock each Thursday morning. Before she could leave with me, she had to perform her morning Quran recital. She would be with me for the rest of the day and had to be back by five or six p.m. on Fridays to get ready for school the next day.

From then on, she came to my house every weekend. It was awesome, a dream, a miracle.

We had a fantastic time the first time she came to my apartment. We had a "Barbie celebration party" with her dozens of Barbies to honor the occasion. We spent time swimming in the pool at the complex and went out to eat and hung out in the apartment. She met some of my friends and made her own friends with children of hospital employees.

After some time, the family began to have their driver bring Aisha to my compound and often pick her up. We would arrange this weekly, depending on what was happening in our schedules.

Before we had started visitation, I had written a letter to the administrator of the hospital, who was an incredibly wonderful Saudi man, asking for permission for Aisha to live with me during her visits. I also asked for medical benefits for her. He agreed that Aisha could live with me and that she was eligible to get the same free medical care I received. Aisha started to have vision, dental, and health checkups at the hospital. Her father was paying nothing whatsoever toward her care; this was a sore subject with her grandfather. The hospital made an identification badge for Aisha to wear around the hospital when she was with me, which she thought was really cool.

Aisha helped me plan her eighth birthday party. The grand event took place in the "party room" of the hospital's recreation complex. We decorated the huge, empty room with brightly colored helium balloons and streamers that splashed the ceiling and walls, and were serenaded with cassette tapes playing popular music throughout the evening. We clapped, danced, talked, and laughed with our many guests of multiple nationalities. We nibbled on hors d'oeuvres, but the huge chocolate sheet cake with thick, delicious chocolate frosting adorned with gaudy decorations of teal and gold took center stage.

When the cassette player blared out "Happy Birthday" to Aisha in Arabic and in English, everyone clapped and sang along. Aisha, wearing the beautiful, expensive, frilly party dress from her dad's wedding, was determined to cut her own cake. A huge knife was presented for her tiny little hands. She fearlessly, unevenly slashed the cake while the crowd cheered her on.

All of my Riyadh friends, coworkers, and some of her relatives came to celebrate not only her birthday but also the victory of having successful visitation at my home that had taken two years to achieve.

Aisha now visited her dad less frequently, as she disliked spending time with him and his new wife. She said they ignored her. Within a year of living in Riyadh, Abdul's wife left him and went back to Jeddah, where her family was. Abdul later left his job in Riyadh and went back to Jeddah to work. Rumor had it that he billed his company more money than he used on his business trips and had been caught. He was given the option to leave on his own or be fired. Being fired would be on his record, and it would have been difficult to get another job. Because of this, Abdul moved back to Jeddah to attempt to rekindle his relationship with his wife. He wasn't around Riyadh anymore, other than infrequent visits when he flew to there to see his parents or his daughter. I was ecstatic with this change. Along this whole journey, somebody I knew or worked with knew of someone who knew Abdul, so I was kept well informed of what was going on with him for years. As the saying goes, "Karma is a bitch."

My life with Aisha continued in Riyadh. I was delighted and still in shock at the miracle of having my daughter spend weekends with me. I finally was able to take her out for an ice cream cone. I would visit her, and she would come over to my home. Siti invited me to Aisha's school events, and I would frequently eat lunch, the biggest meal of the day, or evening meals with them. I had become part of the family. It was important to me for my daughter to know who her mother was. Her dad was slowly fading out of her life.

After one school play, Siti invited me to have lunch with their family. Abdul called, and Siti mentioned that I was there and had gone to the school play. Abdul lost it and said that I had no right to be in their house. This was one time that I understood what Siti said back to him in Arabic: "This is *my* house. You have no right to tell me who can come to my home." I realized then they knew I was the responsible parent who wanted to be with Aisha and participate in her care. They saw my dedication and I saw theirs. They fell in love with her, and I with them. My biggest stumbling block was that Siti and I didn't share the same language—my Arabic was improving, just not fast enough—but we understood the language of a mother's love.

Out of respect, I did my best not to talk negatively about Aisha's father, though that was often difficult. I wanted to set a good example and worked hard to be positive when I was around her. One day Aisha said, "Do you know what, Mom? My dad is a liar." I looked at her and said that was not nice to say. Her reply was, "Well, it is true." I asked her why she would say that. She said, "My dad says he will call me, and he never does. I call him, and they say he is not there, but I know he is." This went on and on.

Aisha's grandfather always teased her about who she was going to marry. He would joke with her, "I am going to marry you to a Sudanese man," and laugh. My daughter replied, "Jedi, I will marry whomever I choose." They bickered and laughed back and forth. We talked politics. We talked about the Gulf War. It was a great to have these interactions with him.

Aisha was a delight, and I loved to watch her experience different cultures and people blending together. Wherever she lived, she merged her worlds together. One day, we were playing on her grandparents' cool marble porch and sidewalk. Aisha gracefully jumped up, stood in front of me, and asked, "I know I'm half American and half Saudi. Which half is which?" I looked at her quizzically and then started to laugh at the question. Still laughing as I watched her turn around with a slight jump, she bent over and smacked her butt. She dissolved into contagious giggles, saying she had decided it was her bottom half that was Saudi, and her upper body was American. Did she say this because of our similar hair and eye color? Regularly, we heard the comment, "You look so much like your mom." Was this Aisha's interpretation of being half Saudi and half American?

My Parents' Visit

Before my parents returned to the States, they offered to help financially, if I wanted to try to get Aisha out of Saudi Arabia.

Three years had passed since my parents had seen Aisha in Jeddah. In the fall of 1993, my parents received visas to come visit. They were offered the use of the home of a couple I worked with, in the family complex, while they were on vacation. It was a perfect fit for all of us, with three bedrooms and two baths. Being in the "couples compound" meant more freedom to come and go.

During my daughter's weekend visits, my parents commented on what a significant difference there was in Aisha's mannerisms from their visit in '89. She was now eight years old, and three years is a lot of time in which to grow up. It was more about how reserved she was, how she behaved toward men—in this case, my dad. She would not get close to my father. He did have a long, bushy beard, and she didn't know him, but this went much deeper than that. She was awkward and self-conscious about giving her grandfather a simple hug, as if it was *haram* (forbidden). It was almost as if she was being taught that it was not all right to do so. This was a behavior I hadn't seen in her approach to anyone else, whether she knew them or not. Her American grandpa and grandma were very concerned about Aisha's well-being, as this was atypical for a child of her age in the States. This was such a big change in this part of her life, one I had not observed, that I wondered if I may have been too close to see it before. Aisha looked at my dad as if she should be cautious of him. I kept reminding her, "He is your grandpa." As time went on, she warmed up to him, but it did give us reason for concern.

My parents' month-long visit was filled with a variety of activities. We all played together. My father taught Aisha to ride a bike, and she taught my mother to dance. Aisha was definitely the life of the party wherever she went. We had a *ma'a s-salāma* party, a mixed-company going-away party, for two women from my work unit who were leaving. Aisha entertained us with accomplished Arabic dancing, dancing with all of us. We had a fantastic time, and maybe thirty to forty employees and family members showed up to celebrate into the wee hours of the morning in this amazingly free compound.

My parents and I participated in events that were held through my employment and at the American embassy and attended various gatherings with friends of mine. We visited my first cousin, an expat from Kansas, who worked in telecommunications. We went out to dinner and took sightseeing trips of Saudi ruins.

We hired a limo to take us out in the desert for a day to visit a camel farm. While in the desert, we were invited into a large white Bedouin tent made of camel skin. We sat on a thick red printed carpet on the floor to drink Arabic coffee that was made from cardamom seeds, a flavor that one gets used to. As it was during Ramadan, the men in the tent were fasting, but they still showed us their incredible hospitality and served us coffee. We didn't see any women around; they may have been back in the city preparing food for breaking the fast. I was grateful for the Arabic I knew and understood enough to carry on a decent conversation.

My dad was often called an American mutawa because he had such a long, graying beard that extended well onto his chest. I teased Dad, "I do not know if you should have that long of a beard here." It was definitely a conversation starter.

When my parents left Riyadh, I had two regrets. I had not invited my daughter's other grandparents to our home to meet my parents, and they hadn't invited us to their home.

Before leaving, my parents talked with me about their concerns for Aisha. They saw a certain brainwashing in how she reacted, and it really bothered them. They mentioned that they would be willing to help financially if I wanted to try to get Aisha out of Saudi Arabia. I was surprised to hear them say this; my mother had never offered to give me any money for anything, period.

They were able to see the drastic cultural differences between the two countries, and they saw how dissimilar to her old self Aisha had become. I understood what they observed. I had become part of it, however, so it wasn't as apparent to me. I noticed it in myself when I went back to the States for vacations. I found myself becoming more self-conscious of what I wore and where I was. My friends started pointing out that, based on the way I talked about things in Saudi Arabia, I had acclimated to a way of life that didn't fit my customary patterns.

New Housing

Aisha could enjoy a more open lifestyle, with an Islamic presentation, but not so strict. We were in heaven with our new liberties.

After a few months of Aisha's visits in my single-female compound, my British neighbor, who worked with the hospital's housing department, suggested I apply to change my housing now that I had regular visitation with Aisha. I applied and was approved to live in the married/family housing compound, which gave us more freedom to come and go.

We shared a three-bedroom townhouse with its own backyard and outdoor patio. The neighbor who had suggested the change became our roommate. Aisha now had her own room when she came for visits, and this new home would provide Aisha with a more liberal lifestyle and a community with streets and playgrounds among mixed nationalities. She could play with friends or ride her bike freely around the compound. The guards at the entrance were less strict about who came to visit our little international community. Men, women, and children from many countries resided there. Families lived together in a wonderful tree-lined neighborhood with a swimming pool. Aisha could enjoy a more open lifestyle, with an Islamic presentation, but not so strict. We were in heaven with our new liberties.

For the first time ever, Siti brought Aisha to my new house. I was sure she came to see where I lived and if it was acceptable for Aisha to be there. I invited her to come in, but she declined. She must have given her approval.

Life in Riyadh

When I asked Aisha if her Ken doll was the boyfriend or a husband for Barbie, her reply was, "No, Momma, he is the driver." Of course. Who else was going to drive the Barbies around, as girls could not do so in Saudi Arabia?

Aisha was raised, I would say, being quite privileged. She lived with a princess mentality that was part of a completely different world from mine, and I did not particularly like it. Her grandparents treated Aisha differently than they treated their own children, more as though she was an American. Times were changing, and she was a grandchild who happened to live with them. Wasn't she supposed to be spoiled?

Aisha changed their lives just by being who she was. When she started to live in the family home, two of her uncles and her aunt were in high school. She became close to her younger uncles, who played with her and teased her; they were interested in her life. By contrast, it was difficult for Aisha's aunt to adjust to all the freedom her niece was given. She showed resentment of her niece's newfound opportunities that had never been allowed before in their home. This was not what she had experienced, as her childhood had been quite strict. There had been no birthday parties; my understanding was that to celebrate a birthday took attention from the religion. Aisha, however, was allowed to have birthday parties at home with her family. She had girlfriends over, with music and dancing, and Aisha and I would make or buy birthday cakes for the family. On one occasion, we got cans of foam spray, and Aisha surprised Baba by shooting him with the foam when he came into the room. Everyone laughed, and it was a wonderful sight to see.

When the other children were younger, photos had seldom been taken, but Aisha's youth was well chronicled. Taking photos had once been forbidden in Islam altogether, though this concept was changing for many, and that included their home, particularly with Aisha. In decades past, though the religious interpretation varied, making an image was thought to be emulating God and idolatry; no object or image was to interfere with their faith. Mosques, the Quran, and at one time even coins were void of human portraits.

Baba would tell me how much he loved Aisha. She would ask him if she could help him. This was who Aisha was. She was her own spirit, quite warm and affectionate. When I asked Aisha's aunt what she wanted to do after she went to college and whether she wanted to get married, her response to me was, "It is up to my father." Unlike Aisha was now experiencing, she had not been encouraged to be her own spirit. It was as if a script had been written for her, and she was to follow it without being inquisitive or curious.

When they wanted something from the kitchen or wanted something done, the family would push a button on the wall in the living room, and one of the three maids would answer the bell to get whatever was needed as quickly as possible. But I encouraged Aisha to get things for herself. Despite my wishes for a change in this behavior, Aisha would leave things all over for the maids to pick up, as everyone did. Hoping to give Aisha gentle direction, I often reminded the maids that if Aisha and I were playing with something, to leave it alone so that we could put it away ourselves when we were finished.

Aisha had many toys, including a little yellow motorized car that ran on a battery, which an uncle had bought for her. She loved her car and learned to drive quite skillfully, piling her dolls in the car and driving around the walled compound. I am sure her car helped later in life when she learned to drive. If she wasn't driving the car, she was riding her bike.

She also had a beautiful toy Barbie RV. My parents had traveled around the US by RV, so they shared this in common with Barbie. My daughter had over twenty Barbies, with plenty of fancy clothes. Barbie dolls were still not allowed in the Kingdom, but this didn't stop them from getting into the country.

Aisha once asked me for a boy doll for a holiday gift, so I bought her a Ken doll. When I asked her if Ken was going to be the boyfriend or a husband for Barbie, she said, "No, Momma, he is the driver." Of course. Who else was going to drive the Barbies around, as girls couldn't drive in Saudi Arabia? They needed a driver, and now they had one.

Once, when I went to pick up Aisha to come to my house, I asked Siti, who was in the outside kitchen, where she was. She said she was upstairs taking a shower in their bathroom. I went into Aisha's grandparents' bathroom; and in the shower, with her clothes on, was one of the maids, washing my daughter. I was embarrassed to see this. I asked the maid to get out of the shower and told Aisha that she was big enough to take her own shower. To me, this was ridiculous. Aisha translated what I said to the maid, who had gotten my gist. However, the maid had been told to bathe Aisha; she was just following orders. I told Aisha it was time for her to do more for herself, that she was becoming a big girl.

Aisha and her friends would "play" covering their heads, standing in front of a mirror and throwing the scarves over their heads and acting so grown up. It reminded me of when I had played with my mother's high-heeled shoes as a kid; it was a rite of passage on the path toward becoming a woman. It wasn't looked at as a negative thing then, and I saw this as being the same for Aisha.

At one party, the wife of Aisha's uncle danced openly in front of a mixed group of people, and she did not cover. While this didn't matter to either of them, when some women married their husbands wanted them to cover, not just with an abaya or a headscarf, but their whole face, and gloves, too. This was difficult for me to understand. Often, their husbands had been educated in Western countries and had what appeared to be a more liberal way of thinking. Was this a power trip? How could it be based on purity or righteousness when the same men might abuse their wives and children?

There was a time when Aisha, one of her girlfriends, and I went to the American embassy for a Christmas dance with festivities for the children. A male friend accompanied me. After dinner, the children were to go to their own area for fun, games, and music. The dancing music started for the adults, and my daughter had a fit that I danced with a man. She got angry with me and wouldn't leave the dance floor. Annoyed, I took her outside and asked her what was going on. She said she was going to call the Mutawa on me because I wasn't married and had danced with this man.

I had never heard her talk like this. I could feel the heat rising in my body, like a volcano ready to spew its hot orange-red lava, and wondered, *How am I going to respond?* I sternly took hold of her and said, "You do not even know what you are saying. If I ever hear you talk like this again, then we may not be able to see each other." I could understand it was normal for her to be jealous, but to threaten to call the Mutawa! I didn't realize she even knew who they were. Who was filling her tiny brain with this way of thinking? Was she becoming a spy and reporting back to the family or her father? I had apparently forgotten where I was living and who had influence on her.

After a weekend morning of Quran recital, Aisha came down the marble stairway of her grandparents' spacious home to greet me. Cheerful and prancing as usual, she said, "Momma, if someone is not a Muslim, will they go to hell?"

A bit baffled, my reply was, "Some people may say this, but it is not what I believe." The question had caught me off guard. I went on to explain my philosophy about religion. "Momma believes that it is not the religion you are, but how you live your life and who you are as a person that matters. I believe that it is more important to be a good person. To be a kind, generous, honest person regardless of your religious beliefs. I believe we share the same God. Some of your relatives are Christians, and they believe they will go to heaven. You will figure it out for yourself one day."

I encouraged Aisha to be herself. It was important to me for her to have a positive experience with her family, regardless of where they came from or their beliefs. Family was extremely important to me; had I not felt that way, perhaps I would have run and hid with Aisha years earlier, before she was abducted.

Six of the boys in Abdul's family and one sister looked alike. They, like Baba, had paler skin, the Turkish blood. Siti had darker skin, as did one of the brothers, and it was often mentioned how different he was from his other siblings. He was so much more open to life and seemed to have a more outgoing, liberal personality. Aisha and I enjoyed spending time with him. When he married, Aisha and I would visit them at their home. I was once asked if I ever wondered if that brother shared the same father as the other brothers; they always joked about this.

In 1993, I learned that Faisal, the brother whom Abdul and I had stayed with in Washington, was moving back home. His job took him back and forth between Saudi Arabia and America. His appearance in the family home always changed the mood of the house and of all who were in it. He thought that because he was the oldest son at home, he was the boss. The whole household was glad whenever he went away, and the home would become happy again. He was unpleasant to be around and created a negative, volatile unrest, which affected the peaceful, warm atmosphere. There was always a sly smile of reprieve when we heard that he had gone back to the States. "*Al-ḥamdu li-llāhi*" (Praise be to God). Our next question would be, for how long? His return was dreaded. He was not so fond of me, and he was worse with Aisha. He was mean to her and disrespectful. I would frequently stand up for her when I was at their home. Grandfather would often ask me to "be nice" to him, and my reply was, "When he is nice to my daughter and to me, then I will be nice to him."

I told Aisha, "Bad people, even those who are family, do not get the same rights as good people." Generally, I did not see people's ethnicity and culture as an obstacle, but there were many frustrating days in Saudi Arabia, many times when I felt a profound need to leave before the country and its ways drove me to insanity. My daughter and I grew up together in it, so she knew how I felt about life there, both the good and the bad.

I was often shocked as I learned more about lifestyles in other cultures from the women I worked with, who shared what life and love was like for them in their countries of birth. Nurses from Egypt, Sudan, Somali, India, Philippines, and other countries had stories that left me in inner turmoil at such cruelty as female mutilation. There were women who wanted to be loved only to find they had become the possession of a man who had the "right" to rape and beat them. There were loveless marriages with no intimacy, only sex, often described as brutal. Many women did not know what their husbands' bodies looked like, as clothes weren't removed during intercourse. What happened to kissing and hugging and love? What a world we live in.

I knew I wanted more from life for Aisha. One day, she and I went to the amusement park with my favorite sister-in-law and her children. We liked to frequent the parks, which were like fairs, with all the carnival rides and games. Different days were open for families, for men, and then there were some days just for females. I enjoyed those days. Women would enter covered, pay, and then uncover once inside. While at the park, I mentioned to my sister-in-law that I dreamed that when Aisha got out of high school, she would come to the States to go to college. She gave me a startled yet sympathetic, loving look and said, "It will never happen."

I looked at her, almost in tears. "Really. Why?" I was shocked at her reply.

"They will never let Aisha leave Saudi unless it is to Egypt for their vacations."

I asked again in disbelief, "Why? She is an American, and she would be old enough. Other Saudi women have left to go to school there. Would they not want her to get a good education?"

"Sorry. That will not happen," she repeated.

This had been one hope I had held on to. What was I thinking? Time to get back to reality. Her words resonated deeply. My child, my offspring, would not be allowed to go to the country of her birth when she grew up. She would be held like a prisoner in their country. I was left pondering the sad twists and turns my life had taken when I had carelessly fallen in love with a Saudi man who was not the person I dreamt him to be.

Lawyer's Visit

I was taken aback when he unexpectedly asked if I would marry him.

At work one day, someone knocked on my office door. I opened the door but didn't recognize the gentleman who was standing before me. It was my lawyer from Jeddah. He was in Riyadh and had come to visit me. Pleasantly surprised, I invited him into my office. I was delighted to see this incredible man who had saved my life, my ego, and my self-esteem in so many ways. I closed my office door and gave him the biggest, friendliest hug I had to give, then reopened the door. I hadn't seen him in months, nor in his full dress before, thus the reason I didn't recognize him.

We talked and caught up on news and events in my life, but I was taken aback when he unexpectedly asked, "Will you marry me?" I had not seen this coming.

Caught off guard, I shyly responded, "What an honor it is that you ask me to marry you. I am so sorry, but I am unable to do this." I really loved him and all he had done for us—he and his son had both been very helpful and encouraging while they worked on my legal case—but marriage was not in the picture.

He replied sadly, "I did not think you would, because I think you like my son." It was true that I did have a crush on his son when in Jeddah, but that was over. His son and I had dated for a short while, and I enjoyed being with his two young daughters, but I was not culturally the right wife for him or mother for his children.

I sat in my office in shock, but genuinely honored that my lawyer had asked me to marry him. He was at least twenty years older than me, but that really didn't matter. He was still married to his first wife. In Saudi Arabia, though not typical, a man could have four wives. My understanding was that the concept originated during wartime, when women and children were left behind, and Mohammed, the prophet, peace be upon him, said it was acceptable for a man to marry more than one woman, since women whose husbands were killed in battle needed someone who could take care of them. In keeping with this concept, if a man chose more than one wife, he was to treat them equally.

At the hospital in Jeddah, we had a "royal suite" on the top floor. One of our male patients in the suite had two wives, and both of the wives would come and see him. The first wife had agreed for her husband to have another wife, and they actually lived in the same home. I wasn't privy to more details, but it was apparently a relationship that worked for them. In the younger generation, it was not readily practiced, but did still occur. I observed that when a man wanted another wife it stirred up jealously and hard feelings. It just seemed so bizarre to me, and usually to the women who experienced it. Perhaps they accepted it, but I knew it would not be my fate.

Do You Want to Play a Game?

I suspected sexual misconduct. I had to get my daughter out of there, and quickly. This was the final straw.

I had adjusted to my lifestyle in Riyadh. Aisha and I had regular visitations at my home, and we went on outings together. I had also become involved in her school activities. The family was comfortable with me being in Aisha's life, and my relationship with her grandparents and relatives was going well.

One day, when Aisha visited, she asked me if I wanted to play a fun game with her. I asked her, "How do you play this game?"

She innocently replied, "You lie on the floor, I get on top of you, and put it in, into your belly button."

Very shocked and enraged, though I tried desperately to stay calm as the heat rose through my body, I asked Aisha, without sounding too hysterical, how she had heard about this game. I did not want to show alarm. Her reply was, "In my uncle's bedroom." The uncle I did not like, Faisal.

I continued to question her, "Why were you in your uncle's bedroom?" She naïvely explained that she couldn't sleep, so she got up from her bed in her grandparents' bedroom. She saw her uncle's bedroom door was open and went in to lie down on the bed. The uncle and the family caretaker/driver, the one who had worked for the family for years, were in the room watching porno films. They didn't stop. Why did they let her watch this? Did they think she had gone back to sleep?

This same evil brother who let her watch porno films would have Aisha massage his back and butt. When the young female cousins visited, she told me, he would have them do the same. Rubbing his back was one thing, but nothing else was acceptable. Who knew if he rolled over? What else they were told to massage? As children, they didn't know the difference. If he said to do it, they were going to do what he asked because they were afraid of him. I was livid, and her story continued; there was more she wanted to disclose.

I quivered with fear, afraid to hear what she would share next. She described overhearing her grandparents in bed while they had sex. Aisha whispered her secret to me: "After morning prayer, my grandfather had no clothes on and got in bed with Grandma." She demonstrated the moans and groans she'd heard from her grandfather.

Again, trying to stay sane and make light of the story, I asked her, "What happened next?"

"My grandma said, 'Get off of me, and leave me alone!'" On the inside, I laughed at this last remark. What could I make of all this information in ten minutes? I was speechless and baffled. I was frightened for my daughter. What now?

Aisha's bed was still in her grandparents' bedroom. They had a large bedroom with a sitting area; and when she had moved to Riyadh, a bed was placed in there for her. She was afraid to sleep alone, as she had recurring nightmares and woke up screaming. Her grandmother's room safely protected her. I asked if they knew she had watched them that night. She said, "No, I had my sheets tucked this way," and she demonstrated peeking out from the sheets, now giggling.

Something was grossly wrong with this picture. I did not know what to do. I was frightened and concerned for my daughter's well-being. She didn't understand what was happening.

Should I speak with her grandparents or should I speak only with Baba? Should I speak with Faisal, the bad uncle? What do I do to change whatever's happening there?

I knew that if I spoke with Faisal, he would make Aisha's life even more miserable because he was such a mean bastard. I was freaking out at what was now poisoning the innocence of Aisha's life.

Not knowing what to do, I first confided with a Jordanian friend and coworker and asked her advice on how to handle my fears for Aisha. She advised me to talk to the father or the uncle, but I felt this would just make things worse.

I worked with a very Westernized female Saudi psychologist. Months earlier, I had consulted with her about one of my friends who was being beaten by her husband. I wanted to know what we could do to help. She just looked at me with her huge, bewildered brown eyes and said, "Not much in this country." If I inquired about my dilemma, what would she say?

I was sick, nauseated, and angry and felt very alone, with few resources to draw on. I was fortunate to have good female friends to vent to who could empathize with me and help me attempt to deal with the problem, but there were no actual solutions.

Before Aisha went on summer vacation, I talked with her about what was appropriate touching and what was not. I asked her if anyone had tried to touch her body. We also talked about her body and the changes that were occurring, as she was slowly starting to develop. I also instructed her that it was unacceptable for her to be in any boy's bedroom at any time, day or night, including her uncle's.

While I was on vacation in the States, I spoke to my therapist about my concerns for Aisha. The therapist said, "Even if she has not been molested yet, it is very likely she will be." He gave me advice to share with Aisha when we both returned from vacation.

Something happened while I was away. When I returned from vacation, surprisingly, the uncle had been moved to the other side of the house. The way the house was designed, there were two bedrooms off the living room in a little alcove with a shared bathroom. Previously, the uncle had had one bedroom and Aisha's aunt had the other. Aisha had now been moved into the uncle's old bedroom, and she had her own room after two years of living in the home, sharing a bathroom with her aunt. They had been given keys to their bedrooms. Wasn't this a bit strange? Something must have happened that I was not privy to. I had shared my concerns with a relative; had they said something? It was understood that the uncle should have no business with the girls. Aisha's aunt, the only daughter, had started college. It made sense for her and Aisha to have this privacy and, perhaps, protection.

Through more discussions with my confidantes, my concerns about sexual molestation increased. I heard that when Abdul was a teenager, he had made one of the younger female relatives touch his penis and was "inappropriate" with her.

Then I recalled that, when Aisha was little, she had once put her tongue in my mouth when she kissed me. Surprised by this, I had stopped her and asked what she was doing. Her response was, "My daddy kissed me like that." I made it clear to her that this was not an acceptable way to kiss. I didn't know how long that had been going on. Now that Aisha's body had started to develop, and I was putting more pieces together, I knew there was no way she would be protected in a country so far behind in dealing with sexual abuse. I had to get my daughter out of there, and quickly. This was the final straw.

Part Seven

First Attempts to Leave

Finding a Way

This was the beginning of the long, spiraling, tenacious saga of many lies to obtain a new outcome.

How was I to know what to do to get my daughter out of Saudi Arabia? There were no instruction books. Once I suspected sexual abuse, however, I decided the time had come for action. My eight-year-old daughter's safety was foremost to me. It was my responsibility to protect her and her changing body.

I started to plant a seed in Aisha's mind about the possibility of going back to America. A select group of close friends and family in the States, and also in Saudi Arabia, were aware of the new developments in our lives. Aisha was quick to know whom she could talk more openly with about what was really happening in this part of her life. Getting my daughter and myself emotionally prepared to make this journey became a roller coaster of unknowns. I had to creatively formulate a plan.

In preparation for the next chapter of our lives, I explained to Aisha, "Mommy would like to go to America to be with my family.

I would stay and live there." I asked Aisha what she thought about coming with me. "You cannot tell your grandparents or anyone. This would be our secret," I said. "No one could know because we would get in trouble." I told her that going to America would mean she would probably not see her grandparents or father for a long time. She was open to and excited about the idea of going to America. It was the "cool" thing to do, especially among her group of young girlfriends with more open, worldly views. Peering into her eyes, I asked one final time, "Can you keep a secret?"

How would I explain what the ramifications of all this could be to an eight-year-old in Saudi Arabia, where our lives could be on the line? Not more than a week had passed when Aisha arrived for her weekly visit. She could hardly contain her excitement as she wiggled up and anxiously informed me, "Yes, Momma, I want to go to America." I reiterated that it would need to be a secret between us, only us. She knew how to keep this secret from her father's family and other friends. She was truly amazing. Aisha, a deep, soulful child, said she understood the risks and what it meant to be quiet, especially with her grandmother, her confidante.

Her grandparents had taken her in when her father was mistreating her. They had fallen in love with her, and she with them. They were the only family she knew, as she had not yet been three years old when she had started living in Saudi Arabia and was six when she moved in with her grandparents.

Overall, they were a great family, and I was grateful that they had invited me into their home and their lives so that I could be with my daughter. Siti knew what it was like to be a mother, so she was empathetic to my circumstances. We had an unspoken bond, mother to mother, and words were not always necessary. We had learned to communicate through nonverbal gestures and eye contact; and with Aisha attempting to teach her siti English, verbal communication became a hilarious game of repetition for the three of us.

The conversation with Aisha regarding leaving that home and starting a new life in a very different country became a recurring topic. She said, "I know, Momma." She understood, but how? She was already a part of both worlds; she hadn't lived in her mother's country long enough to remember it, but she still felt the connection through me.

In a nod to the insane climate of the country we were in, we adopted a gesture for whenever we talked about taking this new journey—especially when it wasn't the most appropriate time to talk about our quest. We jokingly gestured by moving our hands across our necks, as if we would get our heads chopped off. This helped point out the serious nature of our scheme.

Sometimes Aisha liked to call our adventure "the Troll." Aisha had a troll doll with wild, neon-pink hair that stuck up straight. I had given this troll to her years earlier, and it continued to have a place in her life. The troll became our mascot.

We would need new identities, so my vacations in the States now dealt with continued research on ways to create new, untraceable identities for my daughter and me to use when we fled Saudi. I'd read many articles on ways to accomplish this, some of them bizarre.

My sister bought us wigs to use for our eventual escape and our makeovers. I put on my long, dark-brown wig to "become another person" as I went to pose for a photo of the new me at a mall that would make identification cards. They were not legal cards, but it was a start, and they looked quite official. I needed a new look and a new name, and I needed to become familiar with this new person. I attempted to get a passport under a new name by jumping through a few hoops, but it didn't work for me.

Hours became days as I laboriously searched through the Mormon's large genealogy library in Houston, Texas. I gathered information from obituaries where birth and death certificates might be used to create new identities. Computers, though in their infancy, were a roadblock instead of an asset, as they were beginning to link data from birth and death certificates, a process detrimental to my efforts. I had heard about people who would assume new identities by using someone's social security number when that person died. I looked extensively to find documented information that might work and then ordered the needed paperwork from Vital Statistics, but something would always be not quite right, and I couldn't use them.

I explored possibilities with friends and family for creating new identities through people they had known and people who had died. My German friend, Anna, used her Cold War contacts. A family unknown to me came forward and offered me the birth certificate of their young daughter who had died. Their daughter was two years younger than Aisha. Sadly, that would not work. My mind spent endless hours sifting through possibilities, but to no avail. All avenues failed, and it seemed hopeless.

As my mother and I contemplated what we could do, we both considered the possibility of some family friends who had attended the same church as us. Their daughter and I were childhood friends for many years, and she had died of a brain tumor a few years before. My mother said that she would talk to my friend's parents about the possibility of using their daughter's birth certificate. Her parents were aware of my plight, so when my mother approached them, their reply was, "We would be honored to let Leah use our daughter's birth certificate to help create her new identity." They applied for a new birth certificate from the Bureau of Vital Statistics for me to use, only to discover, to our dismay, that her death information had already been merged. The birth certificate arrived with the word "Deceased" stamped in bold red ink across the front of the document. That would not work.

Her parents graciously gave me her frail original birth certificate, then over forty years old. With this document, I was able to get a new driver's license, using a new name and birth date. In doing so, I had to claim it was the first time I had applied for a driver's license. I even had to take the driving test. Her parents also gave me her social security number in case it became necessary in the future. This was the beginning of a long, spiraling, tenacious saga of many lies to obtain a new outcome. This was the beginning of the "new me" on paper.

My efforts to get my hands on a birth certificate to use for my daughter, other than the one with a two-year age difference, had been unsuccessful. I was unable, at that time, to secure documents to establish her new identity.

Undeterred, I remembered that, months earlier, a woman I worked with in Saudi had mentioned that she and her husband knew someone, an "ex-Marine, Special Forces, CIA kind of guy," who was willing to help get Aisha out of the country. She said if I ever wanted his assistance to let her know. It was time to tap into her resources.

First Attempt: Turkey, 1994

It was unsettling to make any plans, though I knew something needed to be done—and soon. It was like shooting arrows aimlessly into the air at an invisible target.

The thought of what could happen to Aisha—that she could be molested and by whom—became a constant terror for me, and I had ample reason for my suspicions. It was time to formulate a plan. The coworker who had approached me months earlier got in touch with "Tom," her contact.

I met with Tom and his friend Andy at my home to discuss my escape options. They had a plan—a plan with a high price tag, of course. After much consideration, though doubtful that they understood what they needed to do, I decided it was my only option. It was unsettling to make any plans, though I knew something needed to be done—and soon. It was like shooting arrows aimlessly into the air at an invisible target.

If this plan was going to work, Aisha would need to meet the gentlemen so she would know them when they approached her. She needed to be comfortable enough to go with them. We made a game of their meeting. She especially liked "Uncle Tom," the name she gave him. They had a sweet, congenial relationship, forever teasing each other. My daughter was a jokester, always having people in stitches, laughing.

Uncle Tom had a plan, but it hit a snag before we even put it in action. Every summer, my daughter's family would vacation in Egypt. Her grandparents had done this for years, and they had their own apartment in Cairo, where Aisha's grandfather had lived and worked many years earlier. Her father was also born in Egypt, as were other siblings. That summer, much to my shock, instead of going straight to Cairo, they planned to go to Turkey first. I knew where they stayed in Egypt, but not in Turkey. Turkey was the country of Aisha's grandfather's ancestry. He had a brother and relatives they had not seen in years who lived there, and they wanted to visit them. Abdul and I had honeymooned in Turkey, and my mother and I had traveled there, but that familiarity would not help in executing the plan.

The shift from Egypt to Turkey threw a wrench into our mission and made it a more complicated undertaking, but we decided to proceed. The men had asked for $50,000 up front. Through my sister's help, I deposited $35,000 into their American bank account, per their request, with more money to come, no questions asked. I obtained the flight information regarding the day and time the family would be leaving Riyadh and when they would arrive in Istanbul. I also found out which flight they were taking later to Egypt, but not the exact date. Generally, these details were not shared, though I was able to extract the information I needed.

Aisha and I became very efficient at figuring out creative ways to get what we needed. We knew the family planned on staying near Istanbul for a week to ten days and would then fly to Egypt, where they would stay until late August. The timing was dependent on the imminent death of Baba's brother, however. He had suffered a stroke, and his health had rapidly declined. Aisha's grandfather would need to return to Saudi Arabia when his brother died.

Meanwhile, I applied for an emergency visa, saying my mother was ill and that I needed to be with her. This allowed little room for prying by the nosey informants my ex-husband probably still had watching me.

The two confident hired men arrived in Istanbul ahead of the family to get everything ready to safely abduct my daughter and get us to the States. I was to take the next morning flight out of Riyadh to meet Uncle Tom and Andy to accomplish our mission.

When Aisha and the family arrived, the men were to follow them from the airport to see where their accommodations were. It wouldn't be difficult to spot a little eight-year-old blonde, blue-eyed, tall, lanky girl with a "covered" aunt and grandmother holding her hand. As they walked through the airport, Aisha was to indicate that she saw the men by giving a prearranged signal: she would rub her eyes. In addition, Aisha had another instruction. The men were to carry a certain Barbie doll, one on whose leg she had written her name. My daughter said, "Whoever has this doll, I know to go with them." This would help her know it was time to go with them or whomever gave her the doll.

Back in Riyadh, I informed my roommate that my mom was sick and I needed to fly to the States immediately. My boss was aware of this possible intervention. It was difficult to contain my nervous, gut-wrenching excitement when I flew to Turkey to get Aisha; a long-awaited dream was unfolding at that moment. I arrived at the airport in

Istanbul, and the two hired men picked me up as planned. We greeted each other and then found a quiet place to sit. I was anxious to hear their good news, but something was wrong; I could feel it in my bones. They did not seem as pleased as they should have been.

"Your daughter is in Turkey," they explained. "We saw her at the airport, but we were unable to follow her." What the hell had they just said? They explained that their car had been blocked in traffic at the airport pickup area, they couldn't get out, and they were unable to follow the family. "We can't find her. We don't know where her accommodations are located. We need to call this mission off."

Outraged, I was about to explode. My heart had been squeezed so tight I didn't know if it was even beating, and I couldn't see through my tears. I wanted to scream at them, "We are *not* going to call this off just like that! How could this happen?" Instead, when I spoke, my voice barely squeaked, "There are other options."

I had already paid them $35,000, and now they thought it was time to quit. I didn't think so.

They had lost the family before they had even left the airport. These two specially trained Marines had parked their *one* vehicle where it could be blocked in and hadn't even hired anyone to help them. I wasn't sure why—it would have been so inexpensive. What was wrong with hailing a cab? Who needed special training to figure this out? They had lost the family as they boarded a shuttle van to leave the airport.

The men tried to explain that when they parked their car, it looked like an easy getaway spot. However, when the time came to leave, the traffic at the airport was congested. They got behind some vehicles that didn't move. The shuttle van had driven away from the airport, and now they didn't know which direction my daughter had gone. They had lost an entire family taking a shuttle van! I could only think them incompetent.

Aisha had seen the men. She had rubbed her eyes so much that her grandmother had asked what was wrong with her. Still, no one took action.

My head was spinning. I felt faint. My heart raced, my mind jumped all over the place, trying to get some sort of control of my panic-stricken thoughts. I was so damn angry. Again I wondered, *Why were there only two men? Why not hire more help? Why only one car? They could have hailed a taxi to follow the van. That is what I would have done.*

I was speechless. I had wanted to believe that this plan would work, and Aisha was even mentally prepared to accomplish our mission. What would we do next?

Still in the airport, the three of us sat in silence. I wanted to scream at those fools. I insisted that we were not finished and that we needed to find out where my daughter was staying, no matter what.

While my "professional and highly experienced" hired help seemed to cower because of their huge mistake, my adrenaline kicked in. "First, we find out all we can about the van. Which van company did they use? Who drove the van yesterday? Where did they take the family?"

The old airport had rows of public telephones, where I located a vacant phone booth with a large, tattered phone book and started jotting down possible relatives, people with the same last name. I hoped someone might know Baba and might give me a lead as to where the family was staying. Finding numerous names and numbers to call was encouraging.

A woman at a phone booth next to me overheard me attempt to carry on conversations in English to possible relatives who spoke only Turkish or broken English. She offered to assist me, but I needed to tell her a story so that she would understand my urgency. Still, I couldn't tell her the actual truth. "I am here to meet up with my husband's family, who arrived yesterday," I said as I cried. "I was unable to join them at that time, and now I've lost the card with the address and telephone number of where my family was staying. I do not know how to find them." She started to make some of the calls and gave everyone who answered all the family details. Some knew of the family, but no one knew where they might be. I began to worry that I might have opened up Pandora's box by calling relatives, starting a chain of events I would live to regret.

We questioned—or, more accurately, interrogated—the van companies at the airport to see if someone might recall taking the family to their accommodations. After describing the family, one van company said they had picked them up. They thought Aisha's family was staying in a small town outside of Istanbul. We were informed it was a neighborhood where many Middle Easterners resided while on vacation.

My less-than-competent hired hands and I drove our rented car to the neighborhood that had been suggested to us. Two hotel rooms were booked so it would appear that we were husband and wife with a brother accompanying us. We explored the community over and over again. I loosely covered with a hijab, abaya, and sunglasses. I didn't want to draw attention to my blue eyes that were so easily noticed in that brown-eyed part of the world, so I tried to blend in in any way I could.

Sadly, the two men with me stood out like sore thumbs. Here were two white, ex-Marine, American men, clean-cut and clean shaven, in their forties, wearing what looked like CIA-issued sunglasses in an Arab neighborhood. They wore blue jeans and white T-shirts. What were they thinking? Couldn't they have worn clothes that might have served as better camouflage, or made some attempt to look like the locals or at least to act like tourists?

For three days, we walked repeatedly through the same neighborhoods, but we had no luck seeing any sign of my daughter and her family. We must have looked very suspicious to anyone who saw us. Who *wouldn't* get suspicious of these men after a couple of days?

I decided to go on my own with a photo of my daughter to see if anyone had seen her. Again, Aisha, with her blonde hair and blue eyes and with Arab relatives in an Arab neighborhood, would easily be noticed. No such luck.

With further questioning of a van company in the neighborhood where we stayed, we found out that an older man who matched Baba's description came in regularly on a different van to a certain stop and would transfer to one of their vans. The van would take this man to the physical therapist several times a week. This made sense; Baba had hurt his back and was getting therapy before taking vacation. I decided I could at least go see if this was indeed Baba.

The revised plan was for me to identify Baba the next morning at the stop without being noticed. If it was him, we would be waiting to follow him on his return van ride home.

When morning arrived, something did not feel right. I was apprehensive and jittery when I woke, and all of our energy was down. I was to go on my own to see if this man could be Baba. It was before ten o'clock when I nervously started my walk, deliberately taking one step at a time to the silver metal hut, a little one-room tin shack used as a van and bus stop.

An overwhelming premonition took over my body; I felt as if a setup was about to happen, an ambush. Something was wrong. Something told me that it was not the right time to do this. Every bone in my body said to run, to abandon my plan.

By then, too many questions had been asked and too much time had passed. Relatives would have let the family know someone was looking for them. Perhaps the van company had forewarned the family that someone had inquired about them. It took every bit of my being, but the decision was made to call off this mission.

Feeling watched, we hurried back to our funky, dirty hotel; packed our belongings; and left as quickly as we could. We headed in dead silence to Istanbul, a forty-five-minute drive. It was not going to happen this time, and I had to admit to failure. What was I going to tell my daughter? I would be unable to talk to her until after her vacation. She must have known by then that something had gone wrong, very wrong. She had prepared to "never return to Saudi."

What a disaster! I was crushed and defeated. Later that day, in a conversation with the men, I found that they had not had any plans in place for after we'd gotten Aisha. They didn't have an exit route planned or a passport for Aisha. How were we going to get out of the country? "We were going to figure it out when it was time," they said.

Supposedly, they were ex-Special Forces Marines and had experience in the CIA. I now had a different image of their abilities and their mentality. What a rude, cruel awakening. Not to mention the blow of the $35,000 that I had already paid, with $15,000 more promised. They had the gall to ask for the remainder.

"You have got to be kidding me. You are not getting it!" I shouted. They had not come through and had made a series of stupid mistakes; and I had made a stupid, expensive mistake by hiring them. What had I been thinking?

When we arrived in Istanbul, we checked into a hotel and spent the rest of the day regrouping. I couldn't take more. I finally said, "I have to go; I need to get a flight to the States. I cannot do this right now." There is a certain amount of trust needed in these situations; how quickly it had vanished. I was weighed down and plagued with deep sorrow as I prepared to leave Turkey. My daughter still waited for us, but we would not come to her rescue as planned.

Later, when Aisha and I talked, I discovered we had been close to finding her. We had been at the ice-skating rink she had frequented, which was also very close to where she had stayed. Our timing was off, however; she wasn't there when we were.

Sometime later, I received a letter from Uncle Tom. He was apologetic and invited us to stay with him whenever we needed to. He wanted to know how he could help. Later, he called to make a new offer, but I refused.

Upon my return to the States, I lay catatonic at my sister's home, not knowing what to do. My crying would not stop. I could not eat. At night, I rolled over and over in my lonely bed, the empty silence killing me from the inside. My daughter's anxious whisper replayed in my ears: "Mommy, where are you?" I wanted to hide, cover up with the blankets, and sleep the days away. I couldn't cope with the disappointment and failure I felt over not getting Aisha out as promised. I was worried sick about her. I knew she would want to know what had happened, what had gone wrong. Why had Uncle Tom not come for her? It would be another two months before the summer was over and Aisha and I could talk.

I had built dreams only to find myself being devastated once again. Every time I got hope that my daughter would be free, another plan to save her would not succeed. What would it take to get out alive with my daughter's hand in mine?

Second Attempt: Turkey

Morning would not come soon enough.
I needed to make a telephone call.

In the middle of the night, a vision came to me while I was asleep at my sister's home in Arizona. It was four a.m. This peculiar vision was an image of a beige cardboard box with paper files. Almost in a trance, I went to the closet. On top of the first box I opened was the business card with the name and telephone number of a private investigator I had contacted seven years earlier. What was the likelihood of finding his card, and on the very top of the box? An omen, a good omen, I desperately hoped.

Shortly after Aisha had been taken in 1987 I had contacted "PI Bob." At that time, however, I could not begin to pay $100,000 for his services. Now, almost seven years later, things were different. I had bought a home, my lifelong dream, which was soon to be sold for money for my cause. Additionally, after my parents had visited Aisha and me in Saudi, they had wanted to help secure my daughter's freedom. I had monetary resources now that I hadn't had before.

After the dream, a comfort I had not felt for days seemed to come over me. Morning would not come soon enough. I needed to make a telephone call. PI Bob's time difference was one hour earlier, and I didn't want to leave a message. Later that morning, without thinking twice, I made the call. I reminded him that we had talked before, some seven years prior. He remembered my story. Who wouldn't? I continued in a controlled breath, "I would like to talk with you about getting my daughter out. I am on my way to California. Do you think we could meet?"

Two days later, we met at a restaurant and got reacquainted. I informed him of my first aborted attempt in Turkey less than a month earlier. He said he actually had some experience with getting someone out of Turkey and asked when I wanted to proceed.

After agreeing to start immediately, we arranged initial payment options. He knew that I needed to sell my house, but he started his work immediately. He wanted to do reconnaissance in Turkey before the family left for Egypt. He got his "group of men" together, one of whom he had worked with in the past. He didn't travel to Turkey himself, and I flew to my parents' home in Kansas to wait for the verdict.

In comparing stories, his men were doing reconnaissance in the same locale I'd been to in Turkey. PI Bob called me at my parents' to tell me that he didn't think my daughter and her family were in Turkey anymore. I knew they were going to be in Turkey for a couple of weeks, and then they were going to Egypt, but he asked if there was a way to find out for sure. I felt confident that I could get this information. I called Abdul in Jeddah.

Abdul was shocked when I called. I hadn't talked with him for months, even at his parents' home, and I hadn't called him for years. "I hope your mother is doing well," he said.

I gasped at his awareness of my mother's made-up illness. How did he know? "Thanks for asking," I said cordially. "She is doing better after surgery." I got to the point. "I am calling to see if I might be able to talk to our daughter."

He replied empathetically, "Honey, she is not here. My dad came back to Saudi because my uncle died. My mom, sister, and Aisha flew directly to Egypt."

I gave my condolences regarding his uncle and thanked him for the information. As I said goodbye, he reprimanded me for taking mail out of the country, which I had done as a favor for some maids. Instead of just hanging up, I replied, "I do not have any problem taking their mail." How had he found out this had even happened? This was typical of the kind of conversations we had.

As we said goodbye, he said he loved me. My ex-husband's bipolar personality was showing through. Though I had not heard of a diagnosis for his illness, I had once seen lithium, which was often used for this condition, among his belongings.

Clearly, he had been surprised to hear from me, but he was already aware I was out of the country. How would he know my mother was sick? I'd had no contact with him or his family.

Later, when I returned to Saudi, I found out from my roommate that Abdul had called to talk with me while I was gone. This was not the norm for us. She was purposely uninformed as to what went on in the secretive part of my life. The excuse I had used when leaving was that my mother was sick and I had to go home to visit. Abdul had called to gather information, as word had probably filtered back to the family that there was a woman who was looking for them in Turkey.

My intuition has helped me throughout my life, and it was likely that my cover had, in fact, been blown and that my instincts were right on the day I had aborted the first mission.

Egypt, Summer 1994

What would happen if we did secure Aisha but could not get her out?
We would be arrested in Egypt, our fates unknown.

I informed PI Bob that Aisha and her family were no longer in Turkey and had left for Egypt, then sent him photos of my daughter and her relatives and the address of their apartment in Cairo. I had not been to that apartment. A confidante had given me the address and telephone number a few years before. My daughter had told me their apartment was close to the pyramids, by the Nile River.

With this information, the hired team found the family apartment. PI Bob joined the team and rented an apartment across the street so they could watch whatever went on. He sent me photos he took so I could confirm that they were watching the correct child. I sobbed when I received the photos showing my daughter. I knew they were on track. PI Bob kept me posted on what they observed, and they attempted to get an idea of the family's patterns. They wanted to arrange the best, safest opportunity to snatch Aisha and run. She didn't know these men, but I would be present when the time was right.

The plan was for me to fly to Egypt so I could be there when she was taken. We all believed that my presence was instrumental because of the psychological dynamics of taking a child. After all, PI Bob was a stranger to Aisha. As she had said before, "You need to give them my Barbie so I'll know they are the correct people who will help me."

Unfortunately, PI Bob didn't have the Barbie.

I was still on vacation in the States, so it was not a problem for me to meet them. Looking up flights to Egypt was my next project. I would leave soon.

Before I booked my flight, PI Bob became concerned by a strange event that occurred at the family's apartment. He said, "I don't know what is going on. Aisha's grandfather was taken to the police station." Maybe the family suspected something. Did they know something was happening, and had they talked to the police? We had no clue.

Again, my heart skipped a few beats. I started to feel defeated, but I knew I couldn't give up.

PI Bob's group did more research. Baba's brother had lived in Egypt most of his life. I had met him a couple of times and knew him to be a very likeable, admirable, and professional man. He had numerous high government positions, as had Abdul's father at one time. The PI's men discovered that my daughter's grandfather had an important military role with the Saudi royal family during King Faisal's rule. I had heard that Abdul's father was an important person, though my ex told me many things. Often, the words out of his mouth were lies; I was not sure what to believe. Numerous times when we traveled, he had attempted to get into airports' VIP lounges because of his father's influence. I never knew if he was telling the truth or not, and Abdul didn't seem to really know what his father did. Nor did I recall discussing the subject with Baba during any of our after-dinner talks.

With this new information, we realized our safety could be in great jeopardy. What would happen if we did secure Aisha and couldn't get her out? We would be arrested in Egypt, our fates unknown. The concern became not whether the team could get my daughter but whether they would be able to move quickly enough to get her out of Cairo in a timely manner. Perhaps there was too much political influence due to Baba's and the uncle's high rank and connections. When the PI shared this information, I was still at my parents' home.

"Can we safely get her out?" was the big question.

It was my decision as to how we were to proceed. I was frightened and anxious. As desperate as I felt, I knew I needed to be wise with our safety and well-being. After hours of beating my head against the wall, debating an emotionally draining subject with my parents and friends, it was decided. The risk was too great. There was no way we could be sure we would get Aisha out of Egypt safely. Attempt number two was aborted. I was whipped and beaten again. How much could a person take?

I hurt more for my daughter than for myself. It was painful for me, but I knew, on some level, that I needed to numb my emotions and hide my hurt and disappointment. I needed to be strong for Aisha. I knew living at her family's home was becoming increasingly difficult for her, emotionally, and I did not trust her uncle.

I was not through yet. I had only been out of Saudi Arabia for six weeks, with the prayer that I would not have to return. Before I had left for the States, my good friend and coworker Mary had told me that if our attempt failed, she might have another plan up her sleeve. At the time, I was not going to consider it. I had needed to believe we would succeed, period.

Mary had wanted me to be aware of some influential people she was willing to talk with who might be able to help get us across the Saudi-Bahraini border if the original plan did not come to fruition. After aborting the Egyptian operation, I discussed this possibility with PI Bob. It seemed viable. We decided to go forward with attempt number three.

This plan would require someone to drive us across the border into Bahrain. PI Bob would intercept and get us out of Bahrain before my weekend visit with Aisha was over. After agreeing to prep for the new operation, PI Bob traveled home from Egypt and I returned to Riyadh, as my "vacation" was over.

I flew back into Saudi, surrounded by a fog of disappointment and with a heavy heart. I arrived back in Riyadh, and my daughter was still in Egypt. Anyone who knew about "the Troll" knew I was *not* supposed to be there and that things had not gone as planned. I needed to hear my daughter's voice, to feel her love and energy, even if it was only over the phone. She needed an explanation, and I needed confirmation that I was doing the right thing in taking these risks to get my daughter to freedom.

Part Eight

Third Time's a Charm?

Failed Outcomes

Both of us felt downtrodden and stripped of our power.
We hung on the phone line in total silence, letting our truth sink in.

It was the end of August 1994 when I returned to Riyadh, depressed and disappointed to face my life there again. I was so down, my mind would not focus; it spun like a carnival ride. Luckily, I returned on the weekend and was relieved to have two days to mourn before I had to put on a happy face and return to work. I walked in a fog, deeply scarred by the failed attempts of the previous six weeks. Aisha consumed my thoughts. It was crucial I talk with her. I had the grandparents' Cairo telephone number, but the family didn't know this. To play it safe, I opted against calling directly. Instead, I called Aisha's grandparents' home in Riyadh, knowing someone would be there.

One of the "nice" younger uncles, whom I had not seen or spoken with in months, answered the telephone. I was both relieved and impatient, but before I got to my reason for calling, I performed the common courtesies—"How are you doing? How are your mother and father?" and so forth—until I had quickly caught up on his life. I had no patience left to speak to nasty Uncle Faisal, or anyone else, for that matter, except my daughter, who could only be feeling as heartbroken as I was.

I told my ex-brother-in-law that I had just returned from vacation and would really like to talk with my daughter. Did he think it would be possible? He sounded positive and said he would check with his father. I was to call him back in ten minutes, and when I did he said, "My father said you can talk with Aisha, but you need to call her." He then gave me their telephone number—the same one I already had. I appreciated being able to call long distance through the hospital's telephone system without leaving my home. My fingers shakily dialed the number.

Baba answered the phone. I quickly got the impression that the phone in their Cairo apartment was located in a place where everybody could hear whatever was said. He asked all the requisite questions to see how I was and then said he had someone who was excited to talk to her mother. This was the first time we had been able to talk while Aisha was on vacation. The first words out of Aisha's mouth were, "Where are you, Momma?" Her words hit me over the head and tugged at my heart; I knew exactly what she meant. She asked me again, louder and with more emphasis, "Where are you, Momma?"

"I love you and miss you, too," I replied. "Mommy is in my house in Riyadh."

There was a long, dreadful silence.

Then, daringly, she asked, "Momma, why are you in Riyadh?"

The disappointment and despondency that came over the telephone line from Aisha took my breath away. To keep her on track, it was imperative to hide my intense sadness.

I firmly replied, "This is something we will have to talk about later, when you return to Riyadh."

Had I been where she could see me, she would have noticed my gesture of a quick hand motion across my throat. She would have known what that meant.

"Momma, what about the Troll?"

More sternly, I said, "It is not going to work this time, Aisha."

"Is this about the Troll, Momma?" she asked again. She couldn't seem to grasp that her dream of getting out of Saudi Arabia that summer was not going to happen.

Sadly, I replied, "Yes, it is."

She would not accept my vague answers and kept asking, "Why, Momma? Why?" She mentioned that she had rubbed her eyes a lot at the airport.

I raised my voice so she would listen, and carefully enunciated the words, "Aisha, we are going to have to talk about all this later, when you return."

Her disposition changed. There was an emptiness in her voice as she came to understand what I had said. She was wise enough to know we couldn't speak openly anymore. Her disillusionment weighed heavily on me. Both of us felt downtrodden and stripped of our power. We hung on the phone line in total silence, letting our truth sink in.

I desperately wanted to hold her in my arms, hug and kiss her, and let her release the built-up tears of sorrow and disappointment that she could not show. No one was there for her in Egypt. No one had a clue what her frail, delicate body was screaming inside.

It broke my heart to think of all she had been through. I reminded Aisha to stay strong and promised her that Mommy would succeed—it would just take a little longer than we had hoped. With some effort, I managed to change the subject, and we were able to climb out of the deep place our wondering had taken us. The rest of our conversation was upbeat, filled with laughter, about what she was doing and her vacation. We talked about Turkey. Some of the places she'd visited were places I had searched for her. Clearly, the timing had been off, and the incompetence of my rescue team hadn't helped.

Aisha laughed and teased about her grandfather being taken to the jail by a policeman in Cairo. When I questioned her further, she said he had called the police to report a noisy neighbor. The policeman had picked him up to go write his complaint. The story was now coming full circle as to why PI Bob had seen Grandpa taken away a week earlier.

We wrapped up our conversation, and a few days later I called again to check in with her. What a strong constitution my daughter had. I was so proud of her ability to cope and move on with life, no matter what was thrown at her. She did it better than I did.

We would be seeing each other in a few weeks, and we could not wait.

Returning to work, however, was dreadful. The few friends who knew of my expedition realized that our attempt had been futile. What a crazy, emotionally harrowing summer. I desperately needed a break from thinking about this disturbing nightmare of an ordeal, though my head relentlessly pounded with the question of what to do now.

It was time to talk with my friend Mary, who knew of an American man that might be willing to help get my daughter to freedom. This man had a diplomatic passport, which gave him more privileges than other people had regarding coming and going in and out of the country. He had a different security clearance, not needing exit and reentry visas; and his passport remained with him, instead of being taken upon arrival in the Kingdom by his employer. The colossal question was whether or not he would still be agreeable to putting his life on the line to smuggle us illegally across the Saudi-Bahraini border. A week later, Mary confirmed that her contact was still willing to help us and that he didn't want a dime for his service. What a miracle—another angel along my path.

Preparation for a Third Attempt

*I needed to regroup and get over the trauma
of not getting out during the summer as planned.*

After the summer, my daughter—now almost ten—was not the same little girl. She had mentally prepared herself to get out of her grandparents' house and live in America. Moving forward, when it was time for her to return from our weekend visits to her grandparents' home, she became fidgety and tearful, especially when she knew that her uncle Faisal was home.

"Momma, I do not want to go home. I hate it there. I need to get out of here, please!" She wrote me notes: "Mom, please take me away from here!"

She would even get stomachaches; obviously, she couldn't take it anymore. I knew then that I couldn't wait too long because she was not coping.

It seemed that Uncle Faisal was at it again. He picked on Aisha. He was degrading and nasty. My bigger concern was over the possibility that he might be sexually molesting her. As a way to handle it all, I suggested that Aisha visualize kicking him in the balls when he was being mean to her. Aisha laughed and said she would try it. She later told me that it worked well.

Aisha would share confidential information from the family she had overheard. She always lowered her voice to a whisper when she told me these things. "I pretend to fall asleep on my grandma's lap in the living room and listen to them talk," she said.

Apparently, she overheard many conversations. She heard her father say that he wished I was out of his life and that he wanted to take me out to the desert and get rid of me. I was so sad that she had heard her father say that about her mother. How very sick this man was. She did say, however, that Baba had defended me and told Abdul he was very stupid to think like that.

PI Bob was ready to keep the momentum going. He wanted to start making plans to get us out of Saudi to Bahrain, but I needed a break—just for a while. I needed to regroup and get over the trauma of not getting out during the summer as planned. Time was needed to mend my heart and prepare for the next grueling mission. What if it didn't work *again*? If we were caught in Saudi, I would certainly end up in jail. I couldn't find the strength to keep the momentum going at that particular moment. As much as I wanted to move forward, I was mentally, emotionally, and physically fried.

Regardless of my wavering stamina, there was preparation to be done. For our next attempt, our exit route would be in the eastern region of Saudi, near the Aramco Compound at the King Fahd Causeway. This four-lane bridge took approximately thirty minutes to cross into Bahrain.

Because it was a more liberal Middle Eastern country than Saudi Arabia, many people would go to Bahrain to vacation and enjoy the freedoms it embraced. Many would go to legally drink, party, and pick up prostitutes. In addition, bootleggers would go to Bahrain to smuggle real alcohol back into Saudi Arabia to sell illegally.

I found it an amusing juxtaposition: "You cannot do that here in the KSA, but we are going to build a causeway over into a place where you will have the liberty to participate in sinful acts, even if it is against our religion."

Throughout the vast, barren Saudi desert, there were many manned checkpoints. Usually, the guards wanted to see your passport if you were fortunate enough to keep it, or they looked at your *iqama*—the work visa. At the borders, there were immigration police and customs officials who would check the identification of those entering or leaving the country. Even to go to Bahrain, an exit visa and a reentry visa were necessary for most expats. This did not apply to people from Saudi Arabia who frequented Bahrain.

Smuggled into Bahrain

*After what seemed like hours, we were at the border checkpoint.
We were in our hidden places. Our hearts were beating
fast and furious.*

It was January 1995; Aisha was now ten. I had had a few months reprieve and was as ready as I could be. The PI agency was in contact with me via my sister who lived in Arizona. We began exchanging cryptic messages to each other about the upcoming mission. With the help of another woman I worked with and my sister, we were able to communicate secretly through hospital faxes, which we determined to be a safe, secure way to communicate quickly. Fortunately, my co-worker had an office with a fax machine she shared with a man from Jordan whom she trusted would not invade her privacy.

We had made new plans. We had many options, dates, times of day, seasons, and safety risks to discuss and consider. We called this mission "the Party," and it would take place during the month of Ramadan, in February.

A few months before making this next attempt, I was introduced to the man who was eager to drive us across the border. This angelic man, our hero, didn't want to be paid for this dangerous, risky task. He just wanted to help my daughter get to freedom.

I confirmed with Aisha that she still wanted to continue. "Yes," was her immediate answer. The new plans were explained to this amazing girl.

She had kept our secret for over a year. Every week, she would bring a few more clothes, dolls, or toys to leave in the suitcase she had picked out. Closer to the time of our departure, our suitcases were moved to a safe place on the compound. It had been arranged for someone to secretly pick them up at night and keep them until we were ready to leave. Other suitcases and boxes of our belongings had already been shipped or taken by expats leaving for the States. Many of our personal items were given away or sold privately. A list was made of people who would receive items, like Aisha's old toys, if we successfully made it to the Party.

Prior to the mission, I decided it was a good idea to go to Bahrain to see what it took to get across the border, having never been there. This helped ease my anxiety. My coworker's husband was going to Bahrain, and he was fine with my tagging along for the weekend. He had a British friend named Oliver who allowed us to stay at his villa. During this visit, I was invited to come again and was told that if there was any way he could help, all I needed to do was ask.

Our departure date and time were determined. The weekend would be in the month of Ramadan (the holy month of fasting). This, to me, would be a great time to make our escape across the border. If the ride was calculated correctly, taking about four hours, we would cross the border about the time to break the fast and for the call to evening prayer—perfect distractions.

Unfortunately, another disappointment presented itself. A couple of weeks before our planned journey, it was put on hold. The

American Embassy announced uprisings in Bahrain. People were fighting for their rights, and a warning was issued which discouraged people from going to Bahrain at that time.

What would we do now? The Party had been arranged, and everyone had been invited and had RSVP'd. If we were going to change plans, we had to figure it out right away, without delay. I would need to stop things in the States before PI Bob and his team started their travels.

We were on the brink of rescheduling when our "driver'" told us to "let the Party begin," despite the announcement from the American embassy. He was familiar with Bahrain, and he and his wife had discussed other options and decided to stick with the scheduled time. His life was on the line for us.

With everything in place, the day arrived. Since it was Ramadan and a weekend, the city was dead. Many people who fasted would sleep all day and party all night, and work hours were reduced. Not wanting my roommate to be privy to any details, I mentioned to her that Aisha and I were going out to the desert for a picnic with friends. My roommate knew nothing about what was happening, though she knew of our eventual goal. She had even arranged British passports for a mother and daughter, which we kept stored on top of our refrigerator as a backup in case they might be needed.

Up to this time, Aisha didn't know when we were leaving. We had it all planned, but she didn't have a clue about the timing. Taking the limo, I picked Aisha up at nine as usual from her grandparents' for our weekend visit, which was meant to last from Thursday morning until Friday afternoon at five o'clock. As we often did, we went to the market. As planned, my friends were there. They invited us to their home, and we rode with them. One of their friends stopped and offered to take Aisha and me for a ride in his decked-out van. He would then drive us "home." Aisha thought that would be cool, so we hugged our friends goodbye.

As Aisha got into the van, she immediately saw the suitcases and panicked. She started to scream: "Oh, my God! Oh, Momma, what are we doing?"

"We're going to America," I said.

She started to cry at the reality of what was about to transpire. Panicky and in shock, she cried, "*Now?* We are going right now?" She continued to sob as I held her shaking body.

I needed reassurance from her. "You want to do this, right?"

She said, "Mom, is this it? Are we really leaving?" The intensity of her crying increased. She was hysterical.

"What's wrong, Aisha? Why are you crying like this?" I asked, trying to understand.

It wasn't that she didn't want to leave; she was simply upset because she hadn't kissed her grandmother goodbye.

I attempted to comfort Aisha and told her, "We can write Siti a letter to say goodbye and tell her know how much you love her. We will let her know we are fine."

Aisha held me tight as she let her body melt with grief over not saying good-bye to her grandmother, and absorbed the reality that now was the time. My heart mourned with her over the loss of her/our Saudi family, especially Siti. They were close, and I recalled in that moment how she had once called her grandmother Omi, meaning "mother."

As we crossed the desert, I was eventually able to comfort Aisha, and our focus shifted to the perilous but hopeful adventure we were on. Using the privileged diplomatic passport of our driver, we breezed through the four checkpoints heading east to Bahrain. He presented our documents with his, but the guards chose not to check our paperwork and waved us through. Aisha and I both had newly issued passports from the American embassy in Riyadh. With the clout of the diplomatic passport on top, we were on our way.

As we neared the Saudi border and the causeway to Bahrain, our driver pulled off the road and stopped. He asked us to get out of the van. Then he pushed a switch and the back seat became a bed. Aisha and I were told to get under the bed. This would be our hiding place for the next thirty minutes. We nervously crawled into this narrow, dark, cramped space. One could discover this hiding place by opening the back door, moving the decoy of pillows, and looking under the bed. We all prayed for our safety and that they would not ask to search the van, as was often done.

My daughter said, in her little giggle of a voice, "Can we sing the song from *Sound of Music* now?" referring to the scene in the film when the family flees Austria and ascends the mountain.

I said, "No, we are not singing now. We are going to keep quiet and not move. We have to freeze and not even wiggle. Our lives are in danger." It was too dark to make the gesture of my hand across my neck, but she knew the seriousness of the moment. She understood what could happen if something went wrong.

After what seemed like hours but in reality was only a few minutes, we were at the border checkpoint. We were in our hidden places, and our hearts were beating fast and furious. I prayed that my daughter would not move or make a sound. The radio was playing to mask any noises. It was time!

My pounding heart was now in my throat. We arrived at the checkpoint just as the announcement to prayer was being called, exactly as planned. Two immigration officials immediately rushed out from their small office building. They clearly wanted to pray so they could break their daylong fast and eat. One person asked for our driver's passport, while the other guard walked around the vehicle. Making small talk in Arabic, our driver gave his passport to the immigration official. He saw that it was a diplomatic passport by the color of its cover, and that he had the necessary visas to continue his journey. He waved him through and wished him a good day, saying, "*Ma'a s-salāma.*" We heard the men hurriedly walk away so they could pray and break their fast.

We could finally breathe. Today, infrared security measures are in place that would have discovered our warm, hidden bodies, but we had gone undiscovered. After we'd driven what felt like a safe distance, I told Aisha she could sing if she wanted to. In less than thirty minutes, we crossed the border. Our driver said, "We are in Bahrain! *We did it!* You are free, together!"

We shouted, "*Al-ḥamdu li-llāhi!*" (Praise be to God).

We had made it! We were out of Saudi Arabia, free and together, after eight years!

Meeting in Bahrain

One could only wonder if our escape boat was really seaworthy, as it looked so old and rickety. I was unsure how it could even float. The paint had been peeling for many years, leaving huge patches of uncolored, worn wood.
It was bare and empty inside.

So far, everything had gone as planned. It was Thursday, around six in the evening. We were out of Saudi Arabia! We had been smuggled illegally into Bahrain with no visas, on our brand-new American passports. PI Bob and an assistant waited for us at the deserted designated parking lot a short distance from the border crossing. It was getting dark, and the parking lot lights had just turned on. Hugs of appreciation were given to our beloved driver, whom we never saw or spoke to again. I heard that he and his wife left Saudi Arabia and were doing fine. He was an amazing man.

We were greeted and quickly escorted with our two suitcases to PI Bob's rental car and then taken to the large hotel south of the causeway in the city of Manama. We all stayed in one hotel room with two queen-sized beds. It was our goal to get out of the country by five o'clock the next day. Aisha's weekend would be over, and she was expected home around six at the latest. We stayed out of the public eye, utilizing room service and hiding in the bathroom whenever anyone came.

The plan that PI Bob thought best was for us to leave Bahrain by boat. This required an additional $5,000 to pay for the boat on top of the $100,000 that had already been paid. My sister was clever in the way she distributed this much money without its being traced. The PI's assistant, Barry, and I were to pretend that we were husband and wife and that we were taking a boat ride to Abu Dhabi.

I was nervous and doubtful of this idea, not knowing the distance by boat. Early the next morning, we would go to the port. I asked what the plan was for getting us visas so that we could get out of the country, but there was none. I tried so hard to stay positive, but my uncertainties got the best of me. Somehow, they thought they could get us out of the country quickly and without any visas. Apparently, PI Bob thought he could talk, pay, pray, or bribe his way through immigration, even though we had no permission to be in the country, let alone to leave it!

I was growing increasingly agitated. Did he really think these officials were that dumb? Time would tell. Angry and disillusioned, I said to myself, "Oh, fuck, here we go again."

On Friday morning, we drove a short distance to the harbor. PI Bob had our new, virgin passports, but no visas at all. He explained that the original boat he had selected had some mechanical problems, so another boat had to be arranged. When we got to the dock, we were taken to this boat. PI Bob had hired an old Indian fishing boat and its crew to take us out of Bahrain to another Arab country.

My "husband" accompanied us to the boat. Aisha and I were distressed when we saw it. One could only wonder if it was really seaworthy. I was unsure how it could even float, it looked so old and rickety. The paint had been peeling for many years, leaving huge patches of uncolored, worn wood. It was bare and empty inside, with no blankets, food, or water. I felt sick, weak, and deeply disappointed. I was immensely frustrated with the plan, but I attempted to hide my nervous feelings from my daughter and make light of the situation.

My "husband" asked us to stay on the boat and said he would be back when we were ready to sail. Our suitcases were placed in the hollow of the vessel, so we would be ready to leave if we managed to get through immigration. Aisha and I were left alone. After an hour, we started to get nervous. Something was wrong. We saw the port police's boat come to shore. Were they looking for us? They seemed to be looking and pointing at us.

The men finally returned, telling us it was too windy to go to sea. We would have to come back that afternoon. We all returned to the hotel room, disheartened. I was freaked out about that boat. They could have at least chosen a decent boat for the price I had paid. Was that the only vessel available? What husband who loved his wife and daughter would take them out on this boat? I knew we were in for another crazy adventure, and it didn't seem very promising. I was so upset that I wanted to yell, scream, and cry, and I wondered again at the competence of my team. I couldn't believe what lay before me, but what were my options?

The weather did not cooperate; it was windy, and the seas remained too rough to go out. All boat traffic was suspended. Every time we went to the boat, Aisha and I would take Dramamine to help our seasickness. The Dramamine made us drowsy, especially Aisha, who would go back to the hotel to sleep. On the plus side, it did calm a nervous, energetic ten-year-old's restlessness. The longer it took to get us out of the country, the more frustrated I became. Our safety was on the line.

Each time Aisha and I went to the boat, the motley crew—who most likely didn't know what they were involved in—had done a few more things to make our journey as comfortable as possible. The longer we stayed at port, the more they cleaned up the boat, putting cheap carpets on the floor where we could sit and sleep. The next time we came, there were blankets. Soon, food appeared—tea, crackers, and juice.

We continued to try on Friday. Repeatedly, we were told, "Bad weather, come later." I wondered if this weather was normal for this time of year. Why had this not been taken into consideration? The goal was to be out of Bahrain by Friday evening, and it was now after five, with dusk quickly approaching. Our time was up; Aisha was expected to be home.

We had successfully made it across the Saudi border, thought to be the hardest task of the whole event. For both Aisha and me, it was a dream come true. We were together and outside of Saudi Arabia for the first time in eight years, and my daughter was an American citizen again. Had I known it could be that easy to at least get across the border with the help of a brave and gracious diplomat, I might have tried it years earlier.

The second phase of the operation was not going so well, however; and I knew, as we went back and forth repeatedly to the rickety boat, that there was still much more to deal with. Why couldn't there have been a second option in the event of poor weather?

In between our fruitless visits to the boat, two men, a bouncy, full-of-life ten-year-old girl who was used to a lot of space, and her mom were cramped into one small hotel room for two nights. There never was a dull moment with Aisha. She embraced all of this craziness with a sense of humor, lifting my spirits with her amusingly high-pitched singsong and an infectious laugh.

Kahlil Gibran has a great poem about children:

"On Children"

Your children are not your children.
They are the sons and daughters of Life's longing for itself.
They come through you but not from you,
And though they are with you yet they belong not to you.

You may give them your love but not your thoughts,
For they have their own thoughts.
You may house their bodies but not their souls,
For their souls dwell in the house of tomorrow,
    which you cannot visit, not even in your dreams.
You may strive to be like them,
But seek not to make them like you.
For life goes not backward nor tarries with yesterday.

You are the bows from which your children
    as living arrows are sent forth.
The Archer sees the mark upon the path of the infinite,
And He bends you with His might
    that His arrows may go swift and far.
Let our bending in the Archer's hand be for gladness;
For even as He loves the arrow that flies,
    so He loves also the bow that is stable.

On the last port visit on Friday, the men went to talk with the officials. It was not permissible for us to be in the country without visas. Surprise, surprise, their planned scenario failed. They couldn't get the exit visas because the passports had not been stamped with entry visas. They were told to go immediately the next day to the visa office to sort out the problem.

If we somehow got the visas we needed, maybe we wouldn't need to sail on that boat after all—maybe we could fly. Meanwhile, things were heating up in Riyadh. Aisha was missing!

The Investigation in Riyadh

It was the end of the weekend. Aisha had not shown up as usual.
We were now "missing" people.

Aisha had not returned to her grandparents' home. It was Friday evening, and she was to be home by six, at the latest. If I was ever late, I would always call; but this time, they did not get a call. Maybe I should have called them, but it didn't occur to me. I could have told them a story: "I am sorry. We are out in the desert"—a true statement—"and we had a flat tire," or, "We got lost and drove to Bahrain. Just kidding." I could have come up with something. The family would be getting concerned as to our whereabouts, especially with no phone call.

It was now seven p.m. We were missing. What had happened at my home in Riyadh as we waited on Friday for the fourth time for our boat ride in Bahrain? It was later revealed to me in a letter mailed to my sister by my ex-roommate. She outlined the chain of events that occurred when we didn't show up.

Lisa, my roommate, came home from being out for the day. The answering machine signaled that there were messages—three from Aisha's family, each questioning where we were and instructing me to call. As far as she knew, we had gone out in the desert for a group hike. As the tone of the messages began to get more anxious and heated, Lisa started to wonder what was happening and why I wasn't home yet. She didn't know what to do.

When the phone rang again, Lisa answered it. They asked her where we were, and she replied, "I really do not know where they are. They were going out in the desert for a hike with some friends. Maybe something happened out in the desert."

Because our apartment looked as it always did, Lisa couldn't tell that we had left for good. Due to the fact that she hadn't heard from me, however, she began to get suspicious, as this had never occurred before. She decided to look on top of the refrigerator and found that the passports she had gotten for us were gone.

I had never talked with my roommate about any details of the past or present attempts to free my daughter. This way, she could plead ignorance.

The family threatened to call the police, and Lisa realized she needed to get the hospital security involved before the public police. She told the family she would call them. Because I was employed at the hospital and my housing was on hospital property, hospital security had jurisdiction. They came over to our home and started the questioning. Lisa told them that all she knew was that we were going on a picnic in the desert. The security officers asked many questions about things like my friends, where I worked, if I had a boyfriend. Then they searched our home for any evidence of our whereabouts.

Lisa learned that our home phone was tapped and that my friends' phones had been tapped, as well. Even my boss's phone and my work office phone were all tapped.

The next day, my Saudi girlfriend Noora, from hospital security, heard what had happened and went over to my director's office. Without saying a word, she motioned for my director to come out of her office. She wanted to let her know her office phones were tapped. She knew they were looking for us.

Everyone around the hospital was trying to figure out what was going on. People I worked with were questioned. An Egyptian friend who lived in the same compound knew about my concerns for Aisha and was aware that I dreamed that Aisha would one day live in my own country. When she learned we were missing, she had a good idea of where we were.

When the hospital's security department found no evidence to reveal what had happened, the Riyadh police department was contacted. They started their investigation into our whereabouts. Could there have been foul play? What had really happened? I became wanted by the Saudi government.

Back in Bahrain

*A nervous, restless feeling that we were not going
to get out tormented me.*

We started our third day in Bahrain and were still waiting for gentler seas and for visas. My outward persona was strong, calm, and cool; but, in reality, I was stressed out, sleep deprived, and paranoid.

It was Saturday, and the official workweek had begun. We returned again to the port, knowing that our futures had been entrusted to these dim-witted men. Maybe they thought it would be their lucky day, since they would be talking with different immigration officials. I was furious.

My hired men presented our passports to the new officials at a seaside hut as we waited, once again drugged with Dramamine, on our soon-to-be floating home. Would we get the necessary visas to get us out of the country? For Aisha and me, it became a game. What else could I do to keep my daughter distracted?

"Where do you think you are going?" the officials gruffly demanded. "You have no visas on these passports to be here. You are not supposed to be in this country. You think you are going to get a visa to get your wife and daughter out of this country?"

The men lamely explained that the officials at the border had forgotten to stamp our passports when we had arrived.

"That does not happen here," replied the officials.

Their explanations to the officials did not work. Fortunately, with the weekend over, the government offices would be open—but with shorter working hours because of Ramadan. The officials in the hut instructed our two men to go to the Bahrain Passport and Immigration Office located downtown. The men dropped us off at the side door of our hotel and went immediately to the office to sort out the visa problems.

Aisha and I finally had the hotel room to ourselves. We could be silly together, sing, dance, and play cards before the Dramamine in our systems put Aisha asleep. It was time to make other arrangements. We needed another place to stay if we were unable to leave that day.

My faith in PI Bob had waned rapidly. Our time was up. Of course it was not all right for us to be in Bahrain without visas. Their stupid scheme would not work, and no one was going to buy their weak excuses. Aisha and I could have done better ourselves, a mother and a crying daughter. The thought of how much money I'd paid started to eat at me.

We had been at the hotel going on three nights. A nervous, restless feeling that we were not going to get out tormented me. No boat trip yet, as it was still too windy and we still had no visas. Hours later, the men returned unsuccessful. We were now known to be in Bahrain illegally, and people were starting to notice us. Saudi police were also looking for us. Something needed to drastically shift.

I decided to contact Oliver, the man I had met the previous month in Bahrain. He was aware of my situation, and he had invited us to stay if we needed to. It was time to move. I mentioned my friend Oliver to Bob. I had to get Aisha and myself out of the hotel so that we were not cramped up in a room with two men for another day. I telephoned my new friend.

We packed up our few possessions and were taken to the British chap's garden villa. This was a perfect place for a ten-year-old; there was room to openly move, make noise, and play music, and there were other children to play with. It was a wonderful place for me. I could eat and legally drink and relieve my stress. It was our third night in Bahrain, with no foreseeable exit plan.

Every day was one more day to possibly get noticed and caught. Oliver had lived in Bahrain for some time, and he had influential friends who might have contacts with a boat we could use. Maybe, *inshallah*, someone could help us. PI Bob asked Oliver if he would ask about obtaining some assistance to free us. Oliver reached out to a few people, but no one was willing to take this risk. Now what were we to do?

On Sunday, PI Bob informed me that our only choice was to go to the American embassy in Bahrain. He said, "I am not going to be able to get you out of the country." Of course, in my mind, I cursed him. Had he really thought his plan was going to work? And why hadn't he considered a backup plan? I had paid this man $105,000; I had sold my house. Conversely, an amazingly heroic, daring man had risked his life to drive us across the border, out of Saudi Arabia, and he had declined any money. PI Bob had been paid handsomely and had accomplished nothing.

The American Embassy in Bahrain

It felt like a rope around my neck, pulling tighter with every minute.

On Sunday, our fourth day in Bahrain, PI Bob went to speak with someone at the American embassy on my behalf. I was afraid to go. The American embassy in Riyadh had lectured me repeatedly and would not help. It had become a broken record. PI Bob had a bundle of documents I had prepared in the States, from the court proceedings eight years earlier, that stated that I had custody of my daughter. There was also information about such things as the kidnapping from the US, my ex-husband's physical abuse, and the restraining order. PI Bob gave all of this information to the consulate and asked for help with our case. Oliver and I waited in suspense for hours to hear the verdict. Bob did not call. I was scared. What had happened?

The next day, day five, PI Bob called. He quickly got an earful from me because of his disrespect in not calling to let us know what had been discussed the day before. He had been informed that I needed to go the US embassy personally to ask for help. Initially, I refused. But what choice did I have? I had no other options.

I struggled to hide my fear over the chain of events. I had to be strong for Aisha. The tension felt like a rope around my neck, pulling tighter with every minute.

Since the American embassy in Saudi Arabia had consistently told me they could be of no assistance in getting us out of Saudi, why would it be different in Bahrain? Aisha and I were familiar faces at the American consulate while we lived in Jeddah. They knew us by name. We went in for new passports; we went in to see what they could do to help us. They were well aware that we were planning to leave, though not of the day. Surely these embassies must have communicated. Did the embassy in Bahrain not know of us through their correspondence? I imagined the American embassy in Riyadh might have already sent messages.

Bob drove me to the embassy in the rental car. "The car I'm paying for," I whispered under my breath with disgust. I recall little else about the ride to the American embassy in Manama, Bahrain. I was focused on one thing and one thing only—getting my daughter and myself to America.

A female Foreign Service officer "interviewed" me, though it was more like an interrogation. My unease and paranoia may not have helped, either. I didn't take my daughter with me for this first encounter because I wondered what they might do to her. Was the embassy from Riyadh in touch with them? No one said. Had they obtained information from Saudi International Police or the Saudi government? Could they take her away from me and send her back to Saudi Arabia? She was an American citizen, though that hadn't made a difference before. As I feared, the embassy spokesperson said, "We cannot help without meeting your daughter. You need to bring her so we can talk with her, to hear from her personally." As a small compromise,

I was told I could remain in the room with Aisha when they spoke with her. That helped calm the horrendous thoughts that were going through my head.

Bob took me to get Aisha from Oliver's house. When we returned to the embassy, Aisha and I were escorted down a few hallways into a narrow room with dark colors; in this room was a long conference table of stained brown wood with maybe twenty black leather chairs on rollers around it. We were offered a seat as the male consulate officer introduced himself. At the beginning of the conversation, I sat right next to Aisha. One of the Foreign Service representatives started to explain to my daughter why she was there and asked if she understood.

The gentleman began his set of questions for Aisha. She looked so small in this big, dark, dreary room. I was proud of her for being so brave. Her courage and determination always amazed me. While I sat, nervous and uncomfortable, listening to her answers, I looked for a way to escape with her if the need arose.

They asked if I was her mom.

"Yes," she replied.

"Do you want to go with your mom?"

"Yes," she replied again.

"Maybe your mom can go to the US, and you will have to go back to Saudi."

How could he make a statement like that?

My daughter's eyes widened, and she began to cry. She immediately jumped out of her chair and onto my lap. She grabbed me and insisted, "I am not leaving my momma. I am not going back to Saudi. They will kill us."

That was what she thought because she knew she was in big trouble and that I was in danger. She mentioned to the embassy official what she had overheard her father tell her grandfather about how he wanted to take me out in the desert and kill me.

After she was questioned for ten more minutes, the American Foreign Service representative said he would present this information to the consul general. He would ask him to represent us and appeal to the Bahrain government on our behalf to get us visas as soon as possible. We left the embassy shaking, still unsure of what the verdict would be. It was brutal to wait and not know.

Finally, late in the afternoon on the following day, after nearly a week on the run and in hiding, we got the call from Bob saying that we had gotten the visas. Entrance and exit visas were stamped on our passports. We would be able to leave together as soon as they could find a direct flight back to the United States. It would cost roughly $4,000 for last-minute flights. Bob didn't offer to assist in buying the tickets. From the $20,000 cash I had in a highly guarded money belt that I wore continuously about my waist, I paid the embassy for our tickets. What remained was all I had left for the rest of our lives.

Leaving Bahrain

I knew we were protected at that moment.

The time had come—we were really leaving. We were both terrified and excited. The embassy officials picked us up at Oliver's. We gave Oliver a heartfelt goodbye and gladly said our farewells to Bob and my "husband." We were driven to the airport and escorted to a hidden, private room, where we stayed for over an hour before our direct flight to New York City. The embassy officials stayed with us. It was day six, Tuesday, February 13, 1995, nine o'clock at night when our flight was called. We were instructed to wait with the officials. They made sure we were the last people on the plane so nothing could stand in our way. We boarded, and it seemed as though the presence of God came over me. I knew we were protected at that moment. If somebody had gotten wind of us leaving, it was too late; we were taking flight. Fourteen hours later, we would arrive in New York City. I knew that God would carry us safely to America, the Land of the Free.

Part Nine

Success: America

America, Valentine's Day

*We registered in our hotel as Jane and Mary Doe
and prepared for what lay ahead.*

We made it!

It was Valentine's Day on Tuesday, February 14, 1995, when we arrived in New York City at six o'clock in the morning. No one met us; no one from the State Department was there to greet us, nor were any of our hired team. We felt extremely lonely, and so tiny among all the people around us, though it felt as if we stuck out for all to see. Bob was to have informed my sister, through our confidential message system, that the "packages" would be arriving safely, and we were told by the American embassy in Bahrain to contact the State Department upon our arrival, but we were on our own.

We would constantly scan our environment and be on a certain level of alert moving forward. We would always survey our immediate area for any signs of danger, suspicious people, or strange conversations. Constantly surveying our surroundings would become a part of our lives.

Nevertheless, we had made it safely to America. With a sigh of relief and elated beyond belief, we jumped up and down, celebrating our newfound freedom. Together at last! Aisha was in America, a Saudi girl's dream and an American mother's dream realized after eight long years.

Though I was physically and emotionally drained, a rebound of adrenaline, jubilation, and euphoria charged through my body. What was I to do next? Would we need to immediately travel to our first of many safe homes as we embarked on a new world of living underground?

We took a yellow cab to our nearby hotel. A fresh morning snow had carpeted the busy city's landscape, offering a brisk, beautiful, and exciting new experience for Aisha, coming from the desert.

We registered as Jane and Mary Doe and prepared for what lay ahead. Self-conscious and holding tightly on to each other, we made our way to the hotel lobby to make a confidential telephone call to announce the arrival of the "packages" through a chain of command. We aborted that idea when the unoccupied telephones were next to Arabs who looked at us suspiciously—or so it felt.

During our first night in America, we alternated between sleep and wakeful hours. Aisha and I watched American television, ate the largest New York pepperoni pizza we had ever seen, and celebrated our victory.

When I awoke during the night, Aisha was awake. I could see and feel the joy overflowing from her ten-year-old body as she practiced writing her new chosen name, the name of her friend, over and over again. Our old identities and lives were about to be buried forever. The next morning, and from that day forward, we would become "new" people, like immigrants starting over in a strange land.

www.ingramcontent.com/pod-product-compliance
Lightning Source LLC
Chambersburg PA
CBHW030107100526
44591CB00009B/304